The Moderate Solution

The Moderate Solution

HOW WE CAN BALANCE THE FEDERAL BUDGET (AND IT ISN'T EVEN THAT HARD)

David B. Wilson

ISBN: 0692481524
ISBN 13: 9780692481523
Library of Congress Control Number: 2015910617
Integer Press, Larchmont, NY

Table of Contents

David B. Wilson earned a degree in economics from Lafayette College in Easton, Pennsylvania, and an MBA from the Harvard Business School, where he was a Baker Scholar. He spent his twenty-five-year career in corporate finance and private investing with E. F. Hutton & Company; Donaldson, Lufkin & Jenrette Securities Corporation; and Fidelity Investments, as well as private investment firms that he founded.

He has always held a very active interest in economic theory and the practical economic issues that affect the United States and the world. He considers himself a fiscal and social moderate with a strong belief in individual freedoms and possibilities.

He lives in Larchmont, New York, with his wife, two dogs, and whichever of his four children happen to be at home at the time.

Preface

IMAGINE THAT YOU ARE THE leader of a country, which for the moment we will call New Atlantis. You are a wise and fair leader, and you care about the country and its citizens. You are not driven by self-serving political considerations; you are a patriot and take your stewardship seriously. New Atlantis happens to be the richest and most powerful country in the history of the world. The size of its economy is twice as large as the next largest in the world, and on a per-capita basis, New Atlantis is among the most affluent nations in human history. Its military might is unrivaled in the world, with spending on national defense nearly ten times that of any other country. Yet, far from being seriously threatened from any major national power, New Atlantis is surrounded by friendly nations and has largely co-opted most of its major rivals into the world order of Pax Atlantica, which has endured for much of the past century.

New Atlantis is blessed with a multitude of natural resources, including abundant fresh water, wood, minerals, metals, and energy sources, and it produces more than enough food to feed its population. The country has more than six thousand miles of coastline bordering its continental area and a multitude of natural harbors suitable for shipping. Its neighbor to the north is a friendly nation with a vast of amount of natural resources that New Atlantis requires for its industry. The 5,500-mile northern border is largely open and unguarded. New Atlantis's southern neighbor is also a friendly nation with a young and growing population. The southern neighbor is still a developing country, and its relatively low wage rate makes it an ideal base for low-cost manufacturing for New Atlantis companies and a potential growth market for export.

While New Atlantis has a very diverse population, the people are united in their common belief in individual freedom, and the country is relatively free from sectarian or other material internal strife. Its citizenry is hard-working and vibrant, and in contrast to many of New Atlantis's fellow developed nations, the population is growing, both from natural birth rates and from immigration, as the country is viewed by much of the rest of the world as the land of opportunity. It is the worldwide leader in innovation, attracting the best and the brightest from around the world to its universities and technology companies. Its currency is the worldwide reserve currency, and the country is considered an investment safe haven in times of world crisis. While New Atlantis has had its problems and economic cycles, the country has always found a way to bounce back, driven by the natural optimism and industry of its people.

Ruling this country requires wisdom and compassion. Does this sound like an impossible job? Hard maybe, with difficult decisions to be made for sure, but it certainly could be worse. All that really has to be done is make use of the country's natural advantages and make sure you don't screw it up.

If you have figured out that New Atlantis is in reality the United States, then congratulations, you are an astute individual and should read this book. If you did not realize that New Atlantis is in reality the United States, then you really *need* to read this book.

"Let's try common sense" was one of the key slogans in President Barack Obama's State of the Union address in January 2009. The Straight Talk Express was Senator John McCain's campaign bus during the 2008 presidential campaign. President Obama's 2013 State of the Union address included this:

> It is our unfinished task to restore the basic bargain that built this country—the idea that if you work hard and meet your responsibilities, you can get ahead, no matter where you come from, no matter what you look like, or who you love. It is our unfinished task to make sure that this government works on behalf of the many, and not just

> the few; that it encourages free enterprise, rewards individual initiative, and opens the doors of opportunity to every child across this great nation. The American people don't expect government to solve every problem. They don't expect those of us in this chamber to agree on every issue. But they do expect us to put the nation's interests before party. They do expect us to forge reasonable compromise where we can. For they know that America moves forward only when we do so together, and that the responsibility of improving this union remains the task of us all.

These are all noble concepts, but it seems clear to me that today's political discourse lacks both "straight talk" and "common sense," important concepts if we are to adequately address the important issues facing the nation today. The United States is the wealthiest nation in the history of the world, and yet we can't come close to balancing the national budget? The problems we face may be large, and the decisions to be made may be difficult, but are the solutions really that elusive? Can we not figure out how to do better with $5.8 trillion of total government spending in 2013 (federal, state, and local) in a $16.8 trillion economy? I would certainly hope so.

Depending on the selected meaning, a politician is "a person experienced in the art or science of government; *especially*: one actively engaged in conducting the business of a government" (*Merriam-Webster*), or "a seeker or holder of public office, who is more concerned about winning favor or retaining power than about maintaining principles" (Dictionary.com). I believe we need more of the former and less of the latter. I expect that for many politicians, both definitions apply to some extent. While I suppose that for many of them, perhaps even most, their motives may be honorable (or at least in their minds they think them honorable), it appears that by and large they end up representing special interest groups or just blowing in the political winds based on the latest public-opinion poll or party position rather than serving as principled representatives.

Perhaps it is the nature of the political system. Eventually, even the most idealistic politicians become jaded, start to fear losing the election rather than guiding the nation, start to pay heed to special interest groups rather than doing what is best for the country as a whole. I have always liked the few politicians who speak their minds and act in a manner consistent with their values, with a little pragmatism thrown in. At least then you know what you get, and hopefully that includes the ability to manage an organization as large and unwieldy as the federal government.

It seems to me that the only way to consistently act in this way is to not care if one wins or loses the next election. How many politicians act in this manner? Not many. No wonder an NBC News/*Wall Street Journal* poll conducted in July 2013 listed the approval ratings of the US Congress as low as 12 percent. A 12 percent approval rating? That is more than a little embarrassing. President Obama wasn't doing much better in late 2013. He claims he has a mandate from the American people to raise taxes on the "rich" because he won the 2012 election by a margin of 51 percent to 47 percent based on the popular vote. Yes, he won the election handily with 66 million votes, but does that mean he can ignore the views of the 61 million Americans who voted for the other guy? Is that margin of victory truly a mandate? I would think not, particularly when one considers that the Republicans retained control of the House of Representatives and that Mitt Romney easily carried those voters earning more than $50,000 a year in income, the group that pays more than 100 percent of all federal personal income taxes (sounds strange, but it's true), and the group who would be most affected by the President's tax-increase proposals. Now if President Obama had carried the segment of the population with incomes over $50,000, maybe that would have meant something mandatewise. And $50,000 is about the median household income in the United States, so it's not like we are talking only about rich people.

As in most national elections in the United States, the verdict is for some type of a middle-ground approach. Our elected leaders must push their party agendas, but they also need to recognize that they each have a responsibility to represent all Americans. And that goes for both sides of the aisle.

Full disclosure here, I must admit that I have a slight conservative/libertarian philosophical bent. I generally believe in personal responsibility, that less government is better government, that this country was founded based on a strong belief in individual freedoms as opposed to governmental control or intervention, and that people are most productive when left to their own ingenuity and energies. However, I also believe that the government has an obligation to set the rules of the game, to be the defender of the oppressed, and, given our national wealth, to provide some sort of a social safety net. I am, therefore, in favor of low taxes; I am also in favor of social services. Who isn't? To deny some of the benefits of government—our national defense, our schools, our parks, our highway system—would be ludicrous. To refuse to offer a helping hand to those truly in need seems heartless. Why not take some of our great productive wealth and use it for the benefit of society at large? Well, clearly we should, and we do. If all of our social programs came without any cost, why not continue to expand them? Of course we know (or we should know) that it doesn't work that way—that in some form or fashion, everything has a cost. And that is what makes it a challenge to balance conflicting goals. That is why we need both "straight talk" and "common sense."

Most politicians frame the debate is an either/or proposition. Either a dogmatic spread-the-wealth mentality without regard for rewarding our most productive citizens, or a cut-taxes-for-the-rich, trickle-down approach. That works great if you are a tax-and-spend liberal or a diehard supply-side conservative. But what about the rest of us citizens? What about the vast number of the independents, the silent majority, those of us who sit somewhere in the political middle trying to actually discern what is the right direction for this country to take? This book is for you, a primer for the independent thinker. Not many people personally want to pay higher taxes, and not many want a complete winner-take-all society either. I know many Democrats, and I know many Republicans. Their basic political philosophies may be different, but in many ways, they aren't really that far apart. They mostly agree that people deserve to keep the fruits of their efforts but also that everyone deserves equal opportunity. It's just a question of balance.

I also have to admit that I am a practical problem solver by nature, as in "let's see what can work for both of us." As you learn in life and in business, sometimes there is no deal, but a good business person knows when a deal can be had and how to get it done. Can we not find a solution that puts the federal government on solid financial footing?

This book deals with the national economy and the impact of government policy and spending. Here is the fundamental issue: The government spends more money than it receives in the form of taxes—currently much more and at a rate that is not sustainable. The United States needs to either raise taxes, cut spending, or both. This is a fact. How to increase taxes and on whom, and where to cut spending and affecting whom, is open for debate. But as I argue in the next chapter, the longer we wait, the harder it gets. Once we accept that something needs to be done, the next question is what. Most of the rest of the book deals with that issue, both in a practical and in a philosophical sense. And despite the continual deadlock in Washington, there is plenty of room for compromise. It isn't even all that hard.

Most of the information and proposals presented in this book are not novel ideas. In fact, I would say that there is nothing new here, just an application of common sense to well-known facts and concepts. I have borrowed many ideas from people much smarter than I. In particular, I have drawn from leading economic thinkers and philosophers throughout history, such as Adam Smith, F. A. Hayek, Ludwig von Mises, Joseph Schumpeter, John Maynard Keynes, Milton Friedman, Robert Heilbroner, and John Kenneth Galbraith, among many others. Maybe you can tell that this list includes both liberal and conservative economists. They are certainly all very smart individuals. In every case, I have attempted to give credit where credit is due. This is not always easy, as, let's face it, good ideas are frequently repeated, knowingly or unknowingly. I am particularly impressed by just how much Adam Smith's writings have stood the test of time and how many of his basic concepts continue to form the basis of our economic system today. I'll spend some more time discussing Adam Smith in Chapter 2, but if you have the time and can manage the 1700s language and writing style, I highly recommend that you read *The Wealth of Nations.*

In addition, I was surprised with just how much data and economic analysis is readily available. From the Department of Labor, to the Department of Commerce, to the US Census Bureau, to the Federal Reserve, there is almost no facet of the US economy that is not tracked in detail. In addition, the Congressional Budget Office publishes numerous "what if" studies detailing the projected impact of alternative policies on the economy and the federal budget. While one can always argue over the details, these studies are generally well thought out, and, I daresay, are literally "close enough for government work." And when we are talking about trillions of dollars, maybe that is all we need. When it comes to fixing the budget, all of the hard analytical work is already done. All we need to do is make the sometimes tough decisions. Honestly, students in a high school social studies class could probably hammer out a balanced budget in a day—and quicker if they were allowed to leave school early when done.

When I first started working on this project, I was a little more worried about the economy and the fiscal position of the United States. Things certainly looked bleak in 2008 and 2009. But as I pushed forward, I became more upbeat, perhaps reflecting the improving economy and national mood. But more than that, the problems began to seem solvable—if the politicians would, in the words of a Keenan Thompson character on *Saturday Night Live* during the height of the financial crisis, "Just fix it!"

As I approach this book, I have two main goals: First, try to keep it simple and to the point. This may be difficult as we deal in national economic issues, but I'll do the best I can. Out of necessity, I do refer to many numbers in order to make a point, but hopefully you, the reader, are not overwhelmed. As former New York mayor Michael Bloomberg has been quoted, "In God we trust. Everyone else, bring data." Numbers overload can be a particular problem with all of the intricacies of the federal budget and deficit. Until very recently, the latest deficits have been hovering at about $1 trillion per year (fiscal years 2009–2012), if you call the $1.4 trillion deficit in 2009 hovering. A trillion dollars here and a trillion dollars there, and pretty soon you are talking about real money. By the way, if you spent $1 million a day, every day, it would take you 2,740 years to spend $1 trillion. Of course if you were able to spend $100 million every day, you could spend $1 trillion in a little over 27 years, so maybe that is more doable.

And second, I will try to provide you with the basic facts so you can come to your own conclusions. At the end, you may disagree with my conclusions, but hopefully you won't disagree with the facts. At least then, we can have a reasonable debate.

Am I qualified to opine on the direction this county is taking? Who is…and who isn't? When the "experts" can't agree, we are left to make up our own minds. When the politicians distort the facts to promote their own agendas, we are left to sift through the informational muck to make up our own minds. That is the nature of democracy, and that is our burden as citizens. I certainly am not a budget expert. Although I have studied the field of economics, I am not an economist. Although I have worked in the field of finance and investment management for twenty-five years, I am not a financial-markets expert. Although I follow politics, I am not a politician. In fact, I don't like politics. What I am is a concerned citizen. And you should be too.

CHAPTER 1

Washington, We Have a Problem

"How did you go bankrupt?" Bill asked.
"Two ways," Mike said. "Gradually and then suddenly."

ERNEST HEMMINGWAY, *THE SUN ALSO RISES*

HERE IS SOME NOT-SO-BREAKING NEWS: the federal government spends much more than it receives in the form of taxes and other revenues. A series of tax cuts enacted in 2001 and 2003, the funding of two foreign wars, continued growth in entitlement spending, and the severe economic downturn in 2008 have taken the federal budget from a surplus in fiscal 2001 to a position of consistent deficits that persist today. The US government ran a budget deficit in excess of $1 trillion for the four straight years of fiscal 2009–2012, ranging from about 7 percent to 10 percent of the gross domestic product (GDP) in each year. (I frequently express government revenues, government expenditures, the federal deficit, and debt levels as percentages of GDP; this is the most relevant fiscal measure since it considers these items as shares of the overall economy.) The last time the United States ran federal budget deficits this big as a share of GDP was during World War II. And, while certainly not as extreme, the deficits are continuing. By the end of fiscal 2014, federal debt held by the public was about two and one-half times the level at the end of fiscal 2007, meaning that more federal debt has been incurred over the past seven years than was accumulated over the entire prior history of the United States, plus an extra $2.5 trillion for good measure. That is a pretty amazing "accomplishment."

And the future is not all that much brighter. All credible forecasts project continued large deficits unless something is done. And yet, very little is done. The December 2010 recommendations of the President's National Commission on Fiscal Responsibility and Reform have largely been ignored in Washington. The federal debt ceiling was raised in August 2011 without a credible plan to deal with the budget. The bipartisan "super committee" established by the Budget Control Act of 2011 failed to reach agreement on a plan to cut projected deficits by $1.2 trillion ($120 billion per year over ten years), which ushered in the "sequester" in 2013, leading to across-the-board spending cuts of approximately $85 billion per year, affecting most discretionary spending categories. So the problem continues to grow. And as a result, the United States has had its debt rating lowered by Standard & Poor's and put on negative outlook by Moody's. The United States is quite literally no longer a triple-A-rated country.

One could argue (as I will) that at least the American Taxpayer Relief Act of 2012 (ATRA) was a step in the right direction, expected to generate approximately $600 billion in new tax revenue over the next ten years compared to the tax rates in effect in 2012. While the ATRA raised taxes, it is called a "taxpayer relief act" because it reduces tax rates from what they would have been if all of the prior tax cuts had been allowed to expire as required under prior laws. Maybe that is a little confusing, but for the moment let's just go with the fact that the American Taxpayer Relief Act increased taxes from the 2012 level.

Which brings us to the question, do federal-government deficits even matter? This is not as straightforward a question as it may seem to those of us trying to manage a household budget. After all, despite the worsened budget outlook and the ratings downgrade, the United States has been able to issue new ten-year debt at an annual interest rate of less than 3 percent. Former Vice President Dick Cheney is reported to have told former Treasury Secretary Paul O'Neil, "You know, Paul, Reagan proved that deficits don't matter." And to some extent, he is correct. That is because, far from overloading our children and grandchildren with burdensome debt, a modest and sustainable public debt need never be repaid. The United States has had a national debt since its founding in 1791, although for a period in the 1830s, the debt was essentially reduced to zero. Much as a profitable corporation can carry debt indefinitely, so can an economically vibrant country such as the United States. To make the debt level sustainable, the lenders need to have faith in the borrower and believe that, theoretically, the borrower *could* pay back the debt if required. However, as securities firms (Lehman Brothers and Bear Stearns), banks (Citibank prior to the TARP bailout and Indy Mac), and many countries (Iceland, Ireland, Greece, and Spain) have recently demonstrated, once this confidence is lost, the results can be sudden and disastrous. The key is to never test the level where 100 percent confidence begins to waver. Where is that level? No one knows for sure, but as a country, we are certainly much closer than we were in 2007.

What level of national debt is sustainable? A common convention is that national governments can handle an annual deficit of 3 percent of GDP and a total debt load equal to 60 percent of GDP. In fact, these targeted levels are in the Maastricht Treaty as a requirement in order to join the European Union, although many European Union countries have failed to meet this requirement in recent years. The simple reason for this convention is that, with an annual deficit of 3 percent of GDP and total national-government debt equal to or less than 60 percent of GDP, the total national debt as a percent of GDP would tend to remain stable over an extended period of time. See the example that follows if you want to review the math

---

Assume a country has total national-government debt of $600 billion and that GDP is $1 trillion (total debt equals 60 percent of GDP). Assume further that the annual deficit equals 3 percent of GDP or $30 billion. As a result, total debt would grow by $30 billion during the year to $630 billion. If nominal GDP grows by 5 percent (a plausible assumption if, say, inflation is running at 2 to 3 percent and real growth is 2 percent), then total GDP now equals $1,050 billion, and total debt of $630 billion continues to represent 60 percent of GDP. Theoretically, this could go on forever, with total debt at a stable 60 percent of GDP. The debt never actually gets paid back, but neither does it get out of hand.

Further, assume that the average interest rate on the public debt is 5 percent (again, a reasonable assumption assuming inflation is running at 2–3 percent, although government rates in the United States and in much of the rest of the world are much lower now). Then the interest cost on the government debt is $30 billion (5 percent times the assumed $600 billion of total debt). This is exactly equal to 3 percent of our hypothetical GDP of $1 trillion. Therefore, in this scenario, if the government is running a 3 percent annual deficit, the entire amount of the deficit is equal to the interest on the national debt. In this case, the government would be said to have a budget that is in *primary balance.* Total revenues would equal total expenses, *excluding* the interest on the debt. Basically, while the total debt would be increasing because of the interest cost on the debt, at least the government is not adding to the problem by running an operating deficit. Again, while the total amount of the debt would be increasing, it would remain constant as a percent of GDP so long as the interest rate on the debt were the same as the rate of growth of nominal GDP, and thus the debt would generally be sustainable over an extended period of time. This is true no matter what the current level of the debt. If the budget is in primary balance and the rate of growth of GDP is at least as great as the rate of interest on the public debt, then debt will not be increasing as a percent of GDP. So far, so good.

Of course, things never work out quite so smoothly. Wars break out. Recessions occur, resulting in reduced GDP, lower tax revenues, and increased government spending, and thus a bigger deficit. This is in fact the case we have faced over the past seven years or so. And if, for example, the rate of interest on the debt is more than the growth of GDP, or if the budget is in primary deficit, then debt can easily get out of hand. For example, suppose that total national debt equals 100 percent of GDP, the budget has a *primary* deficit equal to 3 percent of GDP, the interest rate on the debt is 5 percent, and the rate of growth in nominal GDP equals 2 percent. In this hypothetical example, total national debt after ten years would grow to more than 165 percent of GDP. As we can see, the problem can snowball quickly if not addressed early.

While an acceptable guideline of total public debt of 60 percent of GDP and an annual deficit of 3 percent of GDP seems reasonable, this is not a hard-and-fast rule that either guarantees stability or predicts immediate disaster at higher deficit or debt levels. According to work done by Carmen M. Reinhart and Kenneth S. Rogoff in their book, *This Time Is Different*, "Ultimately, default often occurs at levels of debt well below the 60 percent ratio of debt to GDP enshrined in Europe's Maastricht Treaty, a clause intended to protect the euro system from government defaults." Conversely, governments sometimes exceed these debt levels with no apparent adverse impact. For example, Japan had a budget deficit in excess of 8 percent of GDP in 2011 and had total public debt of about 200 percent of GDP in 2010, and yet Japan continues to be able to issue ten-year bonds at interest rates of less than 1 percent. This is despite ratings of AA- from Standard & Poor's and Aa2 from Moody's (the fourth-highest rating and the third-highest rating, respectively).

On the other hand, recent events in Europe can demonstrate just how quickly an apparently stable situation can change. Italy has had public debt in excess of 100 percent of GDP for a number of years with no discernible adverse effect—until late 2011, that is, when rates on Italian government debt reached 7 percent and spreads over German debt widened precipitously within a couple of months. This is despite the fact that the estimated 2011 budget deficit for Italy was only 3.7 percent of GDP, compared to a budget deficit of 9 percent of GDP for the United States. Greece has also had total debt of greater than 100 percent of GDP for a number of years. The budget deficit was 5.6 percent of GDP in 2005 but in 2010 increased to 10.5 percent of GDP. Greece has already required numerous bailouts, and its ten-year bonds were yielding almost 30 percent at one point in 2011. Even Spain, which had total government debt of less than 50 percent of GDP prior to the financial crisis, saw its public finances collapse, with the deficit climbing to 9.4 percent of GDP in 2010 and government bond yields climbing drastically. In 2011, the unemployment rate reached 21.6 percent in Spain and 17.7 percent in Greece.

As Hemingway rightly pointed out, bankruptcy occurs gradually at first—and then suddenly.

So what is the situation in the United States? Well, better than during the depths of the recent recession but still not great. Gross federal debt at the end of fiscal 2014 was approximately $17.8 trillion, or about 103 percent of GDP. A more relevant measure, total debt held by the public (which excludes federal debt held by the government itself), was at $12.8 trillion, or about 74 percent of GDP at the end of fiscal 2014. This is the highest level of debt held by the public relative to GDP since 1950 and more than double where it stood as recently as 2007. The chart below shows total debt held by the public as a percentage of GDP since 1940. As the chart indicates, since 1953, debt held by the public was below 60 percent of GDP until it surged past that level in 2010. Debt held by the public excludes debt held by federal-government accounts (primarily the social security "trust fund") since that represents federal debt held by the federal government itself. Debt held by federal accounts at the end of fiscal 2014 was approximately $5 trillion, or approximately 29 percent of GDP.

Most economists look at debt held by the public as the more meaningful federal debt figure since that represents the "net" debt level of the government, and I tend to agree that this is the best measure. Of course, the flip side of this position is that the federal debt held by government accounts, including the social security trust fund, doesn't consist of actual financial assets that could be sold for cash in order to meet obligations; these accounts effectively hold, rather, internal IOUs with no real tangible value. In a way, the $5 trillion of federal debt held by federal-government accounts represents future liabilities of the government that will need to be financed with future taxes or additional debt held by the public. So I agree that we should leave that debt off the liability side of the ledger, but then we need to exclude it from the asset side of the ledger as well; unfortunately, one can't have it both ways.

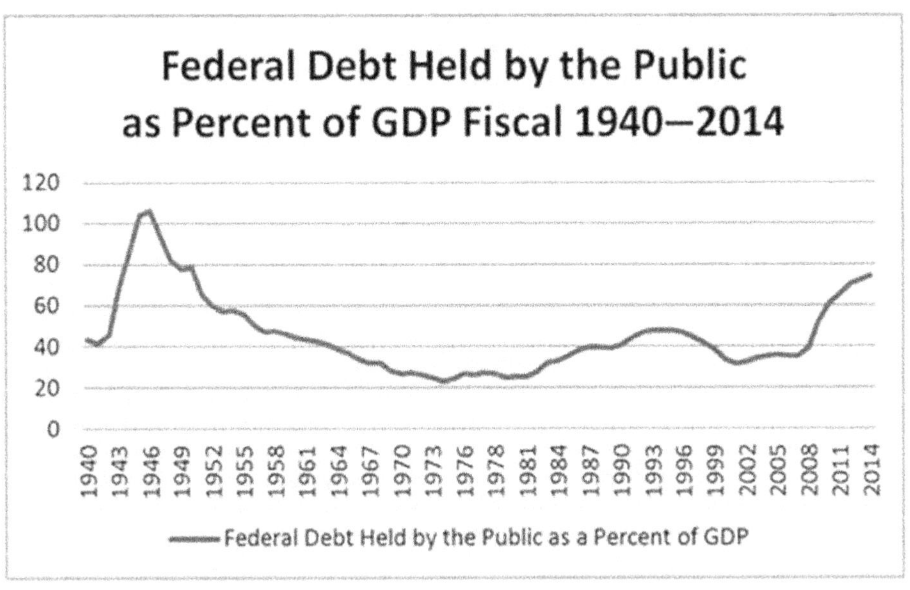

In addition to the reported federal debt, the United States is on the hook for additional liabilities related to commitments, guarantees, and social-insurance promises. Some of these liabilities actually show up on the US government balance sheet. For example, as of September 30, 2014, the federal government had $7.9 trillion of liabilities on its balance sheet in addition to the $12.8 trillion of government debt. By far the largest category is $6.7 trillion (yes, trillion) in federal employee and veteran benefits payable. This is primarily the present value of future pensions, retiree health care, and other benefits for civilian and military federal-government personnel—basically unfunded pension and retiree medical obligations of the federal government. Other liabilities on the balance sheet include environmental and disposal liabilities, insurance and guarantee liabilities, loan-guarantee liabilities and liabilities to government-sponsored enterprises (the mortgage companies Fannie Mae and Freddie Mac). By the way, the balance sheet of the US government as of September 2014 shows total assets of $3.1 trillion and total liabilities of $20.8 trillion, for a *negative* net worth of $17.7 trillion.

In addition, the federal government has a number of liabilities that do not appear on the balance sheet. Not surprisingly, these are referred to as "off-balance-sheet" obligations. By far the largest of these are the promises the federal government has made for social security, Medicare, and similar programs. The government estimates that the present value obligations (over a seventy-five-year projection period) for social insurance for the "closed group" (generally, current participants, assumed to be at least fifteen or eighteen years of age) as of September 2014 to be a staggering $56.7 trillion. This, by the way, is the *net* obligation, after accounting for all future projected tax contributions. This "closed" group is essentially all of the people who are currently receiving benefits or paying into the social security system. Including future participants (those not yet working, or even born, for that matter) appears to help the numbers somewhat because many of these future participants will be paying the required social security and Medicare payroll taxes, but they will not have received much in the way of benefits over the seventy-five-year forecast period. (They will, however, *after* the seventy-five-year projection period.) However, even including these future participants, the net present value obligation over the next seventy-five years is still $41.9 trillion. That is a future liability of the federal government that will have to be met by higher taxes since the current tax rates are already included in the calculation.

Other off-balance-sheet liabilities include outstanding loan guarantees as of September 30, 2014, totaling $1.8 trillion, primarily related to housing programs (such as FHA-HUD) and education loans. The government has additional exposure to housing through its program to backstop the liabilities of Fannie Mae and Freddie Mac; although the expected liability is on the balance sheet, the potential exposure is much larger. This is also true of the Pension Benefit Guaranty Corporation and the various deposit insurance funds as well. For example, while the government reports a liability of $13.2 billion for the Federal Deposit Insurance Corporation funds, the FDIC had estimated insured deposits of $6.2 trillion. So the potential liability is much larger than the recorded liability. Is your mind a little numb now? Don't worry, it should be. The point is that the *known* future liabilities are huge, and the *potential* liabilities are even huger (best word available).

So in total, the federal government on September 30, 2014, had $12.8 trillion of debt held by the public, $7.9 trillion of other on-balance liabilities, and perhaps $55 trillion of various off-balance-sheet liabilities (a bit of a guestimate). The total liability, as a percent of GDP, comes in at about 450 percent of GDP. That is more than a little scary.

So that is the current situation. Not too reassuring. The annual deficit for 2014 was about 2.8 percent of GDP, an improvement from the 2013 deficit of 4.1 percent of GDP and much better than it had been in the prior five years. We should take some encouragement from this improvement, but we are not out of the woods yet, due to the fact that federal debt levels are excessive and budget trends are against us. Over the longer term, things get a little murky depending on what assumptions one wants to make. The CBO's long-term budget outlook (June 2015) shows the annual deficit declining to 2.4 percent of GDP in fiscal 2017 and then gradually increasing to 3.8 percent of GDP in 2022, with debt as a percent of GDP reaching 78 percent in 2025.

Not great but maybe not too bad. Problem solved? Unfortunately, that is not the case, as these projections are based on current law, which, among other things, includes the automatic spending reductions implemented at the beginning of March 2013, as well as certain policies that have been routinely amended in the past. In addition, even under relatively rosy assumptions, the budget deficit grows over a longer-term forecast period as spending on health care and social security increases with the aging population.

I use analysis from the Congressional Budget Office for much of the budget information and projections referenced in this book because I have found it to be reasoned and well thought out. Presumably, the members of the Congress and the White House also review their analysis. The following is from the CBO website:

> Since its founding in 1974, the Congressional Budget Office (CBO) has produced independent analyses of budgetary and economic issues

to support the Congressional budget process. The agency is strictly nonpartisan and conducts objective, impartial analysis, which is evident in each of the dozens of reports and hundreds of cost estimates that its economists and policy analysts produce each year. All CBO employees are appointed solely on the basis of professional competence, without regard to political affiliation. CBO does not make policy recommendations, and each report and cost estimate discloses the agency's assumptions and methodologies. All of CBO's products apart from informal cost estimates for legislation being developed privately by Members of Congress or their staffs are available to the Congress and the public on CBO's website.

CBO provides the Congress with budget projections that go beyond the standard 10-year budget window. Those projections typically span 25 years but can extend as far as 75 years into the future. The projections show the impact of long-term demographic trends and rising health care costs on federal spending, revenues, and deficits. CBO also projects the economic impact of alternative long-term budget policies.

Unfortunately, the CBO's long-term analysis of the deficit and federal debt projects a worsening of the fiscal balance. In June 2015, the CBO projected that by 2040, the deficit would reach 5.9 percent of GDP and that debt held by the public would reach 103 percent of GDP—hardly reassuring levels, considering that the CBO long-term forecasts do not include any economic recessions or other unforeseen unfortunate events. Even under this baseline scenario, federal spending would increase to 25.3 percent of GDP by 2040, compared with 20.5 percent in 2014 and an average of 20 percent of GDP over the past fifty years. The dramatically deteriorating fiscal situation results entirely from increased spending on social security and the government's major health-care programs, as well as an assumed increase in interest rates from today's unusually low levels, which results in higher interest expenditures on the federal debt.

In addition to the baseline case, the CBO considers an "extended alternative fiscal scenario" (which includes the continuation of certain government policies that have routinely been continued in the past), in which case total debt held by the public would hit 156 percent of GDP by 2040. According to the CBO, the extended alternative fiscal scenario "incorporates the assumptions that certain policies that have been in place for a number of years will be continued, that some provisions of law that might be difficult to sustain for a long period will be modified, and that federal revenues and certain categories of federal spending will be maintained at or near their historical shares of GDP." With that in mind, "The scenario, therefore, captures what some analysts might consider to be current *policies* as opposed to current *laws*."

The actual specifics can be a little confusing to the non–budget expert, but the extended alternative fiscal scenario is at least an attempt to illustrate how federal finance would react if the United States were to continue with its current overall tax and spending policies. And the end result is that with total debt held by the public at more than 150 percent of GDP in 2040, the United States would be more indebted than Ireland, Iceland, Greece, Spain, Italy, and just about every other nation (with the notable exception of Japan, which is kind of a special case).

From 2040 on, things really get dicey. The CBO extends their revenue and outlay forecast out to 2090. In the extended alternative fiscal scenario, the annual primary deficit (the deficit before interest costs) reaches 11.6 percent of GDP in 2090. The CBO does us a favor by not presenting the total debt level or interest on the federal debt once the debt reaches more than 250 percent of GDP in 2055, but suffice it to say, it wouldn't be good (debt to the public possibly close to 600 percent of GDP by 2090). Obviously, this can never happen since the United States would have defaulted long before debt reached this level, but the trends are illustrative nevertheless.

Just for fun, here is a graph using the actual data from 1988 through 2014, the CBO extended alternative fiscal scenario from 2015 through 2054, and a combination of the CBO projection together with my debt extrapolation through 2090.

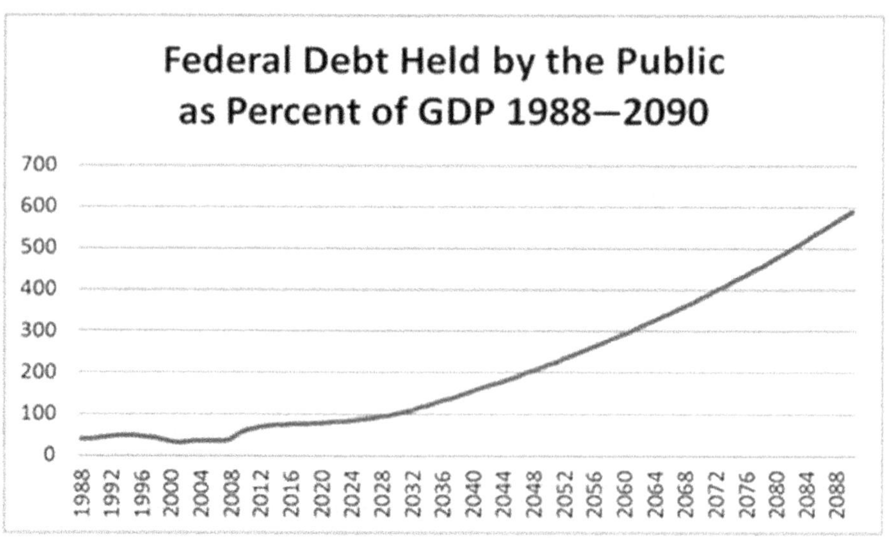

Source: CBO Extended Alternative Fiscal Scenario through 2054, with my debt calculations thereafter.

I have thrown a lot of numbers at you, and future projections, by their nature, are always subject to wide variations depending on economic performance and policy changes, which are not easy to predict. However, this much is certain: we are already at or near the maximum prudent level of federal-government debt. In addition, the US government has made social welfare promises to its citizens that *guarantee* that the federal debt will increase in future years if other tax and spending policies are unchanged. And there is no world economy large enough to bail out the United States. Economically speaking, if we go down, the world goes down. True, the United States does have one huge advantage that is not available to many other debtor nations in that the United States borrows in its own currency. As such, the United States can "print" money as a way to reduce the debt burden. The government doesn't have to acquire gold or euros, yen, or yuan to repay our debts held by China or Japan, for example (they each hold over $1 trillion of US federal debt as of December 2013). Just print up a bunch of $100 bills and send them over. Or better yet, send over a $1 trillion coin, which was proposed by some as a way to avoid the debt ceiling in 2011 (plus a number of $100 bills to come up with the exact amount, or even better, send over two coins and ask for change back). I recognize that it wouldn't actually work this way (transfer of physical currency), but the effect would largely be the same. The United States, presumably, would actually never default but would have a de facto default as the creditor claims are largely inflated away through the creation of more money. So I close this chapter with this from Adam Smith:

> When national debts have once been accumulated to a certain degree, there is scarce, I believe, a single instance of their having been fairly and completely paid. The liberation of the public revenue, if it has ever been brought about at all, has always been brought about by a bankruptcy; sometimes by an avowed one, but always by a real one, though frequently by a pretended payment. The raising of the denomination of the coin has been the most usual expedient by which a real public bankruptcy has been disguised under the appearance of a pretended payment. (Adam Smith, *The Wealth of Nations*, 1776)

Obviously, a de facto default would not be a good thing either. The point is that the fiscal soundness of the United States is a serious matter. Financial crises always seem to crop up at inconvenient times, so let's address the problem now. A little long-term planning never hurt anyone.

CHAPTER 2

The Power of Freedom

With all these blessings, what more is necessary to make us a happy and prosperous people? Still one thing more, fellow-citizens—a wise and frugal government, which shall restrain men from injuring one another, shall leave them otherwise free to regulate their own pursuits of industry and improvement, and shall not take from the mouth of labor the bread it has earned. This is the sum of good government, and this is necessary to close the circle of our felicities.

Thomas Jefferson in his first inaugural address, March 4, 1801

According to the system of natural liberty, the sovereign has only three duties to attend to; three duties of great importance, indeed, but plain and intelligible to common understandings; first, the duty of protecting the society from the violence and invasion of other independent societies; secondly, the duty of protecting, as far as possible, every member of the society from the injustice or oppression of every other member of it, or the duty of establishing an exact administration of justice; and, thirdly, the duty of erecting and maintaining certain public works and certain public institutions, which it can never be for the interest of any individual, or small number of individuals, to erect and maintain.

Adam Smith, *The Wealth of Nations*, 1776

The previous chapter explored the current fiscal crisis facing the United States. Some might argue whether we are actually in a "crisis," so let's call it a debt "problem" in the sense that we are currently in a fiscal position at or worse than the level that is generally acceptable as a sustainable debt and deficit level. Eventually, the hard choices will have to be made, and something will have to be done.

Now here's the good news. Sometimes we forget just how many advantages we have as a nation and just how rich we are in a relative and historical context. Literally, we've never had it this good. The US economy is the largest in the world, accounting for nearly 25 percent of world production in 2013. By contrast, the United States has less than 5 percent of the world's population. We are certainly producing and consuming more than our fair share of global output. As of 2012, the US economy was still about twice as large as the next-largest economy, China, and over 2.5 times as large as the third-largest economy, Japan. And China has a population more than four times larger than that of the United States. Of course, in 2009, the US economy was almost three times as large as China's, so the gap is narrowing. The European Union, taken as a whole (twenty-seven member countries), has an economy slightly larger than that of the United States, although maybe that won't last for too much longer since the United States has a higher overall growth rate. Despite all of our hand-wringing, the United States is still the world's economic superpower.

What accounts for the economic success of the United States? A number of factors to be sure, but the fundamental dynamic foundation of the Unites States is our combination of political freedom and economic freedom. This has not been the defining characteristic of most of the world's civilizations throughout history, having been something that has largely developed over the past three hundred to four hundred years. For our purposes, conveniently, 1776 is a great place to start this discussion, for that is the year the Declaration of Independence and Adam Smith's classic *An Inquiry into the Nature and Causes of the Wealth of Nations* were penned. While the Declaration of Independence set forth the concept of our political freedom, *The Wealth of Nations* espoused the concept of economic freedom. The two are inextricably linked and might be referred to as the "system of natural liberty." How novel (at the time) and yet how logical—a philosophy that allows people to conduct their personal and economic lives as they see fit.

A recent book by Daron Acemoglu and James A. Robinson, *Why Nations Fail*, examined many nations across the world throughout history and found this:

> Inclusive economic institutions that enforce property rights, create a level playing field, and encourage investments in new technologies and skills are more conducive to economic growth than extractive economic institutions that are structured to extract resources from the many by the few and that fail to protect property rights or provide incentives for economic activity. Inclusive economic institutions are in turn supported by, and support, inclusive political institutions, that is, those that distribute political power widely in a pluralistic manner and are able to achieve some amount of political centralization so as to establish law and order, the foundations of secure property rights, and an inclusive market economy.

If you want an excellent example of this, just look at the marked contrast between the relative economic success (and democratic political system) of South Korea and the economic destitution (and familial dictatorship) of North Korea.

Political Freedom

In general, Americans cherish our political freedom and have proper appreciation for the principles guiding the founding of the United States, beginning in 1776 with the Declaration of Independence. Most of the Declaration of Independence is a listing of the grievances of the colonies against the king of England, a justification for declaring independence. However, the most powerful passage, which we all know but frequently bears repeating (and so I repeat it here), is as follows:

> We hold these truths to be self-evident, that all men are created equal, that they are endowed by their Creator with certain unalienable rights, that among these are Life, Liberty and the pursuit of Happiness. That to secure these rights, Governments are instituted

> among Men, deriving their just powers from the consent of the governed.

These are powerful words indeed—and revolutionary in a time when almost all of the "civilized" world lived under some form of a hereditary system of government. (It's hard to believe, but many countries still do today.) The words speak for themselves, but to me two general themes are clear: the belief in individual rights (and opportunity) and in a system of government that derives its legitimacy from the consent of the governed. I didn't invent the concepts, but they sure work for me.

Once the Revolutionary War was over and the states got to work on devising a system of government, the Constitutional Convention drafted in 1787 the Constitution of the United States of America, which was eventually ratified by all of the states, together with the Bill of Rights, in 1791. This event was, I would think, fairly unique in world history up to that time—a system of national government created essentially by and with "the consent of the governed."

And what is this federal government created by the original states? The preamble to the Constitution states the following:

> We the people of the United States, in Order to form a more perfect Union, establish Justice, insure domestic Tranquility, provide for the common defense, promote the general Welfare, and secure the Blessings of Liberty to ourselves and Posterity, do ordain and establish this Constitution for the United States of America.

The Bill of Rights comprises the first ten amendments to the Constitution and shows the deep concern of the people toward an abuse of governmental power. We are most familiar with the First Amendment right of freedom of religion, speech, press and assembly, but all of the amendments deal with the rights of individuals versus the state.

> **First Amendment: Freedom of Religion, Press, Expression.** Congress shall make no law respecting an establishment of religion,

or prohibiting the free exercise thereof; or abridging the freedom of speech, or of the press; or the right of the people peaceably to assemble, and to petition the government for a redress of grievances.

Second Amendment: Right to Bear Arms. A well regulated Militia, being necessary to the security of a free State, the right of the people to keep and bear Arms, shall not be infringed.

Third Amendment: Quartering of Soldiers. No Soldier shall, in time of peace be quartered in any house, without the consent of the Owner, nor in time of war, but in a manner to be prescribed by law.

Fourth Amendment: Search and Seizure. The right of the people to be secure in their persons, houses, papers, and effects, against unreasonable searches and seizures, shall not be violated, and no Warrants shall issue, but upon probable cause, supported by Oath or affirmation, and particularly describing the place to be searched, and the persons or things to be seized.

Fifth Amendment: Trial and Punishment, Compensation for Takings. No person shall be held to answer for a capital, or otherwise infamous crime, unless on a presentment or indictment of a Grand Jury, except in cases arising in the land or naval forces, or in the Militia, when in actual service in time of War or public danger; nor shall any person be subject for the same offense to be twice put in jeopardy of life or limb; nor shall be compelled in any criminal case to be a witness against himself, nor be deprived of life, liberty, or property, without due process of law; nor shall private property be taken for public use, without just compensation.

Sixth Amendment: Right to Speedy Trial, Confrontation of Witnesses. In all criminal prosecutions, the accused shall enjoy the right to a speedy and public trial, by an impartial jury of the State and district wherein the crime shall have been committed, which district shall have been previously ascertained by law, and to be informed of the nature and cause of the accusation; to be confronted with the witnesses against him; to have compulsory process for obtaining witnesses in his favor, and to have the Assistance of Counsel for his defense.

Seventh Amendment: Trial by Jury in Civil Cases. In suits at common law, where the value in controversy shall exceed twenty dollars, the right of trial jury shall be preserved, and no fact tried by a jury, shall be otherwise re-examined in any Court of the United States, than according to the rules of the common law.

Eighth Amendment: Cruel and Unusual Punishment. Excessive bail shall not be required, nor excessive fines imposed, nor cruel and unusual punishments inflicted.

Ninth Amendment: Construction of Constitution. The enumeration in the Constitution of certain rights, shall not be construed to deny or disparage others retained by the people.

Tenth Amendment: Powers of the States and People. The powers not delegated to the United States by the Constitution, nor prohibited by it to the States, are reserved to the States, respectively, or to the people.

All told, the original Constitution, which lays out our system of federal government, is comprised of 4,543 words (excluding amendments). It is the shortest and oldest national constitution in use in the world today. For that, as a nation, we should be proud. The current IRS code has nearly four million words; the Affordable Care Act, popularly known as Obamacare, has 974 pages. Obviously, our government has gotten a little unwieldy over the years, but by and large, the basic philosophy espoused in our founding documents remains today.

These are the principles upon which our government was founded. Are these principles worth sustaining? I believe so. This was not a system of government thrust upon the citizenry by a king, an emperor, or some other form of a dictator. This is a system of government devised by a representative body, designed to limit governmental power and abuse, designed to protect individual rights and opportunity. It is not a static government either, the Constitution having been amended twenty-seven times, most recently in 1992.

Most of us are descendants of people who immigrated to the United States specifically for these political freedoms and for the freedom of economic opportunity. Our ancestors came, we stayed, and, in general, we prospered. Recognizing that there are certain exceptions, we have all more or less bought into this concept of individual freedom and opportunity, and most Americans still believe this. For example, a 2012 poll conducted by the Pew Research Center found that roughly two-thirds of Americans believe that hard work still pays off. We desperately need to maintain and broaden that mindset. And to this day, the appeal of the United States as a destination for those seeking political freedom or economic opportunity remains as strong as ever. There is a reason we have approximately ten million illegal immigrants living in the United States today (or, as they are called officially, "undocumented residents"), and that is primarily that these people want to be participants in the American dream. I daresay most undocumented residents would gladly become US citizens if given the opportunity. They believe in the hope of the United States of America. And so should we.

Economic Freedom

At the same time that the colonies were fighting for political independence, a seminal work was released in England in 1776, when Adam Smith published *An Inquiry into the Nature and Causes of the Wealth of Nations.*

Adam Smith was a fairly well-known professor and moral philosopher in England. He is also generally credited as being the father of capitalism. This is not to say that he is the father of capitalism in the same sense as George Washington is called the father of our country. Adam Smith had no active role in the development of capitalism. He was not a businessman, a financier, or a trader. He was a very astute philosopher and observer of the world about him, not just in his current time, but as a student of history. What he observed was that society benefits when its members act in their own economic self-interests. "It is not from the benevolence of the butcher, the brewer, or the baker, that we expect our dinner, but from their regard to their own interest."

He fervently believed in free markets and that any restraint to the free market—whether in the form of monopolies, cartels, political inequalities, or restraint of labor or of free trade among nations—would reduce production and hence the benefits to society. He recognized that all the factors of production were valuable (labor, stock, and rent) and that each would naturally earn a portion of the return from the value created. Far from being a mercantilist, or one who believed in the accumulation of gold as a measure of wealth, Smith believed that the point of production was to maximize consumption. "Consumption is the sole end and purpose of all production; and the interest of the producer ought to be attended to, only so far as it may be necessary for promoting that of the consumer. The maxim is so perfectly self-evident, that it would be absurd to attempt to prove it." As the economist Robert Heilbroner states in his classic book *The Worldly Philosophers*:

> Nonetheless, this is a democratic, and hence radical, philosophy of wealth. Gone is the notion of gold, treasures, kingly hoards; gone the prerogatives of merchants or farmers or working guilds. We are in the modern world, where the flow of goods and services consumed by everyone constitutes the ultimate aim and end of economic life.

Adam Smith also observed the dramatically increased production to be had from the division of labor into its component parts. He used pin production as his example, but another example is the simple pencil, which is the subject of a 1954 essay by Leonard E. Read, "I, Pencil." I have included that essay in the appendix at the end of this book. It is an excellent read.

Adam Smith also believed that economic society under this system would continue to progress—that as additional capital was accumulated, additional labor productivity would ensue, and production, and thus consumption, would grow. Tying all of this together would, of course, be the famous "invisible hand" of competition—that if, for example, the people desired more gloves, prices of gloves would increase, leading to increased profits for the glove manufacturers. This would, in turn, lead the glove manufacturers to increase production to maximize profits, or would induce other entrepreneurs to enter the glove business, thus leading to the increased production needed to meet the increased demand. This is what makes the capitalist system so efficient; the market takes care of itself. What is necessary to make all this work is a lack of monopolistic practices, such as actual monopoly, collusion among producers, or government policies that restrain free trade.

What is remarkable is that, writing over two hundred years ago, Adam Smith has been proven so right, even more so than he could have possibly imagined. In Adam Smith's time, subsistence living was the norm in most parts of the world, including in Europe. As he wrote, "It is not uncommon, I have frequently been told, in the Highlands of Scotland for a mother who has borne twenty children not to have two alive." In fact, his theory of wages and the demand for labor was based on subsistence wages as the normal compensation for unskilled labor. Any lower and (by definition, I guess) the available labor would decline; any higher and the supply of labor would increase as infant mortality declined and life spans increased, thus depressing wages to a subsistence level. He recognized that continued economic growth would be necessary for continued wage growth.

Although prescient in many ways, Adam Smith underestimated just how powerful capitalism would become as an engine of progress. The amount of wealth in the western world is truly staggering when looked at from a historical perspective. Yes, there is poverty. However, the quality of life for the vast majority of Americans, while perhaps not opulent, is certainly not drab either. Food is plentiful; the people are clothed and, by and large, sheltered. The consumer goods available to the average (or even low-income) American family comprise a fairly long list: brand-name clothes, color TV, car, computer, cell phone, and on and on. In all of the prosperous nations of the world, capitalism in one form or another has won the economic battle, while the world's totalitarian regimes are mired in economic failure. Even communist-ruled China has many characteristics of a capitalist society, including the formation of private wealth (as well as significant income disparity).

Looked at over a longer period of time, humans truly have never had it so good. Let's assume we can use population as a proxy for the overall state of the human condition (a fairly reasonable assumption for most of human history). For most of our existence, the human species barely survived. Based on information provided by the US Census Bureau, the total world population at AD 1 may have been somewhere between 170 million and 400 million people. At 10,000 BC, depending on the study, it may have been as low as one million or as high as ten million people. Today, the world population is estimated at about seven billion. That is a lot of people. Graphically, it looks something like this:

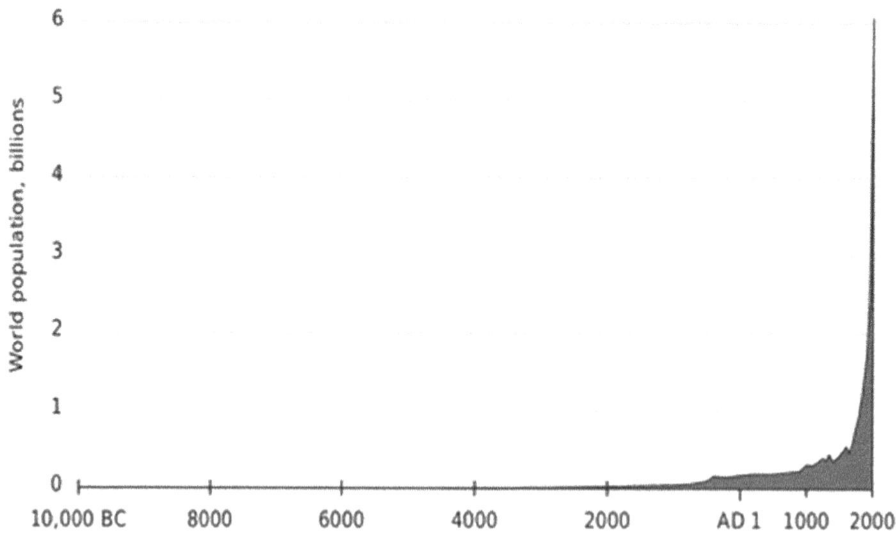

Source: Graph from Wikipedia. I spot-checked the numbers with the US Census Bureau data.

As you can see, for most of human history, it was a fairly rough existence. Now, based on the graph, it looks like we should be hitting a population of infinity pretty soon. Fortunately, current projections indicate that world population will stabilize at approximately ten billion people in the second half of this century.

The Evidence for Our Success

The underpinnings of the capitalist system are the concepts of free markets, free trade, incentives for savings and investments, and the rule of law in respecting property rights and civil contracts. Add in some entrepreneurial spirit, and the results can be dramatic. Let's review the results.

The broadest measure of the output of the US economy is gross domestic product, the output of goods and services produced by labor and property located in the United States. A similar concept, gross national product is "the goods and services produced by labor and property supplied by US residents." GNP includes, and GDP excludes, net receipts of income from the rest of the world (receipts less payments to the rest of the world). We will concern ourselves mostly with GDP since that measure considers output in the United States without regard to who owns the productive assets. After all, if you work at a Honda plant located in the United States, it should matter little to you whether the plant is owned by US residents or by a foreign company. It is still economic activity undertaken in the United States. GDP was $17.4 trillion in 2014.

The vitality of the US economy has truly been impressive. Real GDP (adjusted for inflation) in 2014 was fifteen times the level it was in 1929, the high point before the onset of the Great Depression. (It wasn't until 1936 that the economy again reached the level of output achieved in 1929.) On a per-capita basis (adjusted for population), real economic output per person in 2014 was *over five times* the level in 1929. Even compared to the beginning of the Kennedy administration, real economic output per person today is nearly *triple* what it was in 1960 and is double the level of per capita output as recently as 1975. Times may be tough, but the overall national income per person today is triple what it was during the good old days of *Father Knows Best* and *Leave it to Beaver*.

The graphs below show total and per capita GDP in the United States since 1929. I use real data since that measure adjusts for the impact of inflation. In case you are interested, inflation since 1929 has reduced the value of the dollar by about 90 percent—that is, it takes roughly $10 today to purchase what $1 would have purchased in 1929.

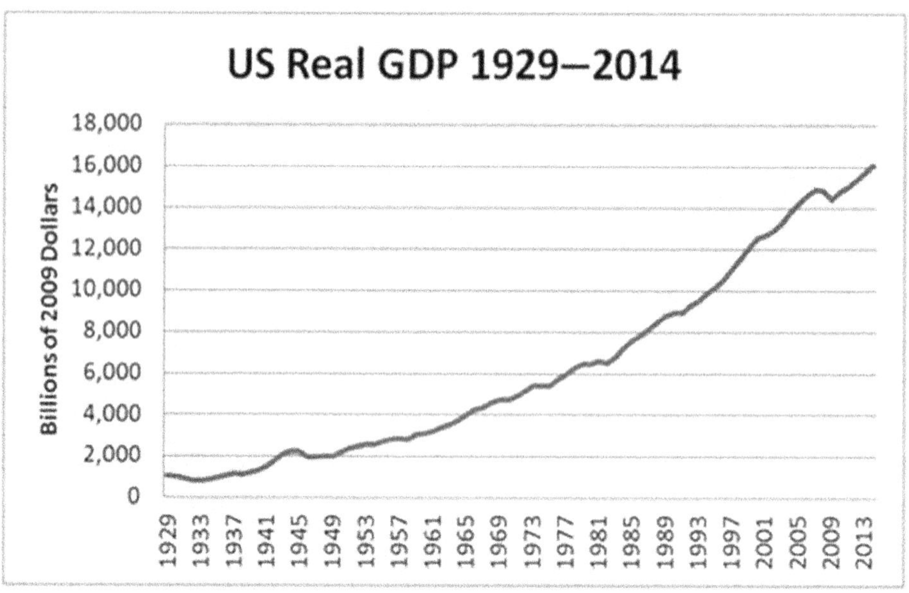

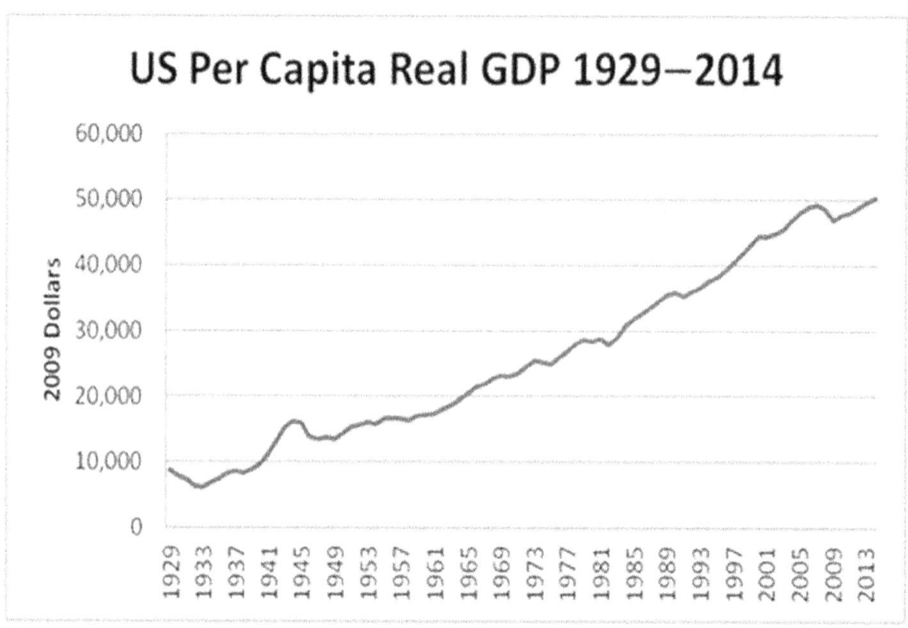

Not to say that our economic progress doesn't have its ups and downs. The US economy has been subject to many business cycles over time—thirty-three business-cycle expansions and contractions since 1854, in fact, according to the National Bureau of Economic Research. Many recessions have been relatively brief and mild, while others have been longer in duration and more severe. The Great Depression was particularly severe, lasting a total of forty-three months, from August 1929 to March 1933. On a calendar-year basis, real GDP was 26 percent lower in 1933 than it was in 1929, and gross private domestic investment was about 80 percent lower than it was in 1929. Even the relatively stable category of personal consumption expenditures declined by 18 percent during that period. People were truly living with less on a day-to-day basis, and businesses were leery of investing in the future.

Since then, recessions have been much shorter and less severe. Prior to the most recent experience, the longest recession since the Depression lasted for sixteen months, and the shortest was a mere six months, although that was the first installment of the double-dip recession of 1980–1982. In contrast, the periods of expansion since the Depression have been quite long. The sixties saw a prolonged period of growth from February 1961 to December 1969, encompassing nine and one-half years. Then the twenty-five-year period of November 1982 to December 2007 saw fairly consistent growth, interrupted by two brief recessions of eight months each, from July 1990 to March 1991 and from March 2001 to November 2001. That period came to be known as the "Great Moderation," which of course led to the "Great Recession" in 2008–2009.

The most recent recession, which began in the beginning of 2008, lasted eighteen months (officially) and saw real GDP decline by 2.8 percent in 2009 from 2008. That is the biggest calendar year-on-year decline in GDP since the immediate post–World War II period, when the US economy was transitioning away from a wartime footing. The most recent recession was certainly severely impacted by housing, and not just because of the resultant adverse impact on the financial markets. From 2005 to 2010, real investment in housing fell by more than half, from 6.5 percent of GDP to only 2.5 percent of GDP, which is the lowest share of the economy represented by residential investment in the United States since World War II. That is a lot of lost economic activity. The recession may be officially over, but it is hard to see how the United States could truly have a strong economic recovery until housing fully recovers (as of 2014, residential investment had rebounded slightly to represent 3.2 percent of GDP). Still, despite the slow recovery in housing, real GDP in 2014 was 12 percent higher than the low point in 2009.

The four primary components of GDP are personal consumption expenditures, gross private domestic investment, government consumption and investment, and net exports/imports. The following table sets forth the components of real GDP for 2007 (prior peak), 2009 (recession trough), and 2014 (in trillions of 2009 dollars and as a percent of GDP):

	2007		2009		2014	
Personal Consumption Expenditures	$ 10.0	67.5%	$ 9.8	68.3%	$ 11.0	68.2%
Gross Private Domestic Investment	$ 2.6	17.8%	$ 1.9	13.0%	$ 2.7	16.8%
Exports	$ 1.6	11.1%	$ 1.6	11.0%	$ 2.1	13.0%
Imports	$ (2.4)	-15.9%	$ (2.0)	-13.8%	$ (2.5)	-15.8%
Government Consumption and Investment	$ 2.9	19.6%	$ 3.1	21.4%	$ 2.9	18.0%
Total Real GDP	$ 14.9	100.0%	$ 14.4	100.0%	$ 16.1	100.0%

Note: Totals may not add due to rounding.

Clearly, personal consumption expenditures comprise the largest component of GDP, accounting for over two-thirds of national output. But private investment (both nonresidential and residential) and government consumption expenditures and investment are important components as well. Government's share of GDP does not include transfer payments such as Medicare or social security payments because there is no good or service provided to the government, just a transfer of funds from one group of Americans to another. However, the consumption expenditures of the recipients of transfer payments are included in GDP. Imports are a deduction from GDP because this represents expenditures captured in other categories that are not produced in the United States and thus not part of domestic production. Similarly, exports are part of domestic production but do not show up in the expenditure categories.

Personal consumption expenditures and government consumption and investment are the most stable components of GDP. Despite the severe recession in 2009, government consumption and investment increased by 6 percent, and personal consumption declined by only 2 percent from the 2007 level. As bad as the recession seemed, Americans as a whole only consumed 2 percent less in 2009 than they did in 2007. And since 2009, personal consumption expenditures were up 11 percent by 2014.

Gross private investment is a much more volatile component of GDP, and this category of production declined by 29 percent in 2009 compared to 2007. This as businesses and individuals cut their investment in capital goods due to excess capacity and a perceived increase in risk for future growth. As a result of this volatility, almost all booms and busts are the result of swings in private investment, and frequently these result from conditions in the credit markets. Fortunately, total private investment has now rebounded in 2014 to exceed the prerecession level in 2007.

International trade is another important component of the US economy. In 2007, exports represented 11.1 percent of the US economy and imports represented 15.9 percent of the economy. The overall level of international trade with the United States is more than double the level during the 1960s. Both exports and imports declined in 2009 from 2007 due to the recession—by 3.6 percent and 15.9 percent, respectively—such that imports accounted for 13.8 percent of the economy and exports accounted for 11.0 percent of the economy. As a result, the net trade deficit declined from 4.8 percent of GDP in 2007 to 2.8 percent of GDP in 2009, where it essentially remained in 2014.

The United States has been in a persistent trade deficit for the past forty years, having last run a trade surplus in 1975. In fact, from 1976 to 2013, the United States ran a cumulative trade deficit of approximately $9.6 trillion, and most of that was in the past fifteen years. Whether this is a good thing or a bad thing depends on your point of view. From a perspective of jobs, it is clearly not a positive as imports represent demand for goods and services that are not produced in the United States. If the United States had met all of its demand for goods and services from domestic production in 2014 (everything else equal, which of course, is never the case), we would have had a

GDP 2.6 percent higher than we did, and probably a condition of close-to-full employment. On the other hand, the United States probably would have had higher inflation since we clearly benefitted from lower-cost imports, which were cheaper than domestic alternatives and probably led to more efficient domestic production as well. In addition, we as consumers had the benefit of consuming $9.6 trillion of goods and services over the past forty years that we didn't have to work to produce. That's not too bad a deal for consumers.

By the way, despite the consistent trade deficit run by the United States, I am generally in favor of free trade, just as I am in favor of all free markets. In my mind, the best argument in defense of free trade was made by the French classical liberal theorist and political economist, Frederic Bastiat in the 1840s:

> PETITION OF THE MANUFACTURERS OF CANDLES, WAXLIGHTS, LAMPS, CANDLESTICKS, STREET LAMPS, SNUFFERS, EXTINGUISHERS, AND OF THE PRODUCERS OF OIL, TALLOW, RESIN, ALCOHOL, AND GENERALLY EVERYTHING CONNECTED WITH LIGHTING
>
> To Messieurs the Members of the Chamber of Deputies
>
> Gentlemen,
>
> We are suffering from the intolerable competition of a foreign rival, placed it would seem, in a condition so far superior to our own for the production of light, that he absolutely *inundates our national market* with it at a price fabulously reduced...this rival...is no other than the sun.
>
> What we pray for, is, that it may please you to pass a law ordering the shutting up of all windows, skylights, dormer-windows, outside and inside shutters, curtains, blinds, bull's-eyes; in a word of all openings, holes, chinks, and fissures.
>
> If you shut up as much as possible all access to natural light and create a demand for artificial light, which of our French manufacturers will not benefit by it?
>
> If more tallow is consumed, then there must be more oxen and sheep...if more oil is consumed, then we shall have extended

> cultivation of the poppy, of the olive...our heaths will be covered with resinous trees.
>
> Make your choice, but be logical; for so long as you exclude, as you do, iron, corn, foreign fabrics, *in proportion* as their prices approximate to zero, what inconsistency it would be to admit the light of the sun, the price of which is already *zero* during the entire day! (Frederic Bastiat, 1801–1850, as reported by Robert L. Heilbroner in *The Worldly Philosophers*)

Sometimes sarcasm is compelling. Here is another one I like from Milton Friedman regarding the fallacy of government jobs programs.

> At one of our dinners, Milton recalled traveling to an Asian country in the 1960s and visiting a worksite where a new canal was being built. He was shocked to see that, instead of modern tractors and earth movers, the workers had shovels. He asked why there were so few machines. The government bureaucrat explained: "You don't understand. This is a jobs program." To which Milton replied: "Oh, I thought you were trying to build a canal. If it's jobs you want, then you should give these workers spoons, not shovels." (Attributed to the economist Stephen Moore from quoteinvestigator.com)

If you think this is not a phenomenon that could occur in the United States, you would be mistaken. For example, Davis-Bacon prevailing wage laws in the United States force local and state governments to spend more than they would need to for various "stimulus" projects funded with federal money. These state and local governments could save money if they were able to competitively bid out these projects at true market wage rates. This saved money could be used for other worthwhile projects, thus giving more workers jobs and giving the public more canals (or more likely today, more roads or fewer potholes). More people with jobs (and at market wage rates that workers are willing to accept), more social benefit, same cost. How does this not make sense? Government logic in action.

The Importance of Savings and Investment

Gross private investment is vitally important to the economy, not only because it is a large component of GDP, but also because this represents the investment in the capital stock of the United States to further economic growth. Based on the Bureau of Economic Analysis statistics, the total capital stock of the United States stood at about $51 trillion at the end of 2014. This includes categories such as fixed business capital, inventories, residential structures, and government productive assets—essentially, the entire capital stock of the United States utilized for the production of goods and services, both public and private (including housing). The physical stock of the United States—combined with the considerable intellectual capital of the population in terms of education, industrial knowhow, training, work experience, and the like—is why the United States has such a productive economy. The physical capital of $51 trillion compares to a total GDP of approximately $16.8 trillion in 2013, so a GDP yield of approximately 33 percent on the capital stock of the United States, if you will. This yield fluctuates over time based on the capital intensity of the US economy as well as changes in the valuation of the capital base, but somewhere in the low thirties range percentage-wise seems to prevail over an extended period of time.

Since this is the case, a long-term increase in the capital base of the United States is a prerequisite for an increasing GDP. The consumption of the capital base (wear and tear) runs at about 4 to 5 percent of the existing base each year, so the United States needs to invest at least that amount just to maintain our existing productive capacity—and more to facilitate continued growth. Fortunately, this has generally been the case as the real capital base has been increasing in almost every year. In fact, net domestic investment (gross investment less consumption of fixed capital) has been positive in every year since the Depression, and net *private* domestic investment has been positive in every year since the Depression other than during World War II, when much of our available resources were devoted to war production. Even in the recessionary year of 2009, when *gross* private domestic investment declined by almost 25 percent from the prior year, *net* private domestic investment remained marginally positive, and the capital stock of the United States increased slightly over the prior year. The importance of capital formation in furthering economic growth is why many economists favor policies that promote savings and capital investment.

Of course, from an economic standpoint, investment requires savings; what is invested in capital goods cannot be consumed out of current production. The biggest source of domestic savings in recent years has been from domestic businesses in the form of undistributed profits. Simply put, businesses as a whole have been funding their own investment needs. Similarly, households and institutions have on the whole been savers, but much less so during the housing boom, as mortgage debt increased dramatically, allowing increased consumption. In contrast, government—and in particular, the federal government—has not contributed anything to national savings over the past decade. The federal government has been a net borrower in every year since 2001, borrowing a net $800 billion in 2008 and an astounding $1.5 trillion in 2009 and 2010, with continued heavy borrowing in the following years. Many people argue that this creates the phenomenon of "crowding out," whereby the borrowing by government "crowds out" the borrowing needs of the private sector, thus having a negative impact on investment. For example, over the twelve-year period from 2001 through 2012, the United States as a whole invested $33.8 trillion and "saved" $27.4 trillion, with a savings shortfall over that period of approximately $6.4 trillion. The biggest contributor to this savings shortfall was the government sector, which was a net borrower over that period of over $11 trillion, with 75 percent of that at the federal level.

If over that period, the United States has not "saved" enough to fund the country's investment in productive capacity, where has the difference come from? It came from the rest of the world, of course. Over that same twelve-year period, foreign investment in the United States in excess of US investment overseas (*net* foreign investment in the United States) was $6.4 trillion. Of that amount, approximately $4 trillion constitutes increases in foreign official assets in the United States, primarily Treasury securities, so foreigners, and in particular foreign central banks, have been a major source of funds facilitating the continued US government deficits. In a sense, one of the largest exports of the United States is dollars, which are used as the world's reserve currency. Charles de Gaulle's finance minister, Valery Giscard d'Estaing, referred to this as America's "exorbitant privilege."

How is it that the rest of the world was able to invest a net $6.4 trillion in the United States over those twelve years? This occurred because, as mentioned earlier, the United States had run a trade deficit of about the same amount over that period. From 2001 through 2012, the United States ran a trade deficit on goods and services of $6.7 trillion (and also ran a current account deficit of $6.7 trillion). By definition, the current account deficit has to be roughly equal to the investment account. So there you have it. Over the twelve years from 2001 to 2012 (just to pick a convenient time frame), the United States over consumed, with a portion of that overconsumption being met by imports, thus running a trade deficit. Also, as a result of our overconsumption, our domestic savings supply was not sufficient to meet our investment needs. The rest of the world, needing a place to invest their dollars from running a trade surplus with the United States, filled the void, and the system was in balance.

Again, whether this is a good situation or not is not an easy question. It is true that the rest of the world finds the United States an attractive investment haven. Does this create a demand for dollars that leads to a higher-valued dollar and thus a trade deficit? Or does this foreign investment help to build the capital stock of the United States, thus helping to grow the domestic economy? Or does our uncompetitive industry (or cheap overseas labor) lead to trade deficits, which result in a surplus of dollars overseas that needs to be invested? In any case, ultimately, the system is in balance.

Finally, it is true that other countries' trade policies have an impact as well. China's massive trade surplus with the United States is partly the result of that country's policy of fixing the yuan rate relative to the dollar at a level lower than would otherwise occur. As a result, the imports from China are less costly than they would otherwise be, and exports from the United States to China are more costly than they would otherwise be. Of course, this seems unfair, and in fact it is unfair. It is unfair to the American worker who has his or her job outsourced to China. It is unfair to the Chinese worker who is not able to consume the true value of his or her labor. However, it is a huge benefit to the American consumer who is able to purchase cheap clothing, televisions, computers, and just about every other manufactured product. In the normal course of events, the exchange rate would be allowed to adjust so that the cost of Chinese imports rises and the cost of American exports declines, but of course China does not allow this to occur due to their critical need to create jobs. However, even this policy has limits in that it can result in increased inflation in China. This leads to increased wages in China and an increase in costs even while artificially pegging the exchange rate. Even now, manufacturers are looking for cheaper costs in the interior of China and in less-developed countries such as Vietnam. Eventually, the system will be self-correcting one way or another.

We Are All Beneficiaries

While the United States may have increased its economic output per person by a factor of five since 1929 and by a factor of about three since 1960, the question remains, who is receiving the fruits of this production? By and large, we all are, or at least most of us are. Median household income (the level at which half of US households have higher incomes and half have lower incomes) was $51,939 in 2013, up in real terms by 19 percent from 1967. While many other Western and prosperous countries have similar or even higher median standards of living, many countries make do with dramatically less. For example, China's GDP per person in 2009 was $3,740, and India and Pakistan were each at approximately $1,000 in GDP per person (compared to over $50,000 in the United States). For many poorer countries, the GDP per capita is below $500. For example, Liberia's annual per capita GDP in 2009 was reported at $220 and North Korea's at $500. Half of all Haitians live on less than $1 per day.

Average household income in the Unites States was $72,641 in 2013, up in real terms by 49 percent from 1967. The *average* household income is more than the *median* due to the impact that very large incomes have on the average (as opposed to the median). Average household income has increased at a faster rate than median household income since 1967 due to the more rapid increase in household income for higher-income households. I address the issue of income inequality in a future chapter, but briefly, it would appear that, indeed, the rich are getting richer, and the poor, while not getting poorer, are basically treading water. For example, the average household income of the second-lowest quintile of households (the group ranging from the 20 percent level to the 40 percent level of all households by income) was $30,509 in 2013, up 13 percent in real terms from the level in 1967, while the average household income for the highest quintile of households (the top 20 percent) was $185,206 in 2013, up 70 percent in real terms from 1967. By the way, I selected the second-lowest quintile for this comparison since it excludes households with very low cash income (not working, for example) in order to focus on what might be described as working-class families or those living on modest retirement incomes. The conclusion is similar looking at other measures of income or share of income in the United States.

The amount of wealth created since 1776 has truly been impressive. The rich are *really* rich, but from a historical perspective, the average citizen hasn't done too badly either. That said, the capitalist system results in losers as well as winners. Not every entrepreneur, business person, or worker is successful. Many individuals don't have the skills or abilities demanded by the marketplace. Some people may be unable to work or find work for various reasons. In the ideal world, we are each responsible for ourselves, and recognizing that, we act responsibly and rationally. In the real world, unfortunately, it doesn't work that way. Some people may be subject to adverse unforeseen circumstances such as illness, may not have an advantaged upbringing with access to quality education and job opportunities, may face the consequences of poor life decisions, or may lack marketable skills or initiative. What are we to do then? That is the crux of the issue that we will deal with in Chapter 12. But first, we return to another basic economic principle in the next chapter.

By the way, *felicities* (in the Thomas Jefferson quote to begin this chapter) means "the state of being happy." I had to look it up.

CHAPTER 3

To Each According to His or Her Work

Opportunity is missed by most people because it is dressed in overalls and looks like work.

THOMAS A. EDISON

NOW THAT WE'VE COVERED THE basic philosophy of the free-market system, let's turn our attention to some of its key aspects. The discipline of economics is "the study of the production, distribution and consumption of goods and services" (*Encarta World English Dictionary*), or as the British economist Lionel Robbins put it, "Economics is the study of the use of scarce resources which have alternative uses." The populace has many needs and wants: food, shelter, clothing, entertainment, leisure time, et cetera, and economics concerns itself with how those needs are met. In a simple feudal system, perhaps the lord of the manor simply told the serfs what to plant, how many sheep to herd, and the like, and the serfs were given a small portion of the resulting produce to sustain themselves. Under a communist or central planning system, the bureaucrats would direct economic activity: how much wheat to plant, how much iron ore to mine, how much steel to produce, and how many tractors to build. We concern ourselves here with a market based economic system, such as is largely prevalent in the Western world and, despite many other systems attempted, still reigns supreme as the most productive economic system by far.

Prices

As discussed in the prior chapter, the whole concept behind the capitalist free-market system is the freedom of producers to produce what they want, how they want to produce it, and the freedom of consumers to consume what they want (and are able to afford and willing to pay for). Obviously, producers strive to produce what consumers want, and if they fail to do this for any extended period of time, they will fail to cover their costs of production and must either change their approach or go out of business. The mechanism that allows this all to work is the role of prices set in a free marketplace.

If the people want more of a certain item, the price of that item will tend to rise, which would have two effects. First, some people that previously desired that item would then have less demand for it—say, substituting some chicken for more expensive beef. Second, in this particular example, the beef producers would tend to increase production, thus satisfying some of the increased demand. Eventually, prices would settle at a level that would equalize the supply and the demand for beef. The process is quite simple and very effective. Similarly, say a major iron-ore mine ceased production due to some accident or other disruption. The price of iron ore would tend to rise. The other iron ore producers would, to the extent they could, attempt to raise production to meet the demand that is now not being supplied from the disrupted mine. Perhaps it would become economical for them to pay their workers overtime or open lower-quality mines due to the increased prices of iron ore. The price of steel would also tend to rise, since one of its main raw materials had risen in price, which could lead to higher prices of cars, appliances, and other end products that use steel. Perhaps the actual demand for cars and appliances would decline because of the higher prices. Perhaps the manufacturers of cars and appliances would substitute some aluminum for steel in their products. Eventually, the various prices would settle at levels that would equalize the supply and demand for iron ore, steel, cars, appliances, and all other affected items. All of this happens automatically by the actions of many people and businesses, all acting independently based on the market signals they receive. And this type of behavior is happening continuously for many commodities, goods, and services.

That is why, so long as we allow the pricing mechanism to work, we see very few long-term "shortages" in the United States. Diamonds may be rare, but there is no shortage of diamonds for sale. We may not all be eating caviar, but there is certainly no shortage of caviar currently plaguing the nation. There is also no shortage of bread, eggs, flour, and other staples, which are generally available at very reasonable prices. This is not the case in many areas of the world, which suffer from market distortions and shortages of many staples. In cases where the United States has experienced shortages—such as with the Nintendo Wii, Cabbage Patch dolls, and the like—the shortages tend not to last very long, and in any case, other alternatives are available that can serve as adequate gifts. Even the gasoline shortages in the 1970s could have been averted if prices had been allowed to increase to levels that would have brought supply and demand into equilibrium.

Where we do have evidence of shortages are instances where the price mechanism is not allowed to work. For example, rent-control regulations may seem like a good idea to control high housing costs in expensive cities such as New York and San Francisco. However, these policies tend to reduce the creation of housing stock, reduce the physical maintenance of the existing housing stock, and encourage people to remain in their apartments longer than they normally would largely because the rent is such a good deal. The result is a tight housing market and the advent of "key money" (basically a form of a bribe to get an apartment lease) and other market-distorting activities. If people are lucky enough to have a rent-controlled apartment, they are receiving a benefit of below-market housing, while those who aren't so lucky pay a higher price for housing than they would otherwise. Similarly, the combination of limiting supply and controlling fares for yellow cabs in New York City has resulted in a system where the taxi "medallions" sell on the open market for more than $1,000,000. Just the right to operate a single taxi is worth over $1,000,000 due to the above market rates charged to consumers and a government-limited supply. However, be careful of market-disrupting developments, as it looks like NYC taxi medallion prices may have come down slightly in late 2014 and early 2015. Is this the result of ride share services such as Uber?

Similarly, we have very few long-term surpluses of specific goods. Again, say a new supply of high-grade iron ore was discovered that was economical to produce. This would add to the overall supply of iron ore, which would tend to depress ore prices. Perhaps some producers would shut down marginal mines or postpone their expansion plans, thus putting a constraint on supply. The price of steel would tend to decline, which might result in additional usage of steel and thus iron ore. Eventually, prices would settle at levels that would result in an equilibrium position in the demand and supply of iron ore.

In non-market-based economies, or in cases where the United States has deviated from free markets, the impact of price controls has played out consistently time after time. In cases of minimum selling prices (or price floors), this has resulted in overproduction of the products in question. In cases of price ceilings, this has resulted in a shortage of the goods in question. That is why people had to stand in long lines to buy bread in the former Soviet Union and why some countries (including the United States at times) have had warehouses stuffed with surplus wheat, sugar, or other food stocks while other citizens do not have enough to eat.

This is not to say that prices are equivalent to "value." While a one-carat diamond may sell for $10,000, to you or me it may not be worth $10,000. Personally, I would rather buy a nice cubic zirconium, which looks much like a diamond, and pocket the remaining $9,900. But of course, the diamond *is* worth $10,000 to the buyer, perhaps exactly because it does cost that much and thus is less available to people of lesser means. Conversely, water is very cheap, but it is very valuable, for we need it to sustain life. If water were not as abundant as it is, certainly the price would be higher. The price of an item is set by its *marginal* use, not its most valuable use. Thus for water, the price is not set by its value as a life-sustaining elixir but by its value for more mundane uses such as watering the lawn or filling the swimming pool. If the price were higher, people might have fewer pools and drier lawns, but we would still have plenty to drink. The bottom line is that water prices are fairly low, and we as consumers are fortunate to have the very high value of a cold glass of water on a hot day at a very low price. Of course, consumers sometimes forgo the relatively free water from the tap and decide to purchase a $1 bottle of water instead—or better yet, spend $2 for a bottle of water imported from Fiji, halfway around the world. That doesn't seem rational to me, but in our system, the consumer is king, and what the consumer wants (and is willing to pay for), the consumer gets. And the rest of us shouldn't care. That is the beauty of it.

Wages as the Price for Labor

Most people in the United States understand the concept of prices and how the pricing mechanism clears the market, whether or not they are consciously aware of market forces. Most people can make the decision that something is either too expensive for them to buy or too good of a deal to pass up. Most people have some sense of what goes into making certain products (a car, for example) and can relate that process to the selling price of that item. Many people have more of a problem relating the same concepts to wages. After all, in the classic system of capitalism, wages are set by the market in the same way that prices are determined for goods and services. If plumbers are scarce in an area, wages will tend to increase to induce other plumbers to enter the market. If wages remain high for an extended period of time, perhaps other workers will switch careers and train to become plumbers. At the same time, the higher wages may induce contractors to raise prices for plumbing work, which may reduce demand for plumbing services. Ultimately, wages will tend to equalize with the supply and demand for plumbers. In concept, it is really no different from the way the pricing mechanism clears the market for goods and services.

Another important concept as it relates to wages is that one's contribution to the economic pie is equal to the wages earned. Thus, if our plumber (let's call him Joe the plumber) earns $49,000 per year (about the median annual wages of a plumber in 2012, according to the Department of Labor), his work contributes $49,000 to the economic output of the country. In a way, Joe the plumber now has a $49,000 claim on the nation's output, equal to the value of Joe's input. Let's say $9,000 goes to federal, state, and local taxes, thus transferring $9,000 of Joe's claim on the economic output of the country to the government. That leaves $40,000 for Joe to spend as he sees fit, such as for housing, food, transportation, et cetera. In the national income and product accounts reported by the US Department of Commerce, gross domestic product, by definition, is equal to gross domestic income (subject to a statistical discrepancy). What is produced is equal to what is earned, and what is earned is equal to what is produced, as shown in the diagram below. In this definition, earnings include all earnings, including profits, which are the earnings that accrue to capital. Joe the plumber's income shows up as wages, and the products or services Joe was involved in producing show up as goods or services produced.

Domestic Production Equals Domestic Income

Expenditures Approach		Income Approach
Personal Consumption		Compensation of Employees
(+)		(+)
Gross Private Investment		Taxes on Production and Imports
(+)		(-)
Exports		Subsidies
(-)		(+)
Imports		Surplus of Private Enterprises
(+)		(+)
Government Consumption and Investment		Surplus of Government Enterprises
(=)		
Gross Domestic Product		
(-)		(=)
Consumption of Fixed Capital		
(=)		
Net Domestic Product	(=)	Net Domestic Income

If our capitalist system works as advertised, Joe the plumber should feel good that he contributed to the country's economic output and that he was rewarded with a commensurate claim on the total goods and services produced. The same is true of all other workers; they are contributing to the size of the economic pie and are being rewarded in the form of wages, which are a claim on the resulting output. In much the same way, retired workers who saved for their retirement are simply spending the fruits of their prior contributions to the economy—while working, they lived without consuming all of the rewards of their past production (assuming they were savers) in order to maintain a claim on the future economic production. And finally, savers are (or should be) rewarded in the form of interest, dividends, and profits for contributing to the capital base of the country.

This may seem obvious, but if you are not working or are not living off of savings from when you were working (and this includes social security and pensions as a form of savings), then you are being supported by everyone else who is working. After all, you still need to eat, need somewhere to live, need clothing and other consumer goods, perhaps need health-care services. The absolute number of people working at least partly on your behalf is quite large, including farmers, laborers, truck drivers, chemists, repair technicians, software developers, lawyers, bankers, doctors, construction workers, et cetera. All of the goods and services that you require are being provided by people who expect to be compensated for their efforts.

Of course, being a plumber requires certain skills and perhaps some state or local certification, and thus not everyone can immediately qualify as a plumber. Other jobs may not require the same level of skills or may have many workers who are able and willing to do the job. Thus, a dishwasher may only earn $18,460 per year (again, the 2012 median according to the Department of Labor). Maybe our dishwasher pays $1,500 in total federal, state, and local taxes, so his take-home pay is $16,960. Although he may work just as hard as Joe the plumber, he may earn less than half as much and thus have a much smaller claim on the nation's economic output. Is this fair? It may be hard to live on $16,960 per year, and nearly impossible to support a family on that income, but our dishwasher is, by definition, earning the value of what he is contributing to the nation's output. The economic pricing signal is that dishwashing is not that valuable to the community relative to some other labor—that if our dishwasher wants to earn a higher wage, he should find a job that pays a higher wage. Maybe our dishwasher is just working until a better job comes along; maybe he will go to plumbing school or some other trade school. Maybe he has few other options, in which case he will have to make do on $16,960 per year. In a way, the price for dishwashing services is similar to the price for water. We really *need* clean dishes; it's just that there are so many potential dishwashers available, so the price of dishwashing services is low.

It may be easy to see the rationale for the wage distinction between a licensed plumber and a dishwasher. One is a skilled trade and the other an unskilled job. But how about the value of teaching as a profession? The median annual income of a schoolteacher in 2012 was approximately $52,000, so slightly more than Joe the plumber, with an after-tax income of, say, $42,000. I would call that a modest living wage, although certainly not a high income (the median annual wage for all occupations in 2012 was approximately $34,750, pretax, so teachers clearly earn more than the average worker). Is it fair that the average teacher earns $3,000 more than Joe the plumber? Both are skilled professions needed in society. One could argue that teaching our children is one of the most important jobs in society and thus should be a highly compensated profession. Also, teachers are generally required to have a college degree and frequently have a graduate degree, so one would think that teachers should earn more than plumbers. But is $3,000 more the right level? I really don't know, but that is what the market has determined.

How about lawyers? The median annual wage for a lawyer is a little over $113,000. Are lawyers worth twice as much to society as teachers? Many would argue not. However, the legal profession requires a law degree and can be a highly specialized profession. If you need a good lawyer and can afford it, you are certainly willing to pay what it takes to get competent representation. A lawyer friend of mine bills her legal services at $950 per hour. That is a lot of money for one hour of work, but that is what the market will bear, and if you are working on a billion-dollar corporate acquisition where the legal services comprise a small fraction of the total dollars involved, that rate is presumably worth it. Otherwise, no one would pay it.

The point is that in a capitalist system, we as a society don't have to make these value decisions; the market makes them for us. And the market *is us*, each of us voting with our dollars every day. If the teacher wants to make more money, he or she could theoretically go to law school and become a lawyer. If our dishwasher wants to make more money, he could potentially go to trade school to become a plumber or pipefitter, or go to college to become a teacher or other professional. If a lawyer is tired of the legal profession and wants more personal fulfillment, he or she could quit the law profession to become a teacher. It is ultimately up to each individual's skills, desires, training, and work effort. The wage rate isn't the only factor that is relevant when choosing a job or career, but it is certainly something that every worker should consider.

A couple of important caveats are in order here. First, the median annual wages referenced above are national medians, without regard for regional differences. Thus a plumber or a teacher in the New York metropolitan area may tend to make more than plumbers or teachers in certain other areas of the country. Second, certain professions have a wide range of compensation. Thus, a lawyer at the top twenty-fifth percentile makes about $168,000, about 50 percent more than the median for lawyers and about 2.5 times what a teacher at the top twenty-fifth percentile of compensated teachers makes. Very highly compensated lawyers can make well into the millions of dollars each year. Plumbers who own their own businesses can make much more than the $49,000 median annual wage rate for plumbers. Alas, dishwashers are subject to a more compact pay scale, with a dishwasher at the top twenty-fifth percentile making only 15 percent more than a dishwasher at the bottom twenty-fifth percentile.

What about very highly compensated individuals? Is their compensation fair? Socially, one could argue that it isn't. Economically it is, however, since they are paid what someone is willing to pay them. Is it fair that Derek Jeter made $16 million a year playing a sport he loves? Maybe not, but it is what it is. Maybe he is worth $16 million per year; at least, that is what the Yankees think. And he is only worth that much to the Yankees because we consumers are willing to pay to watch him play, and enough television advertisers are willing to pay for advertising during Yankees games. How about hedge-fund managers and other money managers? Some of them make $20 million in a year and much more, particularly since many earn a portion of their compensation in the form of a share of the profits generated. John

Paulson is reported to have earned over $1 billion in a single year. I personally don't think many hedge-fund managers' work is worth what they are paid (and certainly not $1 billion in a single year) since, on average, their investment track record as a group is probably about average. For example, John Paulson's investment record, as well as that of many other hedge-fund managers, has been decidedly average since 2009. But if you have a successful investment record and manage enough money, the personal upside is huge. And by and large, they are getting paid these sums either by other professional money managers (at pension funds or university endowments, say) or by *other rich people*. I guess if one already rich person wants to pay another rich person a sizable sum to manage his or her money, why should we care, particularly when the government gets a cut in the form of income taxes?

Finally, from an economic standpoint, it is important to note that, perhaps more so than prices for goods and services, wage rates are often subject to restraint. This can take the form of minimum-wage laws, unions, licensing requirements, et cetera. Thus, certain low-wage jobs may pay higher than they would otherwise through minimum-wage laws. Likewise, teachers who are subject to a collective bargaining agreement may earn higher wages than they would in the absence of such an agreement. Licensed plumbers may earn more than they would if there were fewer restrictions on plumbers entering the field. And chief executives of major corporations may earn more than they would if their pay were not set by their friendly peers on their boards of directors.

So what if we want to make it so that our dishwasher earns more than the "natural" level of compensation? The only way to do this is to somehow take resources from the other members of the society. One common approach is the use of minimum-wage laws. We could, for instance, pass a law that all workers, including dishwashers, must be paid at least $10 per hour. As of the date of this writing, the current federal minimum wage is $7.25 per hour and has been in effect since July 24, 2009. President Obama has proposed raising the minimum wage to $10.10 an hour. In early 2013, President Obama proposed raising the minimum wage to $9.00 an hour, which went nowhere politically, so I guess if you can't get it raised to $9.00, try for $10.10.

Raising the minimum wage above the current prevailing wage rate would certainly be good news for the dishwashers. However, this would cause the costs of restaurants to increase, assuming they currently pay the minimum wage. Restaurants would, to the extent they could, increase their prices. Thus, all of us restaurant goers would pay more for our meals out. Perhaps we would tend to dine out less often. Maybe some restaurants wouldn't be able to remain in business due to the higher costs and less overall dining demand. This would result in the unemployment of some dishwashers as well as other restaurant workers. While the remaining employed dishwashers would be better off, the rest of society would be marginally worse off. Plus, now we have made dishwashing a more attractive job, when the reality is we already have a surplus of dishwashers and potential dishwashers.

Of course, if we limited this to just dishwashers, it wouldn't be so bad. So what if we had to pay an extra dollar each time we dined out? This wouldn't dramatically affect our lifestyle. But of course, it wouldn't be limited to just the dishwashers. We would want to include the busboys and other restaurant workers, all of the retail cashiers, all of the factory workers—in fact, all workers. Then the impact would be more apparent, resulting in higher prices and lower employment in all of the affected occupations. And this is even before considering the impact on occupations that are subject to foreign competition (we'll assume that the restaurant dishwashers are fairly safe from this, but the factory workers are not). Setting a minimum wage higher than the natural wage rate would tend to result in more of the affected work shifting overseas as domestic producers find it harder to compete with their foreign rivals. What we do know for a fact is that individually, every worker is willing to work for the wage being paid. Otherwise he or she either wouldn't be working or would seek a higher-paying job.

Similarly, unions can indeed increase the wages of their members (although not in all cases). Of course, this is at the expense of jobs, for again, if wages are above their natural rate, then costs of producers are higher than they would have been otherwise, prices for consumers are higher than they would have been otherwise, and as a result, production and employment are lower than they would have been otherwise. And this takes place in a closed economy. In a primarily open economy such as the United States, the impact is magnified as foreign, or nonunion, competitors are able to win market share due to their lower cost base. This scenario has played out time and time again in the Unites States. For example, membership in the United Auto Workers peaked at almost 1.5 million members in 1979—but in 2010 was down to about 380,000. Over one million union jobs were lost. Fortunately for the United States and for a number of US automotive workers, automotive employment has been greatly augmented by the nonunion US workforces of such foreign auto companies such as BMW, Toyota, Honda, and the like. Thus, total employment in motor vehicles and parts manufacturing in the United States remained above one million persons until the middle of 2007, when it began a recessionary decline down to 624,700 in June 2009, before beginning a slow climb back to 915,000 by April 2015 (seasonally adjusted). Including motor-vehicle and parts wholesalers and retailers and automotive-repair and maintenance workers adds another 2.8 million domestic workers, so the auto industry is still a very important source of jobs in the United States.

At one time, unions played an important role in the United States, serving as catalysts for better hours and working conditions. In addition, they were effective in capturing a portion of the excess earnings in a number of oligopolistic industries for their members in the form of higher wages. Now, however, we have government-mandated worker protections from the US Department of Labor, OSHA rules and other regulations. Many of our formerly secure domestic oligopolistic industries now have significant foreign competition, and the US competitors are struggling under the burden of above-market union wages and outdated work rules. To be sure, as consumers, we have all benefited greatly from this foreign competition through better quality and lower prices, both from the foreign companies and the increased competitiveness of US producers. However, both the US producers and their union workers who no longer have jobs have suffered. As a result, total union membership in the private sector as a share of employment has declined from 16.5 percent of employment in 1983 to just 6.9 percent in 2010.

The story is different in the public sector, however, as the share of public-sector employment held by union members has remained relatively steady, at 36.7 percent in 1983 to 36.2 percent in 2010. This is not surprising, since government hasn't had to face competition (foreign or domestic), and the politicians have every incentive to be union friendly. After all, it is not the politicians' own money they spend, particularly when it comes to public-pension promises, which don't require current funding but put a strain on future public finances. Of course, it may reach a point where government budgets are under stress, and the taxpayers say no more taxes. Are we at that point now? Possibly we are, as evidenced by the rise of the Tea Party and other antitax sentiments.

So we can see that we have a number of non-free-market features of the labor market, including price floors and restraint of free trade in the form of collective bargaining agreements, as well as a general stickiness of wage rates. As a result, we may have employment at lower levels than would occur naturally. The supply/demand function of pricing is not allowed to clear the market. Perhaps some of this is inevitable. I myself am not entirely against having minimum-wage laws or raising the current minimum-wage level modestly. An extra $1 an hour for someone making $8 an hour may have a much higher social value than the extra prices paid by consumers and the potential loss of some low-wage jobs. We have many other distortions in our economy, including many that benefit very highly compensated individuals, so it is hard to get all worked up about modest minimum-wage laws.

Savings and Investment

Overlaying the production and consumption of goods and services are the concepts of savings, investment, profit, and return. In a society without a capital base, what is produced gets consumed. This would be the case, for example, with a primitive hunter-gatherer society. The day's bounty would be consumed. But even in this case, the tribe may "invest" in some shelter. When some of the members of the tribe are out hunting, others may be building a log shelter. In addition, maybe others are making tools for hunting or cooking. Thus, even in this rudimentary society, capital investment is taking place. To be able to produce capital goods means not to consume a portion of society's output. For an individual, he may save some of his catch for the day to consume tomorrow. Then, tomorrow he can spend his time making some tools. Or, alternatively, he can share some of his hunt with the tool maker, who will trade some of his wares with the hunter for food. The hunter is making this trade because he can now reap a return from his newly "purchased" tools in the form of better hunting (if a weapon) or an enhanced ability to clean the kill (if a skinning tool). Thus the society builds a capital base, which allows it to increase its production of goods for consumption. If all of the individuals of the society had to spend all of their time tending to their immediate needs, the society could not advance.

This is much the case today as well, although we have managed to advance beyond the hunter-gatherer society, and the existing capital base in the United States is quite large. To go back to one of our earlier examples, if the demand for steel were to increase, the steel producers would be induced to increase production. If the industry were already at capacity, the steel producers would need to add new plants and equipment to meet the new demand. Of course, they would not do this unless they had a reasonable expectation of earning additional profits from the investment, and this investment may require a long time to pay off since steel making is a relatively capital-intensive business (i.e., it requires much capital investment per dollar of new sales). They would need to have a reasonable expectation that the increased demand would be a permanent increase so that they could project the demand into the future. They would need to know that the investment they would be making would be protected under the law and that the expected profits would not be subject to too high of a tax rate, so the expected profits would cover the cost of the required investment. Also, they would need to have an expectation that the profits would result in a return greater than their cost of capital (interest costs and cost of equity capital). Otherwise, they shouldn't make the investment and either not borrow the required money or, alternatively, pay out any surplus corporate funds to shareholders.

Economically, society would be devoting some of its economic resources to building a new steel plant. All of the workers who are building the plant, all of the workers who are building the equipment to go into the plant, and all of the raw materials that are going into the construction of the plant are not involved in producing consumer goods. But these workers still need to eat, still need clothing. As a result, this activity can only take place by society not consuming all of its production but instead saving a portion to allow capital investment.

To go back to our Joe-the-plumber example, if Joe saves $4,000 of his earnings and deposits it in the bank, he is not consuming $4,000 of his rightful claim on the output of the nation. Assume the bank takes his $4,000 (and the savings of many more people) and lends it to the steel company to build the new steel plant. Then this claim on the output of the nation has been transferred from Joe to the steel company, which uses it to hire the resources to build its plant, and the workers building the plant then earn a claim that they can use to purchase consumer goods. In the future, Joe may need to utilize some of his savings to consume. Maybe his earnings have fallen from previous levels, or maybe he wants to buy a car or help his children attend college. Then he will be a "negative saver" for a period of time, and his extra consumption will need to be offset by the savings of others since Joe will be consuming in excess of his contribution to the economy.

Our system is thus complete. Producers produce what the consumers want in the quantity that they want, at prices that they are willing to pay, and at prices that allow the producers to earn a (long-term) profit. Workers are rewarded for their efforts in the form of wages that reflect the economic value of their contribution to the economy. Consumers may either consume in the present or save some portion of their earnings, in which case they are rewarded in the form of a return on their investments and the ability to consume in excess of their wages in the future. All of this takes place automatically without the need for central planning or government direction.

Finally, the society needs to look forward to the future to make all of this work. Fortunately, at least it seems to me, the human condition lies generally toward optimism, and this optimism is an important component of the underlying engine that fosters economic growth. If, in general, we believe that as a nation we will continue to prosper, individuals will be more inclined to save and invest for the future. Consumers will be more inclined to borrow (to purchase a car or a house, for example) if they believe that their jobs are secure and that their wages may be subject to future increases. Producers will be more inclined to build factories for future production if they believe that the economy will grow. Hope springs eternal—until a recession hits, anyway, at which point optimism turns into a desire to retrench. Without optimism, we are left with a lack of investment, which leads to a lack of economic and wage growth. Fortunately, most recessions tend to be brief, but it doesn't necessary have to be that way. The Great Depression lasted for over ten years. And, as John Maynard Keynes reportedly observed, the Dark Ages lasted for over five hundred years. Now, that is a long time to go without any significant improvement in the human condition!

CHAPTER 4

It's Not about the Money

Our president took such a dry subject as banking...[and] he made everyone understand it, even the bankers.

Will Rogers

"Lenin was certainly right. There is no subtler, no surer means of overturning the existing basis of society than to debauch the currency."

John Maynard Keynes, *The Economic Consequences of the Peace*

I came across a survey conducted by Tesco Mobile in 2010 asking four thousand British consumers what they thought were the world's greatest inventions of all time. Number one on the list was the ever-popular wheel, followed by the aeroplane and the light bulb. From there, things get a little dicey. The iPhone was number eight, followed at number nine by the flushing toilet. Another all-time favorite, sliced bread, was down the list at number seventy. Surprisingly not on the list was money (well, actually not that surprising on this particular list, given that the all-important invention of hair straighteners came in at number thirty-four). Apparently, this sample of consumers didn't appreciate the fact that our consumerism depends on the existence of money as a medium of exchange to facilitate economic transactions. Money in and of itself has limited usefulness, but much like the wheel is a critical component to most of the mechanical world, money sure is helpful if one wants to get an iPhone ($400 at the Apple Store at the time of this writing). If money didn't already exist, it would certainly have to be invented.

Without the use of money, we are left with the barter system, which, of course, can be a little cumbersome. In a simple economy, perhaps, the farmer can trade some corn for blacksmith services. Today, it is hard to imagine a lawyer trading some legal services to Apple in exchange for an iPad. The famous economist John Stuart Mill explained it thus over a century ago:

> There cannot, in short, be intrinsically a more insignificant thing, in the economy of society, than money; except in the character of a contrivance for sparing time and labour. It is a machine for doing quickly and commodiously, what would be done, though less quickly and commodiously, without it: and like many other kinds of machinery, it only exerts a distinct and independent influence of its own when it gets out of order.

That is why the previous chapter focused on the production of goods and services as opposed to money. Money in and of itself has no usefulness other than as an accounting of how to allocate production and resources. It is a measurement device. Most people complain that they don't have enough money. Creating more money doesn't create more production or jobs. (Although, as John Stuart Mill said, and as we shall see later in this chapter, money can create real economic problems "when it gets out of order.") The real lament should be, "If I only had a job," or "I wish I were paid more for my work," or "I wish I had saved more of my prior pay as compensation for my contribution to the production of the nation."

Ask yourself if we would all be better off if the government sent every adult American a newly printed $100. Your first reaction might be yes, since everyone has an extra $100 to spend. But all that has really happened is that the supply of money has increased. There has been no actual increase in the production of goods and services, so as a nation, we are no better off than we were before. While not all will agree, I will grant you that in times of recession without inflation, a modest boost in the money supply in the form of such "stimulus" may help prime the pump and supply some deficient demand. So I ask this question: what if everyone was given $10 *million* in new bills? Are we all better off then? Well, clearly not. Again, there has been no increase in production. All that has been accomplished is a massive devaluation of the currency and a transfer of relative purchasing power from those who have worked to accumulate some capital to those who haven't. If you had worked your entire life to save $1 million for retirement, I expect you would be a little ticked if everyone got $10 million for free. Most likely, the value of your now $11 million would be worth materially less than your original $1 million savings due to severe inflation. As Ludwig von Mises wrote, "The great inflations of our age are not acts of god. They are man-made or, to say it bluntly, government-made. They are the off-shoots of doctrines that ascribe to governments the magic power of creating wealth out of nothing and of making people happy by raising the 'national income.'"

In addition to its function as a common medium of exchange, money helps to bridge the time gap in producing goods and consuming goods. Let's say I am a plumber earning $1,000 per week. That means that I am contributing services to the overall economy each week valued at the equivalent of $1,000. Instead of trading my services for the specific goods and services that I require, I receive $1,000 that I may spend on other items (ignore taxes for the moment). Almost any good I may desire is expressed in terms of the common medium of exchange—money. However, maybe I want to save some money for a vacation or my kids' college or my retirement. If I save $200 per week, I am effectively banking my work effort now so that I may consume more at a later point in time. A person living off of his or her savings (say in retirement) is consuming the value of the work effort expended in prior years that was not used for immediate consumption. You have to agree that there is a certain simplicity and fairness in this, and that is why the importance of maintaining the value of the currency shouldn't be taken lightly.

Originally, most forms of money had intrinsic value. In ancient times, it is reported that items were valued in terms of cattle. Other commodities that have served as money include salt, sugar, cognac, and tobacco (in the colony of Virginia), among many others. In some cases, money had little value in use, but relative scarcity gave it value in exchange. The island of Uap (Yap), as reported by William Furness III in his book *The Island of Stone Money*, used large stones as money as described in the following excerpt:

> This medium of exchange they call fei, and it consists of large, solid, thick, stone wheels, ranging in diameter from a foot to twelve feet, having in the centre a hole varying in size with the diameter of the stone, wherein a pole may be inserted sufficiently large and strong to bear the weight and facilitate transportation. These stone "coins," if I may so call them, are not made on the Island of Uap, but were originally quarried and shaped in Babelthuap, one of The Pelao Islands, four hundred miles to the southward, and brought to Uap by some venturesome native navigators, in canoes and on rafts over the ocean.
>
> Another noteworthy feature of this stone currency, which is also an equally noteworthy tribute to Uap honesty, is that it is not necessary for its owner to reduce it to possession. After concluding a bargain which involves the price of a fei too large to be conveniently moved, its new owner is quite content to accept the bare acknowledgement of ownership and without so much as a mark to indicate the exchange, the coin remains undisturbed on the former owner's premises.
>
> My faithful old friend, Fatumak, assured me that there was in the village near-by a family whose wealth was unquestioned,—acknowledged by everyone, and yet no one, not even the family itself, had ever laid eye or hand on the wealth; it consisted of an enormous fei, whereof the size is known only by tradition; for the past two or three generations it had been, and at that very time it was lying at the bottom of the sea! Many years ago an ancestor of this family, on an expedition after fei, secured this remarkably large and exceedingly valuable stone, which was placed on a raft to be towed homeward. A violent storm arose, and the party, to save their lives, were obliged to cut the raft adrift, and the stone sank out of sight. When they reached home, they all testified that the fei was

of magnificent proportions and of extraordinary quality, and that it was lost through no fault of the owner. Thereupon it was universally conceded in their simple faith that the mere accident of its loss overboard was too trifling to mention, and that a few hundred feet of water off shore ought not to affect its marketable value, since it was all chipped out in proper form. The purchasing power of that stone remains, therefore, as valid as if it were leaning visibly against the side of the owner's house, and represents wealth as potentially as the hoarded inactive gold of a miser of the middle ages, or as our silver dollars stacked in the treasury at Washington, which we never see nor touch, but trade with on the strength of a printed certificate that they are there. (Quoted from *The Island of Stone Money: Uap of the Carolines* by William Henry Furness, although I originally read this in Milton Friedman's *Money Mischief.*)

The relative convenience of large immovable stones notwithstanding, eventually metals became the most popular basis for money. They can be kept without spoilage, are relatively easily divided into smaller parts, and in some cases, have a high valuation relative to weight or bulk. According to Adam Smith, iron was the common medium of exchange for the ancient Spartans, copper among the ancient Romans, and, of course, the precious metals gold and silver among many nations. At some point, it became convenient to trade warehouse receipts representing gold (or silver or tobacco) held in storage instead of the actual metal for larger purchases. This was, in effect, the advent of paper money, although theoretically, at any time a holder could have demanded the actual commodity by presenting the warehouse receipt.

Eventually, governments got into the act by coining precious metals into known weight and fineness, thus avoiding the constant chore of weighing and assaying the underlying metal for each transaction. Governments could also issue paper money backed by precious metals. Over history, governments have repeatedly debased the currency, either by reducing the purity of the underlying metal or by changing the weight that constitutes a given denomination of money. Prior to 1526, the English pound sterling was equivalent to one Tower pound of silver of a known fineness (92.5 percent silver). English pennies contained a pennyweight of silver, or a twentieth of an ounce. A Tower pound is fifteen-sixteenths of a troy pound, which contains twelve troy ounces; thus, one pound sterling was equivalent to approximately 10.4 troy ounces of pure silver. In early 2015, one pound sterling could purchase less than one-tenth of one troy ounce of silver, although, of course, there is no official tie of the pound sterling to silver or any other precious metal.

One of the earliest and most popular forms of money in the Unites States was the Spanish dollar, or "pieces of eight." The Spanish dollar could be divided into eight pieces, each called a bit, as in "two bits, four bits, six bits a dollar, all for the (insert favorite team nickname here), stand up and holler!" The Coinage Act of 1792 established the US silver dollar as 27 grams of standard silver, or 24.1 grams of pure silver. This specification was based on an average weight of worn Spanish silver dollars, so the US silver dollar had the same amount of silver as a typically worn Spanish silver dollar. The Spanish dollar remained legal tender in the United States until 1857. Much as the Spanish silver dollar once served as the world's currency, the US dollar in many countries serves that role today. In fact, in 2006, the US Treasury estimated that 60 percent of all US banknotes in circulation, or about $450 billion of the $760 billion in circulation at December 2005, was held abroad.

Eventually, most of the Western world adopted gold as the official basis for the money supply. The United States was on the gold standard until 1933, although not continuously. At that time, one troy ounce of gold was set at $20.67, or the equivalent of one dollar being set at 23.22 grains (0.048375 ounces) of pure gold. Gold coins were minted as official legal tender until 1933, and silver was included in the dime, quarter, and half dollar until 1964. The silver content in a 1964 half dollar was worth approximately $6.50 in early 2015. The final, somewhat loose, connection of the US dollar to gold came in 1971 when President Nixon closed the "gold window," thus denying the ability of foreign governments to convert their dollars into gold. At the time, the dollar was officially pegged at $35 per troy ounce of gold, although gold traded at more than $35 per ounce in the open market. During 2011, gold reached a high of a little over $1,800 an ounce, and as of early 2015, one troy ounce of gold was worth about $1,200.

Today, the United States has a purely fiduciary fiat monetary system, *fiat* because dollars are not convertible into any commodity or anything else of any intrinsic value, and *fiduciary* because its value is dependent on the public's trust that it has value and that the government won't inflate the currency. As Milton Friedman put it:

> The pieces of green paper have value because everybody thinks they have value, and everybody thinks they have value because in his experience they have had value...The social convention or the fiction or what you will is no fragile thing. On the contrary, the social value of a common money is so great that people will stick to the fiction even under extreme provocation—whence, of course, comes part of the gains that can be obtained from inflation by the issuers of the money and hence also the temptation to inflate. But neither is the fiction indestructible: extreme variation in the quantity of the green paper—as in the US Revolutionary War or in the hyperinflations in various countries after World Wars I and II—or moderate variation in its quantity plus legally and effectively enforced ceilings on nominal prices—as in Germany after World War II—can render the paper formerly serving as money worthless and induce people to seek substitutes—like the cigarettes and cognac which for a time became the medium of exchange in Germany after World War II.

The Appeal of the Gold Standard

From this, one can easily see the appeal of the gold standard. For a country under a strict gold standard, the government monetary authority committed to redeem notes it had issued for the proscribed amount of gold. The government could increase the amount of money in circulation by buying gold at the set rate in exchange for the issuance of new notes. This system worked so long as the government had sufficient gold reserves to redeem any note presented for conversion, and so long as the population had sufficient faith in the government's ability to do so. The beauty of the gold standard, and why some people still advocate such a system today, is that the government is limited in its ability to artificially inflate the money supply to finance deficit spending; theoretically, the government stood ready to redeem every note it had issued for gold. This doesn't mean, necessarily, that prices are stable. The only price that is stable is that of gold, which is fixed by the monetary authorities. Throughout the history of the gold standard, there were periods of worldwide inflation and deflation depending on the discovery of new gold reserves or more efficient mining techniques (but no severe inflations). After all, any new gold discovery made its way into the money supply simply by its being sold to the government at the predetermined price. This new gold would tend to increase the money supply and lead to increased prices. Worldwide prices would tend to decrease during periods of limited new gold supply and increasing economic growth. When the economy would grow, the money supply had limited ability to grow with it, leading to a "shortage of money" and declining prices, or put another way, an increase in the value of money relative to other goods.

Pegging the currency to gold also had an appeal in regards to international trade. Under a worldwide gold standard, each country would fix its currency relative to gold, and thus by definition, fixed relative to each other. For example, during the 1920s, the dollar was set at $20.67 per troy ounce of gold (23.22 grains per dollar), and the British pound was set at £4.25 per troy ounce of gold (113 grains per British pound). Therefore, by definition, the dollar/pound exchange rate was fixed at $4.866 per British pound. International trade was conducted on the basis of fixed exchange rates, and the system tended to have a built-in mechanism in the event that the balance of trade was not in equilibrium. If a country ran a trade deficit that was not offset by foreign investment, gold would tend to flow out of that country as the surplus trade nations redeemed the deficit nation currency for gold. As a result of the outflow of gold from the deficit nation, its domestic money supply would decline, leading to declining prices and cheaper cost of production relative to other nations. Similarly, the country with increasing gold flows would tend to have increasing money supply, prices, and wages.

This would make imports more expensive to the deficit nation and exports cheaper, leading to a return to a trade balance. Thus, while perhaps painful from a domestic point of view (people don't like declining wages and producers don't like declining prices), the system eventually leads back to a stable price/trade relationship.

Many people today—particularly of the conservative/libertarian sort, such as Ron Paul, among others—advocate a return to the gold standard in the United States for the reasons stated above. If you are against big government, then it makes sense to favor a monetary system that is independent of government, and a true gold standard is by nature independent of government since it is a commodity system. Money is gold, and gold is money. Despite my somewhat conservative/libertarian leanings, I don't favor a return to the gold standard for a number of reasons. Perhaps I am an optimist, but a well-managed fiat currency system can function as well as a gold standard without the cost of the gold standard.

To quote Adam Smith, "The substitution of paper in the room of gold and silver money, replaces a very expensive instrument of commerce with one much less costly, and sometimes equally convenient. Circulation comes to be carried on by a new wheel, which it costs less both to erect and to maintain than the old one."

Or as Winston Churchill said in a speech to Parliament, "Gold is dug up out of a hole in Africa and put down in another hole that is even more inaccessible in Europe and America."

Or as Warren Buffet is reported to have said many years later, "Gold gets dug out of the ground in Africa, or someplace. Then we melt it down, dig another hole, bury it again and pay people to stand around guarding it. It has no utility. Anyone watching from Mars would scratch their head."

Here is the point. Much like the fei on the island of Yap, gold has value because it is limited in supply and expensive to mine (and it also has a pretty yellow color). If the monetary authorities managed the money supply properly, a fiat money can be limited in supply as well, and *inexpensive* to create. Why should we pay people to mine gold as a source of the money supply when we have a cheaper alternative?

Finally, even on a gold standard, the government can, and governments frequently (and always eventually) have debased the currency by either suspending the convertibility of the currency into gold or by devaluing the currency in terms of gold. Governments will do whatever is convenient or deemed "necessary" at the time. So let's do away with the fiction. From 1933 to 1974, it was illegal for Americans to own gold bullion without special licensing. Now, any American can buy physical gold or shares that represent gold held in a vault, and therefore hedge against the dollar losing value in terms of gold. However, consider this: after gold peaked at about $850 per ounce in 1980, gold suffered through a twenty-year bear market and traded down to about $250 per ounce in 1999, until rallying to finally surpass its previous high in 2008, reaching a little over $1,800 in 2011. With gold at about $1,200 per ounce in early 2015, which direction will it move next? I really don't know, but you can make your bet just as you can with any other commodity.

The Complication of Fractional Reserve Banking

So that is a simple monetary system. Once we add the banking system, things get a little complicated. As of December 2014, the US money supply was $1.3 trillion, or $3 trillion, or $11.7 trillion, or perhaps an even larger amount. The first number consists of currency in circulation; the second number is known as M1, essentially currency plus demand deposits (checking accounts); and the third, much larger, number is known as M2, essentially M1 plus savings deposits and retail money-market funds. What is the most relevant definition of *money*, and where does one draw the line between *money* and *short-term investments*? It was pretty easy hundreds of years ago when money consisted of metal coins in your pocket. Today's complex financial system makes it a more difficult question. M1 might be representative of transactional money, or money that is required to conduct one's daily and monthly commerce, while M2 might include money held as reserves, or a store of value, though the distinction is fuzzy.

How do these different definitions of money arise? Over time, most economies, including that of the United States, developed fractional reserve banking systems. This allowed the expansion of credit and the creation of money by the private banking system. The process works as follows.

Say the banking system holds $100 million of deposits from its many customers in the form of vault cash. At any time, the banks are obligated to deliver currency to any depositor who demands to withdraw funds from his or her account. But the banks know that under normal circumstances all of their depositors will not demand to withdraw all of their funds at the same time. Thus, maybe the banks are comfortable holding only 20 percent of their deposits in the form of currency to meet withdrawal requests. As a result, in our example, the banks could comfortably lend out $80 million of their vault cash in the form of loans.

If all the borrowers kept the proceeds of their loans in the form of currency, the banking system would have $20 million in vault cash, $80 million in loans, and $100 million in deposits. However, instead of lending out currency, the banks typically make loans and credit the borrowers with checking accounts at the bank. As a result, the banks would then have $180 million in deposits and still hold $100 million in vault cash (assuming all of the borrowers leave their funds on account at the banks). Over multiple iterations, the banks end up with $500 million in deposits, $100 million in vault cash, and $400 million in loans outstanding, and they are in an equilibrium position. Thus, from a base of $100 million in currency, or "high-powered money," the banks have created an additional $400 million in demand deposits.

The financial system has $500 million in money in the form of demand deposits, plus whatever currency is in circulation. If we assume that currency in circulation is $100 million, then the total money supply in our example is $600 million. If the population desires to hold more currency relative to deposits, the banks suffer withdrawals, and the process works in reverse. For example, if we assume that the banks suffer $25 million in cash withdrawals, they must reduce their loans by $100 million and deposits by $125 million to maintain the same reserve ratio, ending up with $75 million in vault cash, $300 million in loans, and $375 million in deposits. Vault cash once again is equal to 20 percent of deposits. Thus, the total money supply has been reduced to a total of $500 million, consisting of $125 million of currency in circulation (the original $100 million plus the additional $25 million withdrawn from the banks) and $375 million of deposits. The total money supply has been reduced by 16 percent through the simple action of the populace converting $25 million of their deposits into currency.

You may have noticed in my example above that the net worth of the banking system is zero—bank assets (vault cash plus loans) are equal to liabilities (deposits). Obviously this simplification is not the case in the real world (hopefully!), but the overall reserve concept still applies.

Historically, this currency/deposit leverage in both directions is a primary cause of the ups and downs of the business cycle. In good times, credit and the money supply expand, and during times of uncertainty, the process works in reverse. This is particularly true if the faith in the solvency of the banking system is shaken. If people are worried about the health of the banks, they will tend to convert their deposit accounts into currency, and the banks will have to dramatically reduce their outstanding loans in order to maintain their desired level of liquidity, or the ratio of currency on hand to deposits. In addition, typically in such a situation, the banks themselves become more conservative and tend to increase their level of vault cash relative to deposits, thus compounding the negative impact.

This was a dramatic factor in the Great Depression. From October 1929 to March 1933, the stock of money fell by over a third. (*Money* is defined here as currency in circulation plus total demand and time deposits held by commercial banks.) Currency held by the public *increased* by over 40 percent (as depositors converted their bank deposits into currency), but total commercial bank deposits fell by approximately 45 percent. While bank reserves (vault cash plus deposits at Federal Reserve banks) declined by 17 percent, the decline in deposits was much more dramatic as banks sought to increase their reserves relative to their deposit obligations. This illustrates the deleveraging process in action. To put a stop to this cycle and to avoid a continued run on the banks, President Roosevelt declared a national bank holiday and closed all banks after midnight March 6, 1933. Banks finally began to reopen a week later, on March 13, 1933.

The overall impact on the real economy from the contraction of the money supply was dramatic. From 1929 to 1933, total loans outstanding of commercial banks declined by over 50 percent. If consumers can't get a loan, they can't buy a house or a car. If businesses can't get a loan, they can't invest in equipment or inventory. As a result, real GDP declined by 27 percent, and nominal GDP declined by over 45 percent (as prices declined by about 25 percent). Other factors were certainly at work, but in my opinion, this dramatic decline in the money supply and credit, more than any other, is what turned a depression into the Great Depression.

The Federal Reserve System

Prior to the creation of the Federal Reserve System in 1913, the United States was subject to periodic and sometimes severe banking crises. The crisis of 1907 saw a general restriction on the ability of the banks to convert deposits into currency and a scramble for liquidity by the banks and the public. This led "Congress to establish the National Monetary Commission, which put forth proposals to create an institution that would help prevent and contain financial disruptions of this kind." The Federal Reserve System was subsequently created in 1913 by the Federal Reserve Act "To provide for the establishment of the Federal reserve banks, to furnish an elastic currency, to afford means of rediscounting commercial paper, to establish a more effective supervision of banking in the United States, and for other purposes." An "elastic currency" was desired to meet the money needs of commerce; "rediscounting commercial paper" was implemented to provide liquidity to the banking system in times of banking stress. Despite the intent of the Federal Reserve Act to help moderate the many banking crises that had occurred over the years, the Fed's record has been mixed (see Great Depression above and note the 2008–2009 financial crisis).

Monetary policy in the United States is conducted by the Board of Governors of the Federal Reserve System, as primarily conducted by the Federal Reserve bank of New York, one of the twelve-member Federal Reserve banks. Today, in addition to its many supervisory, lending, and financial-services roles, the primary role of the Federal Reserve System is to conduct United States monetary policy. The Fed does this by setting the reserve requirements and pegging certain short-term interest rates, as well as through open market operations (buying and selling government securities), which influence the level of bank reserves. Bank reserves include vault cash (as in our example above) plus member bank deposits held at the federal banks. The current legal reserve ratio, as applied to most demand type deposits, is 10 percent, implying a tenfold multiple of deposits to reserves.

One of the key powers of the Federal Reserve is the ability to "create" money. It generally does this by buying US government securities and crediting the seller's account balance at the Federal Reserve bank. There is no corresponding reduction of another deposit account, which would be the case if, say, you or I were to buy a government security. For example, if I sell you a $10,000 Treasury security (for $10,000), then my cash is increased by $10,000 while your cash is reduced by the same amount. If the Federal Reserve bank of New York buys $100 million in Treasury securities (assume from a member bank), then the selling bank's account at the Federal Reserve is increased by $100 million, and there is no reduction on the other side—$100 million in reserves, (high-powered money) has been created. If the selling bank so chose, it could request that the Fed deliver Federal Reserve notes (paper currency) to the bank and reduce the bank's account balance at the Fed.

The sum of total currency outstanding and bank balances with Federal Reserve banks is known as the "monetary base" or "high-powered money" and comprises the vast majority of the Federal Reserve's liabilities. In essence, the monetary base is "real" money. Not real in the sense that gold coins or currency backed by gold or another precious commodity is real. But real in the sense that under our fiat money system, this is the true money created by the government. All other forms of money in the United States are, in the words of Ludwig von Mises, "circulation credit." Your checking account at the bank is really an obligation of the bank to deliver to you dollars equal to the balance of your account. However, using your checking account does not require that you first convert the total to actual money. "For everybody they therefore are really money-substitutes; they perform the monetary function in the same way as money" (von Mises). Today, the existence of FDIC insurance greatly facilitates the equivalence of bank deposits with actual money since a government agency generally provides $250,000 in insurance per depositor against a failure of any participating bank (raised from $100,000 in October 2008). Even then, bank failures can and do occur, and in some cases, they result in a loss for depositors. IndyMac bank failed in July 2008 after suffering mortgage-related losses and a run on deposits. In a scene reminiscent of the Depression, jittery depositors lined up outside the bank's branches to withdraw their money. While the FDIC made good on its insurance, some depositors did lose money, initially 50 percent of the value of their accounts that were in excess of the FDIC coverage limits.

In December 2007, before the financial crisis, the monetary base was $836.4 billion, consisting of $8.1 billion of reserve balances with Federal Reserve banks, $54.7 billion of vault cash, $763.8 billion of currency in circulation, and approximately $10 billion of other items. The chief asset of the Federal Reserve banks are government securities, so effectively government securities owned by the government itself and forming the foundation of the monetary base.

Also in December 2007, total bank reserves were $43.5 billion, consisting of $8.1 billion of reserve balances with Federal Reserve banks and $35.4 billion of vault cash used to satisfy required reserves. Excess reserves totaled $1.8 billion, or roughly 4 percent of required reserves. Total checkable deposits (funds in checking accounts) at commercial banks and thrifts were $623.1 billion, or 14.3 times the reserves. By December 2014, total bank reserves had ballooned by more than a factor of fifty to $2.6 trillion. Excess reserves were approximately $2.5 trillion, or approximately thirty times the required reserves. Total checkable deposits at commercial banks and thrifts were $1.7 trillion, or only 63 percent of reserves. What a change from December 2007! The monetary base in December 2014 was $3.9 trillion, about 4.7 times the level in December 2007.

So why are checkable deposits currently at less than one times the reserves, implying that the requirement of banks to hold reserves of at least 10 percent of checkable deposits is meaningless? This situation is unprecedented since the founding of the Federal Reserve System in 1913 and is probably the result of a number of related factors. Ultimately, the increase in reserves, and thus the increase in excess reserves held by the banks, was driven largely by the Federal Reserve policy in response to the financial crisis. This includes the Federal Reserve's emergency-liquidity programs established during the height of the financial crises, as well as the more recent policy of quantitative easing, each of which have added reserves to the banking system. As a result, the Federal Reserve System's assets have increased from approximately $925 billion in December 2007 to approximately $4.5 trillion at the end of 2014, which, in 2014, included approximately $1.7 trillion of mortgage backed securities. Of course, if assets of the Federal Reserve system have increased, so have the liabilities, and in fact, deposits of depository institutions held at the Fed have increased from $40 billion in 2007 to $2.4 trillion in 2014. As we know, deposits held at the Federal Reserve qualify as reserves of the banks.

So the question arises, why are the banks holding the excess reserves instead of dramatically expanding their balance sheets through making loans? Well, for one, for the first time in its history, the Federal Reserve began paying interest on reserves beginning in October 2008. As a result, the banks have less of an incentive to lend out their reserves since they can earn a return on their excess reserves. In addition, it is not feasible in the short term for the banks to absorb the dramatic increase in reserves (increasing by more than four times from 2007) by expanding their balance sheets. Also, because of the credit losses taken by the banks during the most recent financial crisis, they were reluctant to lend to all but the most credit-worthy borrowers. And the recession had taken a toll on the number of credit-worthy borrowers. Finally, the health of banks is dependent on their solvency as well as their liquidity. The concept of required reserves is based on a concern for a bank's liquidity—that is, how quickly a bank is able to convert its assets into cash. Obviously, vault cash is totally liquid. If a customer demands his or her deposits in the form of currency, the bank has its available vault cash to satisfy withdrawal requests. Similarly, reserve balances on deposit with Federal Reserve banks are available to satisfy electronic or check withdrawals, or they can be quickly converted into currency to satisfy cash withdrawals. In addition, the Federal Reserve can lend additional reserves to the banks to accommodate withdrawals in a tight situation.

The most recent financial crisis was precipitated more by a concern about solvency than liquidity, although a concern about solvency can quickly become a liquidity issue. Whether a bank is solvent depends on whether its assets exceed its liabilities, while whether a bank is liquid depends on its ability to satisfy its customers' demands for withdrawal of cash. For example, assume a bank has $1 billion in assets, consisting of $200 million of vault cash and reserves on deposit with Federal Reserve banks and $800 million in other loans, and has $900 million in deposits and no other liabilities. Such a bank would have a net worth of $100 million, or the amount by which its assets exceed its liabilities. It would also be very liquid, with $200 million of cash and equivalents, and maybe twice as much legal reserves as required.

If, however, its $800 million of loans are really worth only $600 million, then the bank's net worth is now $800 million minus $900 million, or a negative $100 million. While still liquid, the bank is actually insolvent as the value of its assets is not enough to satisfy its liabilities. If its depositors attempt to withdraw their deposits, the bank becomes both insolvent and illiquid.

Now suppose that the value of its total assets were $950 million. Then the bank's net worth is $50 million. While still solvent, the bank may be constrained from making new loans and incurring new liabilities because its capital cushion (net worth) is too thin. A bank in this position would attempt to constrain its loan growth and try to build up its capital cushion for a time. It would also want to maintain an extra level of liquidity (excess reserves) to prevent a run on the bank in the event that depositors were to lose faith in the financial health of the bank. In 2008, much of the financial system, bank and nonbank, was in this situation. Banks in truly dire straits are sometimes referred to as "zombie banks," the walking dead.

Fortunately, the health of the banking system is much more robust now than it was during the height of the financial crisis, when the Treasury instituted the Troubled Asset Relief Program (TARP), and the Fed implemented its various emergency-liquidity programs. Things were so bad in 2009 that investors were willing to buy short-term Treasury securities with a negative yield—in other words, at that point, investors would rather take a sure small loss on a government security rather than leave their funds on deposit in the private banking system. Now that the crisis has passed and the banking system is no longer capital constrained and flush with excess reserves, the question is, are we setting ourselves up for a massive inflation of the currency?

Money and Inflation

Periodically, the United States has seen bouts of moderate to more-than-moderate inflation. Most typically, this has been during or immediately following wartime. For example, during the Civil War, wholesale prices increased on average almost 25 percent per year. Over the period from June 1914 to May 1920 (roughly corresponding to World War I), wholesale prices in the United States increased by approximately 150 percent, and overall prices nearly doubled. Similarly, wholesale prices roughly doubled during World War II and immediately thereafter (September 1939 to August 1948), while overall prices as measured by the GDP price deflator increased by about 70 percent. Since World War II, the United States has had an annual inflation rate of 3.3 percent, which, while that doesn't sound too bad, means that prices in 2013 are 7.8 times higher than they were in 1949. During the inflationary period of the seventies and early eighties, prices were rising at an average annual pace that would result in a doubling of prices every ten years.

Why is inflation bad? Consistent and moderate inflation isn't so much the problem (although not recommended). After all, then people can plan for the moderate loss in purchasing power of their financial assets. Interest rates would tend to be higher to reflect the fact that a portion of the rate of interest is to compensate the creditor for the loss of purchasing power of his or her principal. In fact, the stated goal of most monetary authorities around the world is to have inflation run at about 2 percent per year. You might call this a little lubricant to help move the economy along. After all, no producer likes declining prices, and no wage earner likes declining wages, both of which are inevitable in some industries or jobs in a total noninflationary environment. A slight general increase in prices helps to mask these factors. For example, if prices and wages increase by 2 percent per year for ten years, then total prices have increased by 22 percent. If you sell your house for 15 percent more than you paid for it, you feel good even if your real sales price is less than you paid for it ten years earlier. Or, if you receive a 2 percent pay raise each year, you might conclude that at least you received something for your good efforts, even if in fact you received no real increase in wages at all.

However, a dramatic, unplanned increase in prices hurts the saver. Remember that savings represents the value of prior work that was not used for current consumption but was "banked" for future consumption. If rampant inflation reduces the purchasing value of my savings, the value of my prior work has been diminished in real terms. That is why inflation is so unfair to the saver. Effectively, the government has expropriated the value of the saver's prior work. As Ludwig von Mises said:

> The assistance of inflation is invoked whenever a government is unwilling to increase taxation or unable to raise a loan; that is the truth of the matter...It is only possible to levy high taxes when those who bear the burden of the taxes assent to the purpose for which the resources so raised are to be expended...It explains why inflation has always been an important resource of policies of war and revolution and why we also find it in the service of socialism.

Much research has been done on the causes of and cures for inflation, and I have no intention of rehashing that here. In the micro sense, prices increase due to an increase in demand or a decrease in supply of a good. For example, a tightening in the supply of oil would typically lead to an increase in prices for oil, gasoline, and other products heavily dependent on oil prices. However, this doesn't mean that prices in general would increase. It is only logical that if people are paying more for energy, then they have less money available to spend on other goods and services. Thus, it is possible that the increased prices of oil may be offset by a small decline in the prices of other goods and through a reduction in actual demand for the now higher-priced oil. In other words, changes in the supply or demand for specific goods and services should not cause a general inflation.

I subscribe to the argument of Nobel Prize–winner Milton Friedman that "substantial inflation is always and everywhere a monetary phenomenon." That is, overall inflation in a country is tied to growth in the money supply that is in excess of the growth of real GDP. As for any commodity, if the supply increases, then marginal value declines. Since the value of money is dependent on its use as a medium of exchange, any increase in money leads to a corresponding increase in inflation as each unit of the money stock loses value. Of course, this impact is not always smooth, and typically the results are felt with a delay (if the money supply were to increase by 25 percent today, prices wouldn't increase by 25 percent today but would work their way up over time). Without me doing any fancy statistical modeling, note the following: From 1929 to 2007, the money supply as measured by M2 increased by 6.5 percent per year, real GDP increased by 3.4 percent per year, and prices increased by 3 percent per year. The quantity of money increased by 3.1 percent more per year than the increase in real output, and prices increased by almost exactly the same amount. Similarly, from 1959 to 2007, M2 increased by 6.9 percent per year while real output increased by 3.3 percent per year, a difference of 3.6 percent. During that period, prices increased by 3.7 percent per annum. A coincidence? I think not.

That is why recent developments are potentially so worrying. From December 2007 to December 2014, the monetary base (high-powered money) has more than quadrupled, M1 has more than doubled (11.4 percent per year), and M2 has increased by 56 percent (6.5 percent per year). So far, overall price increases have been modest, with the GDP deflator up about 11.7 percent (1.6 percent per year), while real GDP is up by 8.1 percent (1.1 percent per year). M1 and M2 have the potential for much greater increases if the credit markets recover because of the high level of excess reserves currently in the banking system. In addition, inflation may pick up if the long-term relationship between the money supply and inflation begins to reassert itself. The Fed says it has the wherewithal to manage the process and to withdraw funds (by selling its portfolio of government bonds, for example) if inflation were to pick up, but what about the political will? This could be difficult if the government continues to run significant deficits, which would require new federal debt at the same time that the Federal Reserve is selling its debt holdings. It took a tightening of the money supply and a brutal recession in 1981–1982 to wring the high levels of inflation out of the economy that were prevalent at that time. Let's not get back to that scenario.

However, despite the dramatic increase in bank reserves and the material increase in the money supply from 2007 to 2014, inflation has been muted and even below the Fed's target rate of 2 percent per year. I for one remain an optimist on the near-term risk of inflation, and so apparently do most investors, as the implied future ten-year inflation rate in early 2015 was about 2 percent per year, based on the relationship of the ten-year Treasury yield and the real yield on ten-year Treasury Inflation-Protected Securities (TIPS). However, we shall see.

CHAPTER 5

The Government Spends

None of us can have as much as we want of all the things we want.

JUSTICE OLIVER WENDELL HOLMES

NOW THAT WE HAVE AN understanding of some basic economic concepts, back to the federal budget. Anyone with basic budgeting sense knows that a budget has spending on one side of the ledger and revenues on the other. If the budget is in a deficit position, the simple math is that revenues are too low, spending is too high, or both are true. To adequately assess the relative merits of raising taxes or cutting spending, it would help to have a basic understanding of the extent of taxation and government spending in the United States. For our purposes, let's start with a look at the spending side of the equation for government.

GOVERNMENT SHARE OF THE ECONOMY

As mentioned in Chapter 2, total consumption and investment expenditures by government (federal, state, and local) in 2013 were $3.1 trillion ($1.2 trillion at the federal level and $1.9 trillion at the state and local levels), representing 18.6 percent of the economy as measured by GDP. These expenditures constitute what we would normally associate with government services—such as national defense, education, transportation (primarily roads), public order and safety (such as police and fire protection), general public services, and the like—and exclude government transfer payments—such as social security, Medicare and Medicaid, unemployment insurance, and similar programs.

Surprisingly, total government expenditures for goods and services have been relatively stable as a share of the economy since 1949, when the government accounted for 18.3 percent of the economy. So basically, government consumption and investment expenditures as a percent of the economy are about where they were more than sixty years ago, and they are materially less than they were as a share of the economy in 2009, when total government consumption and investment represented 21.4 percent of GDP.

Prior to 1949, the share of the economy accounted for by all levels of government ranged from a low of 9.2 percent in 1929 (the first year of the NIPA data series) to a high of 48.4 percent in 1944, when a staggering 43.3 percent of the country's output was for national defense. The following graph shows total government spending for goods and services from 1929 through 2013. This is what it takes to run the federal, state, and local governments in the traditional sense.

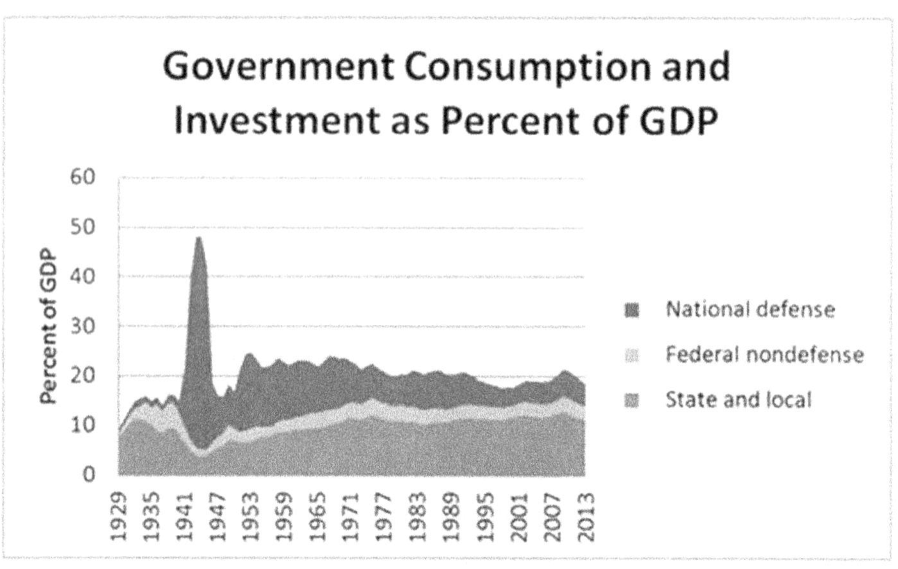

It is hard to see any troubling trends here. Since 1949, the government share of the economy has ranged from a low of 16.9 percent in 1950 to a high of 24.9 percent in 1953 (Korean War) and then declined to less than 18 percent of GDP during each of the last three years of the Clinton administration. Of this amount, federal spending on goods and services has ranged from a high of 18 percent of GDP, again in 1953, to a low of 6.1 percent in 2000, the last year of Clinton's presidency. I once read a quote in *Newsweek* that I remember as something like this: "Bill Clinton—delivered on what Reagan promised," which is actually not too far from the truth. Republicans might not like Bill Clinton much, but from a fiscal standpoint, he may have been one of the best "Republican" presidents ever.

Federal spending for consumption and investment was $1.2 trillion in 2013, or 7.4 percent of GDP. Total federal expenditures in 2013 were $3.9 trillion, or 23.1 percent of GDP (details on the missing $2.7 trillion of federal spending to come). The biggest and most volatile component of federal spending on goods and services is for national defense. Since 1949, spending for national defense peaked at 15.7 percent of the economy in 1953, declined to 6 percent of GDP in 1979, before increasing modestly during the Reagan administration, hit a low of 3.8 percent of the economy in 2000 (the "peace dividend"), and settled in at 4.6 percent of GDP in 2013.

Despite the increase in defense spending since 2000, spending on national defense as a share of the economy is still roughly half the level prevalent during the 1950s and the 1960s. If you are keeping up with your math, you may have realized that federal spending for consumption and investment for nondefense (such as general public service, pubic order and safety, economic affairs, and recreation and culture) represented 2.7 percent of the economy in 2013 and has in fact been very stable, ranging between 2.2 percent and 3.3 percent of GDP since 1960. Ironically, this is the category of federal spending that is frequently targeted for spending cuts—the high-hanging and relatively small fruit. This is essentially meaningless in terms of the overall budget, unless, of course, you are prepared to cut nondefense discretionary spending in half, and not many are proposing to do that.

Most of the government spending for goods and services takes place at the local and state level. State and local governments spent $1.9 trillion on goods and services in 2013, representing 11.4 percent of the economy, four times greater than the federal nondefense total of $462 billion. Clearly, this is where the vast majority of government services are provided, and roughly two-thirds of it is provided at the local level rather than at the state level. Of the $1.9 trillion in consumption and investment expenditures at the state and local levels in 2013, education was by far the largest category, accounting for 43 percent of total spending. The next three largest categories of expenditures include economic affairs (the biggest component of which is transportation), public order and safety (including police and fire), and general public service (the actual cost of running the government), all at more than 10 percent of total state and local spending. Again, spending by state and local governments on goods and services has been relatively stable over the last forty years, ranging from a low of 10.3 percent of GDP in 1984 to a high of 12.4 percent of GDP in 1975, to 11.4 percent of GDP in 2013.

These are government services one can actually see. Lucky me, I am fortunate to live in a state that has one of the highest tax burdens in the country (New York) and in a community that has some of the highest levels of property taxes in the country—the average homeowner pays $20,000 or more in annual property taxes. The upside to this high tax situation is that, in this case at least, the residents receive some tangible government services for their taxes. Our children are educated at the local public schools, which in general do a decent job. Our garbage gets picked up twice a week (plus recyclables on Wednesday). The roads are plowed when it snows, and the potholes are fixed in the spring (eventually). Our children play in the local sports leagues and use the town and school sports facilities. The police take pride in their work, and the community is generally free from serious crime. Are the property taxes too high? Most people would agree that they are, but communities such as this are still considered very desirable places to live despite the high tax levels. In some ways, at least at the local level, you get what you pay for.

Here is a summary of the composition of federal and state and local spending on goods and services in 2013:

Total Government Spending on Goods and Services in 2013

	$ in billions	% of GDP
Federal		
National Defense	$ 769.9	4.6%
Nondefense	461.6	2.8%
Total Federal	1,231.5	7.3%
State and Local		
General Public Service	199.1	1.2%
Public Order and Safety	316.0	1.9%
Economic Affairs	319.9	1.9%
Housing and Community Services	53.6	0.3%
Health	86.6	0.5%
Recreation and Culture	36.1	0.2%
Education	824.2	4.9%
Income Security	76.7	0.5%
Total State and Local	1,912.2	11.4%
Total Government	$ 3,143.7	18.7%

Total Federal Spending

So far in this chapter, we have been reviewing the total government spending (federal, state, and local) on goods and services (excluding transfer payments), which has generally been in the range of 20 percent of GDP for the past fifty years. Total *federal* spending on goods and services (again, excluding transfer payments) has been in the range of 7–8 percent of GDP, so why was the *federal net borrowing* in both 2009 and 2010 at about 10 percent of GDP, before declining to about 5 percent of GDP in 2013 (and about 3.5 percent of GDP in 2014)?

Well, two primary reasons. The first is temporary, which is the severe recession that began in 2008 and really hit hard in 2009. This had the twofold impact of reducing federal receipts (which were down by 11 percent in 2009 from the prior year and down 16 percent in 2009 from the 2007 level) and increasing federal-government expenditures (which were up 12 percent in 2009 from 2008). The second and more systemic reason is the ballooning cost of government social benefits and other transfer payments (including interest on the national debt), which represented over two-thirds of total federal spending in 2013. Essentially, the federal government has two main roles: national defense (which constitutes approximately 5 percent of GDP) and the transferal of funds from one group of Americans to another (representing approximately 14 percent of GDP in 2013), with the entire rest of the federal government constituting less than 3 percent of GDP (plus a similar amount for interest on the federal debt). As a result, total federal expenditures were in excess of 23 percent of GDP in 2013, and total federal, state, and local government expenditures were about 34.5 percent of GDP. On this basis, the size of government in the United States doesn't look so modest.

The chart below shows federal total receipts and total expenditures since 1929 and the resultant net federal borrowing, all as a percent of GDP.

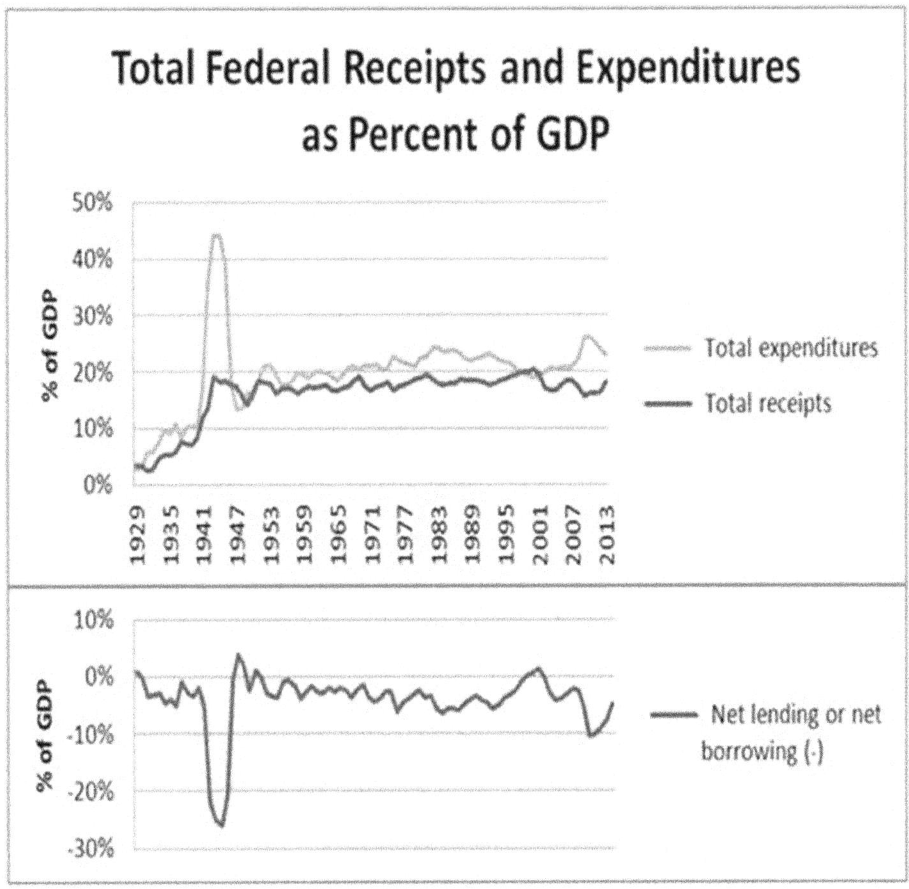

And the chart below shows the main components of federal spending as a percent of GDP since 1929.

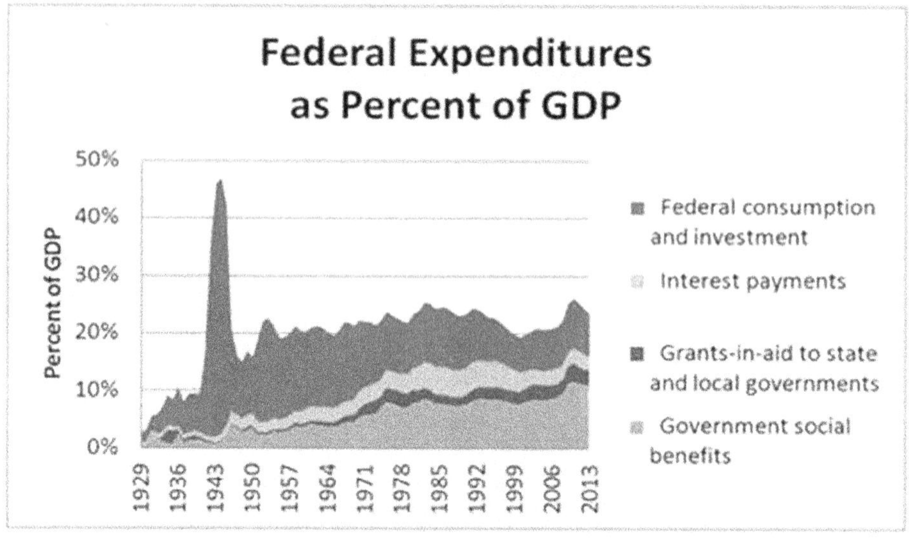

As a share of total federal expenditures, the graph looks like this:

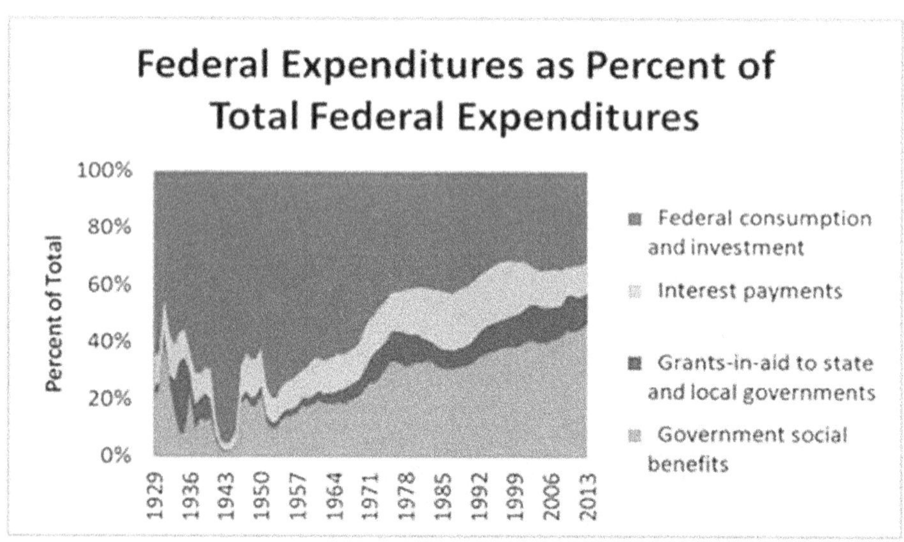

As the charts show, the big components that drive the increase in federal spending are primarily federal social benefits and transfers to state and local governments. These categories combined accounted for roughly 3 percent to 4 percent of GDP in the 1950s and now are at about 14 percent to 15 percent of GDP, roughly increasing by a factor of five times and by more than 10 percent of GDP over the past sixty years or so. This is a huge increase and a fundamental long-term shift in the role and function of the federal government over the past sixty years.

Aid to state and local governments is the smaller component of the growth in total federal transfer spending, accounting for 2.7 percent of GDP in 2013, down from 3.4 percent of GDP in 2010 (lower GDP and the impact of the various stimulus programs in 2010) but up from less than 1 percent during the 1950s. The largest component of these transfers is for Medicaid, which comprises over 50 percent of the total federal transfers to state and local governments. We will cover Medicaid later, but this is largely a federal social-benefit program administered by the states.

Federal government social benefits have increased dramatically over the past sixty years, from about 2.5 percent of GDP in the early 1950s to about 11 percent in 2013. As the table below shows, by far the largest components of this are social security and Medicare. In particular, Medicare has increased dramatically from zero in 1965 to 3.4 percent of GDP in 2013, with further growth destined to come. In addition, recent years have seen an increase in certain temporary social programs such as unemployment insurance, which peaked at 0.9 percent of GDP in 2009 and 2010 before declining to 0.4 percent of GDP in 2013. Despite some recent declines due to the improving economy, there is no question that government spending on social benefits has reached a new permanent high.

But let's take a step back and look at all federal spending in 2013. The table below shows all federal spending in slightly more detail. The numbers presented here may not precisely match other figures presented elsewhere for the same categories of spending due to different source materials, slightly different time periods, or slight definitional differences. However, in all cases, the conclusions are the same.

Total Federal Spending in 2013 by Category

	$ in billions	% of GDP
Nondefense Goods and Services	$ 462	2.7%
Defense	770	4.6%
Total Goods and Services	1,232	7.3%
Social Security	799	4.8%
Medicare	572	3.4%
Unemployment Benefits	62	0.4%
Veterans Benefits	78	0.5%
SNAP (food stamps)	75	0.4%
Refundable Tax Credits	83	0.5%
Other Social Benefits	138	0.8%
Total Government Social Benefits	1,807	10.8%
Grants to State Governments	450	2.7%
Other	106	0.7%
Interest	417	2.5%
Total Spending	$ 4,012	23.9%

Note: Totals may not add due to rounding.

Let's deal with each of these in turn.

Nondefense Discretionary Spending

According to the Bureau of Economic Analysis, the federal government spent about $462 billion on nondefense discretionary spending in 2013, comprising approximately 2.7 percent of the economy. This is spending by the various recognizable federal agencies such as the Departments of Health and Human Services (which is a large user of funds, even excluding the approximate $800 billion distributed under Medicare, Medicaid, and other mandatory programs), Education, Housing and Urban Development, Justice, Agriculture, Energy, and NASA. Without a doubt, money can be saved by each of these departments, but as I've said before, this area of spending has been relatively consistent over the past sixty years (as a percent of GDP) and is actually projected to decline as a share of GDP in the future. So I will not dwell too much on the details here.

Defense Spending

According to the National Income and Product Accounts published by the Bureau of Economic Analysis, the United States spent a record $835 billion on defense in 2011, representing 5.4 percent of GDP, declining to about $770 billion in 2013, or about 4.6 percent of GDP. The official US budget for fiscal 2015 details $875 billion in spending in fiscal 2013 for national security, including the Department of Defense, Atomic Energy Defense Activities, Homeland Security, Veterans Affairs, and Department of State and other international programs. The discretionary spending for the Department of Defense in fiscal 2013 was approximately $608 billion, including over $80 billion for Overseas Contingency Operations (OCO), essentially expenses for the wars in Iraq and Afghanistan. The key components of spending for security agencies are as follows:

Detail of 2013 National Defense Spending

	$ in billions
Department of Defense	
Military Personnel	$ 150.8
Operation and Maintenance (Includes OCO)	259.6
Procurement	114.9
R&D, Test and Evaluation	66.9
Other	15.5
Total Department of Defense	607.7
Atomic Energy Defense Activities	17.6
Homeland Security	57.2
Veterans Affairs	138.9
International Affairs	46.4
Other Defense Related	8.0
Total Security Agencies and Related	$ 875.8

Source: Fiscal Year 2015 Budget of the US Government, Table 28.1 and 29.1

Of course, not all of the spending detailed above is directly related to national defense. For example, the veterans affairs spending includes pensions and medical care for veterans, which does not provide any current defense capability, although it does represent a long-term cost of maintaining our military. The Department of Homeland Security includes the Federal Emergency Management Agency (FEMA), which includes disaster-relief spending, which would seem to be a mostly domestic concern. Homeland Security also includes the coast guard, which does represent national defense. In any case, the total spending above gives an idea of how much the United States spends for national defense, broadly defined, and the NIPA figure of $770 billion would seem to be a representative amount for total direct national defense spending in 2013.

I won't try to pinpoint precisely how much the United States needs to spend on national defense, basically because I don't have the expertise to properly evaluate the world risks and required military structure of the United States, but the total doesn't seem out of line one way or the other. However, I will make some general observations.

The first observation is the very high cost of the wars in Iraq and Afghanistan and related operations. While under $100 billion in 2013, the budget for Overseas Contingency Operations came in at almost $160 billion, or more than 1 percent of GDP, in 2011. I have seen various reports totaling the cost of the various wars at about $1 trillion. A March 2011 report issued by the Congressional Research Service estimates total war related spending of approximately $1.3 trillion through 2011, which could grow to a total of $1.8 trillion by 2021. Other more inclusive estimates of the total costs of the wars (for example, including long-term veteran medical and disability costs) range north of $4 trillion. Whether you believe the number is closer to $2 trillion or more than double that, $2 trillion to $4 trillion sure is a lot of money. As a point of comparison, $2 trillion represents nearly twenty years of the current defense-procurement budget and represents more than twenty years of the current cost of the food-stamp program. As I said before, a trillion dollars here and a trillion dollars there, and pretty soon you are talking about real money. And, of course, this does not include the very real human costs of war, including military and civilian fatalities, the large number of wounded and disabled veterans and civilians, and the strains on military families. Not to mention that after more than ten years of war in Iraq and Afghanistan, the United States' strategic goals have not been achieved. War is *always* more costly than expected! And it is a very serious matter, not to be taken lightly.

Second, one must look at United States defense spending in the global context. In 2009, the United States spent more on defense than any other country in the world—by a factor of almost ten times using official budgets at exchange rates. While some analyses put the advantage of the US defense spending over countries such as Russia and China at something closer to eight to one (with the margin probably shrinking, as Russia and China increase their military spending), that is still quite an impressive margin. In addition, the US defense spending represents about 44 percent of the global total, and the rest of NATO spending represents an additional 21 percent of the global total, so total NATO spending on defense is about two-thirds of the global total. Obviously, things can change, but there is currently no country that is even remotely a general threat to the United States, now that Russia and China are largely members of the worldwide community. And here's hoping that it stays that way, which is maybe a little less certain, given that, as of this writing, Russia has troops active inside Ukraine, and China has become more assertive in Asia. Countries such as Iran and North Korea are threats on a limited basis, but their military capabilities are dwarfed by the United States', and they have very limited abilities to project power beyond their immediate geographic areas. It is a fact that the United States is the world's military superpower.

Now, I am a big fan of a strong defense, since the best wars (and also the cheapest by far) are the ones that never need to be fought. And current defense spending, excluding the overseas contingency operations, is at the lower end of historical norms. But still, if we are trying to bring balance to the budget, it seems that well-planned long-term savings in defense spending has to at least be on the table.

Government Social Spending

Now we get to the big and growing category of federal spending on social programs. The chart below shows spending by the federal government by major social program (excluding certain payments made through the states) as a percent of GDP since 1929.

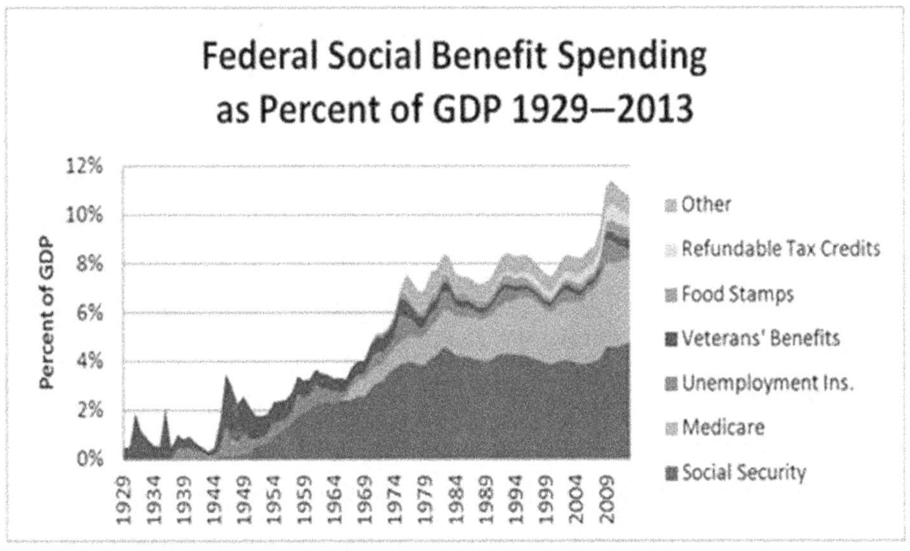

Note: Excludes Medicaid and certain social-transfer payments through the states.

Clearly, social security and Medicare constitute a large majority of federal social-benefit spending. These two programs are the largest federal programs, accounting for 41 percent of federal expenditures in fiscal 2013. Spending on Medicare, and spending on health care in general, are important issues and will be discussed further in a separate chapter. Social security itself consists of two main programs, the Old-Age and Survivors Insurance Trust Fund, which is what we typically think of when referring to social security, and the Disability Insurance Trust Fund, which pays disability benefits to disabled workers and dependents. The Old-Age and Survivors Trust Fund outlays in fiscal 2013 were $679.5 billion, and the outlays from the Disability Insurance Trust Fund were $143.4 billion, for total outlays of $822.9 billion. At the end of fiscal 2013, the combined trust funds had assets of over $2.7 trillion. All of these assets are invested in special nonmarketable securities of the US government (money the government owes to itself). This is roughly equivalent to keeping IOUs from yourself in your cookie jar at home in case of an emergency. The thought may be there, but the practical benefit of the "fund" is dubious.

Social Security's expenditures have exceeded noninterest income since 2010, and the trustees estimate that expenditures will remain greater than noninterest income throughout the seventy-five-year projection period. The trustees also estimate that the combined trust-fund reserves will be exhausted in 2033 (although, again, the reserves are loans by the government to the government).

Social Security, established in 1935, is the federal government's largest program, with 58 million people receiving some form of benefits in December 2013. Of those receiving benefits, 70 percent were retired workers and dependents, 11 percent were survivors of deceased workers, and 19 percent were disabled workers and dependents receiving benefits under the Disability Insurance program. Total benefit payments and administrative costs in 2013 were $823 billion (including the Disability Insurance program).

We will focus on funding for Social Security in more detail in the chapter on taxes, but the main source of funds for Social Security comes from payroll taxes paid by employees and their employers. As such, Social Security is a self-funding program, and by statute, benefits can only be paid out of the fund's revenues and trust funds. The payroll tax only applies to taxable earnings up to a maximum, which in 2013 was $113,700. Until very recently, total Social Security revenues have generally exceeded total benefits, thus leading to the growth in the trust funds to more than $2.7 trillion at December 2013.

Most people know that Social Security is the mandatory retirement program run by the federal government, but probably not many are familiar with the actual details. Basically, workers are eligible to receive retirement benefits if they are sixty-two or older, although benefits are reduced for workers who begin to collect before reaching the full retirement age, currently sixty-six years. To be eligible for benefits, a worker generally must have paid a sufficient amount of Social Security taxes for at least ten years. Benefits are determined by a formula that takes into account lifetime earnings of each worker; specifically, benefits are calculated based on the average of the highest thirty-five years of earnings that are subject to Social Security taxes. This is expressed as the averaged indexed monthly earnings (AIME). For retirees, earnings before age sixty are indexed for inflation and the economy-wide real growth in earnings, while earnings after age sixty are taken at their actual amounts. For workers who have worked fewer than thirty-give years, the "missing" years are included at zero. Thus, for a worker who had earnings for twenty-five years, benefits would be based on the twenty-five years of earnings and ten years with zero earnings. Of course, such a worker would have only paid twenty-five years of Social Security taxes, so the treatment is consistent. Therefore, to maximize your social security benefits, it pays to have thirty-five years of earnings so that there are no zero-earnings years in your AIME (upon which your benefits are based). On the other hand, working an additional ten years (to a total of forty-five) may not raise your AIME at all (assuming those extra years are average income years), even though you would have paid an additional ten years of social security taxes.

The calculation of Social Security benefits is based on a fairly progressive formula because of the factors that are applied to each worker's AIME. For 2014, the primary insurance amount (PIA), or the monthly benefit payable to a worker who begins to receive Social Security benefits at the age at which the worker is entitled to receive full benefits, is calculated as 90 percent of the first $816 of the AIME, plus 32 percent of the AIME between $816 and $4,917, plus 15 percent of the AIME above $4,917.

As a result, a worker who retired at the full retirement age and who had an AIME of $816 ($9,792 annualized) would receive a monthly benefit of $734 ($8,813 annually), or basically 90 percent of their indexed thirty-five-year average earnings. By comparison, a worker with an AIME of $4,917 ($59,004 annualized) would receive a monthly benefit of $2,046 ($24,552 annually), or 42 percent of their indexed thirty-five-year average earnings. Finally, a higher-income worker with an AIME of, say, $8,000 ($96,000 annualized) would receive a monthly benefit of $2,509 ($30,108 annually), or 31 percent of their indexed thirty-five-year average earnings.

Thus, while the higher-earning worker would receive a greater benefit, the benefit would replace a much smaller percentage of that worker's preretirement earnings. Since Social Security taxes are applied as a constant percentage of taxable earnings, Social Security is a much better deal for lower-income workers than it is for higher-income workers. Again, for earnings in each year that are in excess of the taxable maximum subject to social taxes ($113,700 in 2013), neither taxes nor calculated benefits apply.

The fact that nearly all workers pay Social Security taxes and nearly all retirees receive Social Security benefits is probably why the program garners so much support. (That, plus the large number of voting senior citizens!) Much of the criticism of the program focuses on the low level of returns on the trust-fund assets, which are invested in federal-government bonds rather than higher-yielding investments, and the claim that it is a bad deal for participants. However, while it may be a "bad" deal for higher-income workers, it is a very good deal for lower-income workers. After all, the money is going somewhere since only 1 percent of Social Security's revenues go toward the costs of administering the program. The rest is paid in benefits or added to the trust fund to pay future benefits. The CBO estimates that for those workers born between 1960 and 1969, the bottom quintile by income will receive approximately 122 percent in lifetime benefits of their lifetime social security taxes paid (in present values), compared to the highest quintile of workers by income, who will receive only 60 percent in lifetime benefits of lifetime taxes paid (in present values). In other words, the bottom 20 percent of workers by income will receive roughly twice as much benefit per their Social Security taxes paid as the top 20 percent of workers by income.

Is this unfair? From a purely return-on-investment point of view, of course it is. From a public-policy point of view, I am not so sure. After all, higher-income earners typically participate in other tax-advantaged savings plans such as defined-benefit pension and 401k plans. While these types of plans may also be available to lower-income workers, the dollars involved and the taxes sheltered are lower on average for lower-income workers. The fact that social security may be the biggest income-transfer scheme in the United States is in my view actually a positive. At least, unlike the case with the federal income tax (which, as we shall see later, only about 50 percent of Americans pay), almost every worker participates and pays taxes into the social security system. So it truly is social insurance; it is a predetermined lifetime income-smoothing plan designed to at least provide a minimum of income in old age for workers and their spouses. The social security system is a big reason why the poverty rate for people age sixty-five years and older went from 35.2 percent in 1959 to 9.1 percent in 2012. That alone is probably worth something from a social point of view.

The Social Security Disability Insurance program has been growing rapidly and is currently in a much more dire financial position than the Old-Age and Survivors Insurance program, running a large deficit and projected to exhaust trust-fund reserves in 2016. Much of the growth in Disability Insurance payments can be traced to the 1984 Social Security Amendments that relaxed some of the prior restrictions and extended allowances to people with certain mental and musculoskeletal impairments (for example, depression and lower back pain) as well as to recessionary periods, when people may be more inclined to seek disability after losing a job. In 2010, mental disorders comprised 32.8 percent of workers on Disability Insurance and people with musculoskeletal system and connective tissue problems comprised 28.2 percent. Obviously many, and probably most, of these workers are truly disabled, but this is also an area ripe for questionable cases, where workers may be able to work despite their conditions, as well as cases of outright fraud. In any case, the $140 billion in benefits from the Disability Insurance Trust Fund in 2013 was more than double the level ten years prior and more than four times the level in 1993. Total outlays in 2013 exceeded total income by $32 billion for the Disability Insurance program. This is clearly an area where spending can be cut simply through better management.

Medicare

Next on our list is spending for Medicare, which was $583 billion in 2013, representing 3.5 percent of GDP. This is up dramatically from $0 in 1965, when Medicare was established, and Medicare will continue to be one of the fastest-growing categories of federal spending for the foreseeable future. In fact, the trustees of the Medicare trust fund project that total Medicare costs will increase to 5.3 percent of GDP by 2035 and will increase gradually thereafter to about 6.9 percent of GDP by 2088.

Medicare generally provides hospital and medical insurance for all persons over the age of sixty-five who have been legal residents of the United States for at least five years. Broader prescription-drug coverage was added on

January 1, 2006. In 2013, 52.3 million people were covered under Medicare. The trustees project that the Medicare Hospital Insurance Trust Fund will be depleted in 2030, at which time dedicated revenues will be sufficient to pay 85 percent of hospital insurance Medicare costs.

Other Government Social Benefits

Other government social benefits from the National Income and Product Account data—consisting of unemployment benefits, veterans' benefits, food stamps, refundable tax credits, and other—totaled about $435 billion in 2013, down slightly from 2010 due to the improving economy but still representing 2.6 percent of GDP, up from 1.5 percent in 2000. Many of these programs are designed to offer relief from job loss or support for low-income Americans. We will spend more time discussing these programs in Chapter 10.

Grants to State and Local Governments

As mentioned earlier, the largest component of federal grants-in-aid to state and local governments are related to health, primarily Medicaid. In fact, of the $450 billion in federal grants to state and local governments in the National Income and Product Accounts in 2013, $280 billion was for health care, of which $267 billion was related to Medicaid. This represented approximately 1.7 percent of GDP. Other relatively large components of this category of federal spending include income security of $89 billion, of which $76 billion is for welfare and social services; education support of $39 billion; housing and community services of $19 billion; and economic affairs of $11 billion. Again, we will cover some of these categories of spending in more detail in Chapter 10.

Interest

Interest payments by the federal government comprise the easy category. It is a function of the level of federal debt to the public and interest rates. Interest payments were as high as 4 percent of GDP and more than 20 percent of total federal expenditures during much of the 1980s due to the high interest rates that were prevalent for much of that period, and they are now running at about 2.5 percent of GDP. Interest payments have actually decreased somewhat in recent years, even as the total federal debt has increased due to the very low level of current interest rates. Obviously, this category of expenditures could increase rapidly if debt levels continue to grow and if interest rates were to increase from their current record-low levels.

Spending Overview

So that is a brief overview of the total $5.8 trillion in all government spending and the approximately $4.0 trillion in federal-government spending. While every area of government spending can and should be targeted for reductions, at the federal level we are forced to consider the big-dollar areas of defense and, in particular, government social spending (including transfers to the states), which combined account for about 75 percent of total federal-government spending. Within the category of government social-benefit spending, the largest and the fastest-growing spending categories, and thus the largest opportunities for long-term savings, are health-care spending (Medicare and Medicaid) and certain aspects of the social security program.

CHAPTER 6

The Government Taxes

The subjects of every state ought to contribute towards the support of the government, as nearly as possible, in proportion to their respective abilities; that is, in proportion to the revenue which they respectively enjoy under the protection of the state.

ADAM SMITH, *THE WEALTH OF NATIONS*, 1776

OKAY, SO ALL LEVELS OF government (federal, state, and local) spent $5.8 trillion in 2013, equal to roughly 34.5 percent of GDP and $47,500 per US household (approximately 122 million households in the United States). Interesting that total government spending per household is almost equal to the median household income, meaning that if all US households contributed equally to funding total government spending, half of all US households would be paying all or more than all of their household incomes in taxes. Obviously that is not the case, so how was this spending financed? The charts below show the sources of funding for total government spending in 2013 (federal, state, and local).

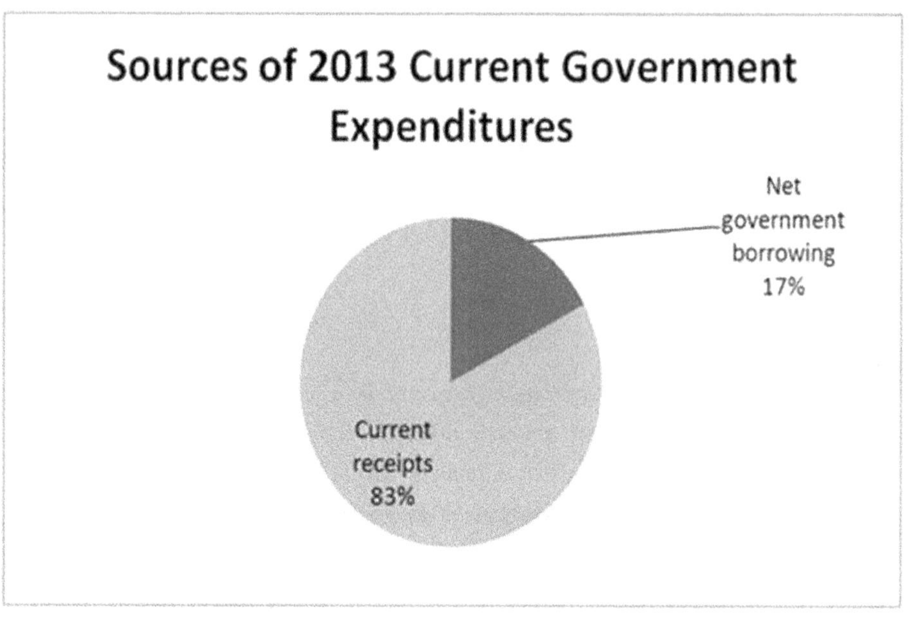
Sources of 2013 Current Government Expenditures
Net government borrowing 17%
Current receipts 83%

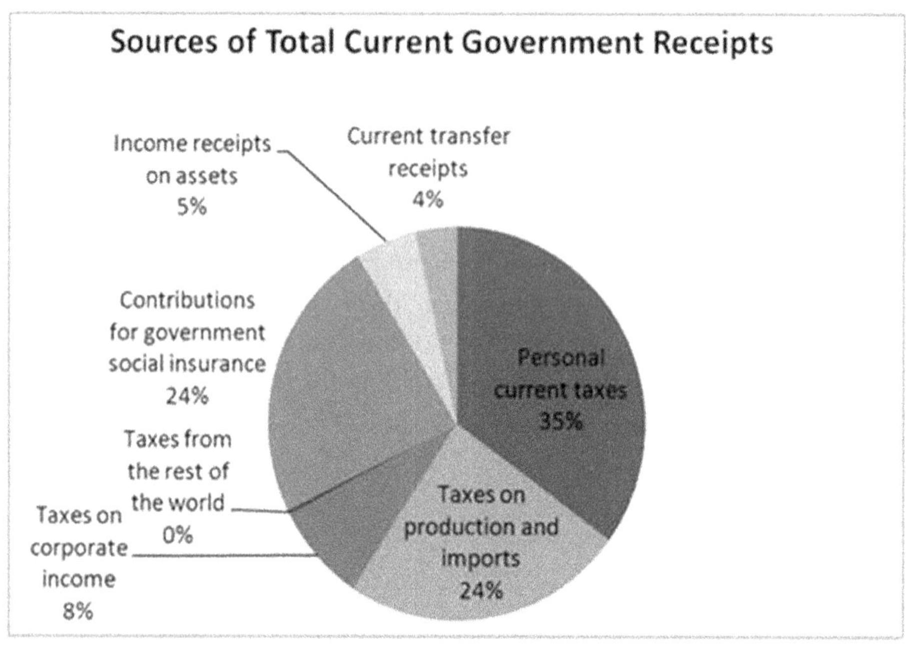
Sources of Total Current Government Receipts
Income receipts on assets 5%
Current transfer receipts 4%
Contributions for government social insurance 24%
Personal current taxes 35%
Taxes from the rest of the world 0%
Taxes on corporate income 8%
Taxes on production and imports 24%

In the aggregate at all levels of government, current receipts were $4.7 trillion in 2013, or 83 percent of current expenditures, and net government borrowing was approximately $1.0 trillion, or 17 percent of current expenditures. Personal income taxes represented approximately 35 percent of current receipts; taxes on production and imports (which includes sales and real-estate taxes) represented approximately 24 percent of total current government receipts; corporate income taxes represented approximately 8 percent of total current receipts; contributions for government social insurance (both from individuals and corporations) represented approximately 24 percent of total current receipts; and miscellaneous other sources represented approximately 9 percent of total receipts.

Total taxes at all levels of government in the United States in 2013 represented approximately 26 percent of GDP. Does that sound like a high number, a low number, or just about right? It certainly seems high, but compared to our Organization for Economic Co-operation and Development (OECD) peers, the United States is on the lower side, with an OECD average of about 34 percent in 2012. The United Kingdom and Germany come in close to the OECD average, at about 35 and 38 percent, respectively, while Sweden, France, and Italy are at about 44 to 45 percent of GDP. Denmark sets the high standard, with total taxes at about 48 percent of GDP, while Mexico is the lowest OECD nation, at about 19 percent of GDP.

Total Tax Revenue as a Percent of GDP

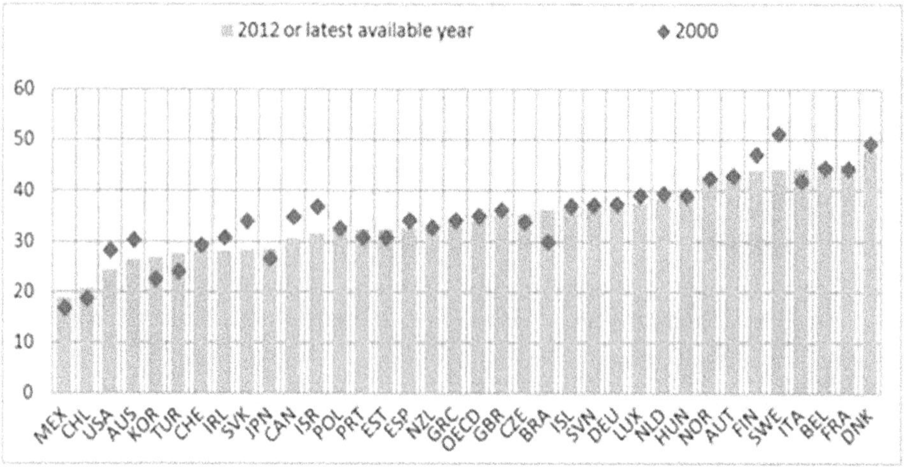

Source: OECD

Interestingly, the OECD reports that the United States is close to the OECD average in terms of taxes levied on income and profits, at 11.6 percent of GDP (excluding social security taxes). Where the United States differs from the typical OECD nation is on taxes levied on goods and services, where such taxes equal 4.6 percent of GDP in the United States, less than half of the OECD average. This is partly the result of value-added taxes (VAT), which are widely used in many countries but not in the United States.

Taxes on Income and Profits as a Percent of GDP

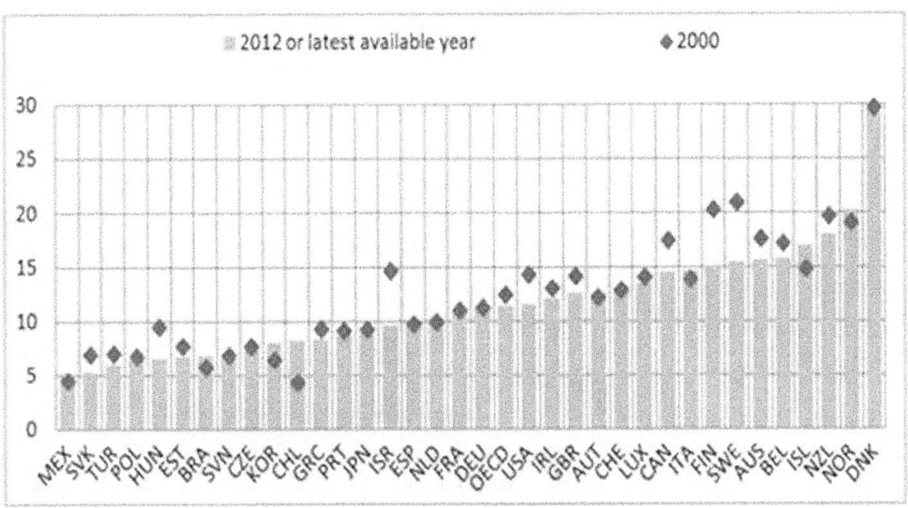

Source: OECD

Taxes on Goods and Services as a Percent of GDP

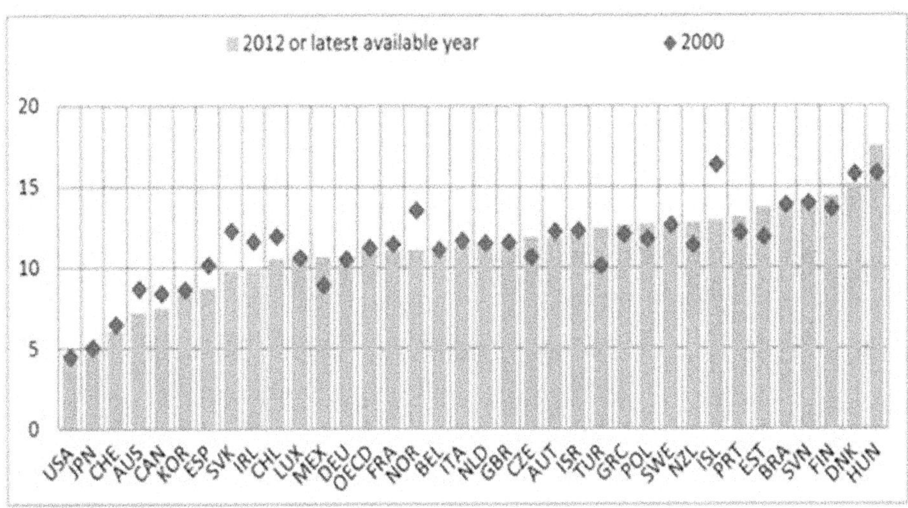

Source: OECD

Of course, the breakdown of US taxes and other revenue sources differs greatly at the local versus state versus federal level, as shown below.

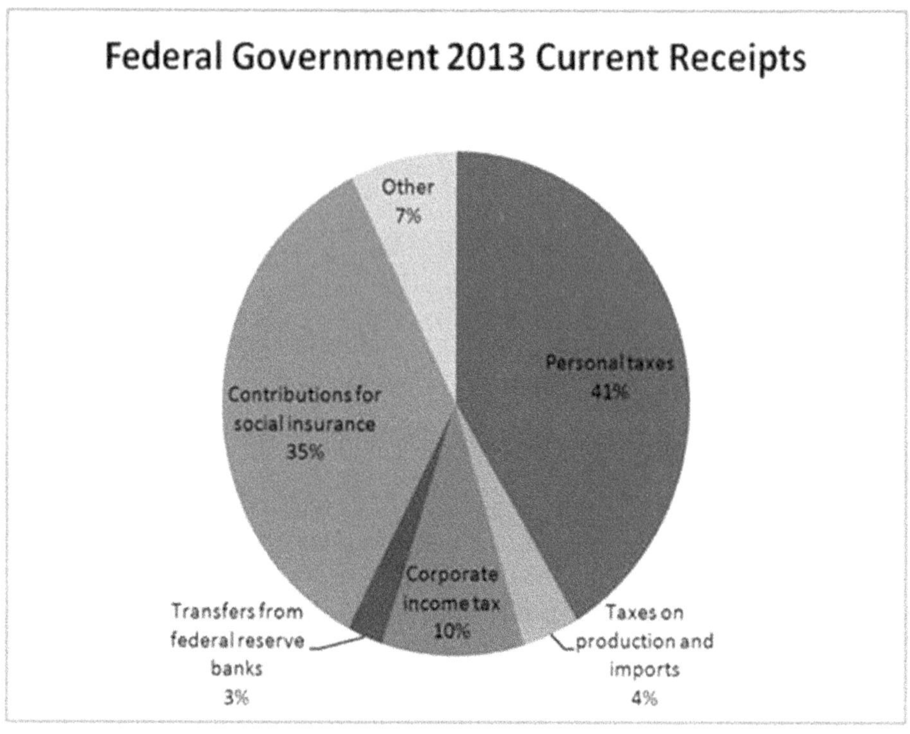

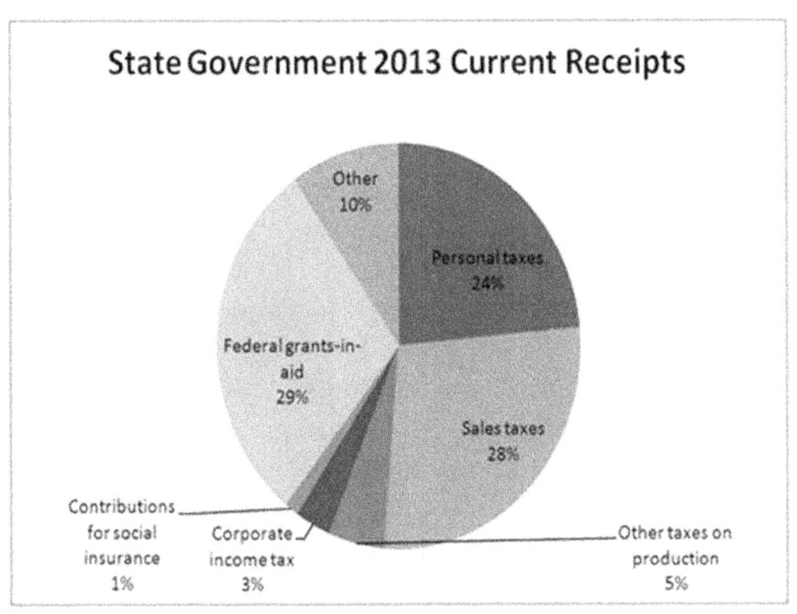
State Government 2013 Current Receipts
Other
10%
Personal taxes
24%
Federal grants-in-aid
29%
Sales taxes
28%
Contributions for social insurance
1%
Corporate income tax
3%
Other taxes on production
5%

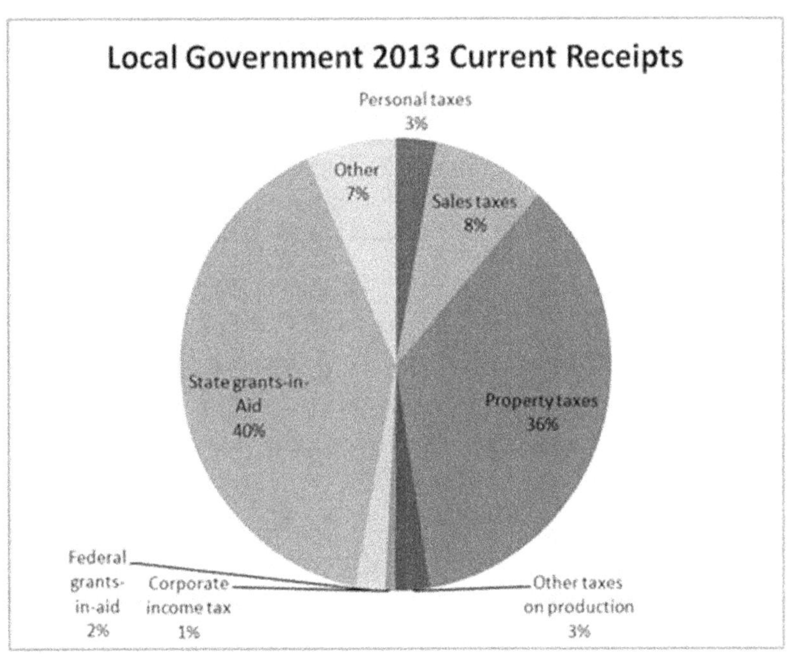
Local Government 2013 Current Receipts
Personal taxes
3%
Other
7%
Sales taxes
8%
State grants-in-Aid
40%
Property taxes
36%
Federal grants-in-aid
2%
Corporate income tax
1%
Other taxes on production
3%

Thus, for local government, tax revenue is dominated by real-estate taxes, which accounted for 71 percent of all local government tax revenue and 36 percent of all local government current receipts in 2013. The largest single source of local funding was grants-in-aid from the state governments, which represented 40 percent of local receipts (the biggest use of these grants are for education). At the state level, the largest sources of tax revenue are sales taxes, which accounted for 47 percent of tax revenue and 28 percent of total current receipts, and personal income taxes, which accounted for 40 percent of tax revenue and 24 percent of current receipts. The largest single source of revenue for the state governments is federal grants-in-aid, which represented 29 percent of current receipts of the states in 2013 (and represented 35 percent of current state receipts in 2010, due to the impact of the economic recession and increased federal support for the states).

The federal government accounted for 55 percent of the total tax burden in the United States in 2013 (66 percent if contributions for social insurance are included—these are, of course, taxes). Based on the National Income and Product Accounts, the federal government raised approximately $1.8 trillion from taxes in 2013, of which approximately $1.3 trillion was from personal income taxes and $385 billion was from corporate income taxes (including about $80 billion in transfers from Federal Reserve banks). Total tax receipts (excluding social security) were down 29 percent in 2009 from the 2007 level, as the economy took a toll on both individuals and corporations, but by 2013, they had increased by 50 percent from the 2009 level to reach a new all-time high. In addition, in 2013, the federal government took in an additional $1.1 trillion in contributions for government social insurance, primarily social security and Medicare taxes, so total federal tax receipts were almost $3 trillion, with the largest source of revenue from personal income taxes. Personal and corporate taxes represented approximately 43 percent of current federal spending, contributions for social insurance represented an additional 29 percent of current federal spending, and net government borrowing represented 20 percent of current federal spending. In 2009, net federal-government borrowing represented 36 percent of current federal expenditures and was the largest single source of government funding. Now that's what I call a deficit! Excise taxes and customs duties, which provided 3 percent of the federal budget in 2013, provided approximately 40 percent of the federal budget in 1929.

The above data is from the National Income and Product Accounts, but the federal data from the Office of Management and Budget is comparable.

History of the Federal Income Tax

Importantly, the federal income tax has undergone many iterations over the last century or so, according to the perceived needs of the government at the time. This is at least partially responsible for the snarled condition of the system today. To illustrate the complexity of this system, this section details some of the major developmental stages of the federal income tax.

Today, the largest source of federal-government revenues is from personal income taxes. While the United States federal government has at times during its history imposed a tax on income, initially in 1861 to help pay for the Civil War, the modern-day income tax was instituted in 1913 following the ratification of the sixteenth amendment to the Constitution, which states, "the Congress shall have the power to lay and collect taxes on incomes, from whatever source derived, without apportionment among the several states, and without regard to any census or enumeration." Prior to that amendment, proponents of an income tax were hampered by the inconvenient language in Section 9 of the Constitution (Limits on Congress) which states that "No capitation, or other direct Tax shall be laid, unless in Proportion to the Census or Enumeration herein before directed to be taken." Does this seem clear? Not to me, but in 1895, the Supreme Court ruled that a tax on receipts from the use of property was unconstitutional (as it was deemed to be a "direct" tax), effectively prohibiting a federal income tax in the United States until the ratification of the Sixteenth Amendment.

When initially instituted in 1913, the tax rate on the lowest tax bracket was 1 percent, and it applied to taxable income of up to $20,000, or approximately $465,000 in 2013 dollars. The highest tax rate, 7 percent, applied to taxable income of over $500,000, or about the equivalent of $11 million in 2013 dollars. By comparison, today's top bracket starts at $400,000 (for 2014 single filer). In addition, in 1913, the personal exemption was set at $3,000 for single persons and $4,000 for married couples (the equivalent of approximately $70,000 and $93,000 in 2013 dollars). As a result, the extent of the impact of the tax was clearly limited in its scope. In the first year, the IRS received a total of 358,000 returns with a total income tax liability of $28 million. It almost seems quaint given more modern practice.

The big impetus to the growth in the income tax was the need to finance the costs of the First World War. By 1918, the income tax rolls had expanded to almost 3.5 million returns, and total tax receipts had increased to over $1.1 billion. The tax on the lowest income bracket had increased to 6 percent on taxable income of up to $4,000 (almost $62,000 in inflation-adjusted 2013 dollars), and the top rate had increased to 77 percent on taxable income over $1,000,000 (almost $15,500,000 in 2013 dollars). The tax schedule grew to include over 50 tax brackets. The income tax had established its credentials as a powerful revenue raiser.

Still, by 1934, personal income taxes totaled only $420 million and represented 14 percent of total federal-government receipts, while corporate income taxes represented a further 12 percent of federal receipts. The largest sources of federal receipts in 1934 were excise taxes, which comprised 46 percent of total federal receipts and "other" (primarily estate and gift taxes and customs duties and fees), at 27 percent of the total.

Once again, it was war, this time World War II, which firmly established individual and corporate income taxes as the primary sources of federal finance. By 1945, the tax rate applied to the lowest income bracket had risen to 23 percent on taxable income of up to $2,000 (approximately $26,000 in 2013 dollars), and the top rate had increased to 94 percent on taxable income above $200,000 (approximately $2.6 million in 2011 dollars). Of course, there were many intermediate brackets in between. Total individual income taxes increased to about twenty times the level paid as recently as 1940, came to represent 8.1 percent of GDP (about the same as in 2013), and comprised 41 percent of total federal receipts. Similarly, total corporate income taxes increased to about thirteen times the level of 1940 and comprised 35 percent of total federal receipts in 1945.

With the end of the war in 1945, defense expenditures began to decline dramatically, and yet total federal-government expenditures and tax receipts had reached a new level. Although total federal-government receipts declined to 14.1 percent of GDP by 1950 (from a peak of 20.5 percent of GDP at the height of the war in 1944), this was still almost three times the level that had prevailed in the mid-1930s. Personal income taxes represented 5.6 percent of GDP in 1950, over five times the level collected in the mid-1930s. Marginal tax rates remained high after the war, eventually settling in at 70 percent at the top tax bracket in 1965 and generally remaining at that level until the Reagan tax reforms in 1981, which dramatically simplified personal income taxes and lowered the tax rate on the top bracket to 28 percent by 1988. Still, despite the decrease in rates in the mid-1980s, total personal income taxes as a percent of GDP generally ran at 8 percent of GDP, not dissimilar to historical trends and roughly the same as in 2013.

Immediately prior to the American Taxpayer Relief Act of 2012, the United States had six tax brackets, with the top rate of 35 percent applied to taxable income over $388,350. Generally, taxes on capital gains and dividend income were limited to a rate of 15 percent. These rates were the result of the Jobs and Growth Tax Relief Reconciliation Act of 2003, otherwise known as the Bush tax cuts. Prior to this, the top tax rate was 39.6 percent per the Omnibus Budget Reconciliation Act of 1993, and in 2000, this rate applied to income above $288,350 (or approximately $385,000 in constant 2013 dollars), and the capital gains tax rate was 20 percent (dividends were taxed at ordinary rates).

Most of the Bush tax cuts were scheduled to expire at the end of 2010, but were extended for an additional two years in December 2010 under the Tax Relief, Unemployment Insurance Reauthorization, and Job Creation Act of 2010. In addition, the estate tax was reinstated at a rate of 35 percent on estates above $5 million, and payroll taxes were cut for working families. The estate tax was allowed to lapse altogether in 2010, but in 2011, it was scheduled to return to its much higher level of ten years prior. Yes, I know this makes no logical sense. Under the American Taxpayer Relief Act of 2012, the top income tax rate for 2013 returned to 39.6 percent for taxpayers with income over $400,000 ($450,000 filing jointly), and the top capital-gains tax rate returned to 20 percent, plus an additional 3.8 percent investment income tax as a part of the Affordable

Care Act. The estate tax was set at 40 percent after a $5 million exemption per person.

The most recent recession had a dramatic impact on tax receipts even though rates remained largely unchanged. Total federal receipts in 2007 comprised 17.9 percent of GDP, of which eight percentage points were from personal income taxes, down from the post-war peak of total receipts of 19.9 percent of GDP and personal income taxes of 9.9 percent of GDP in 2000. These percentages declined further by 2010 to 14.6 percent and 6.1 percent, respectively, as the economy put a crimp in incomes before recovering in 2013 to reach total tax receipts of 16.7 percent of GDP and personal income tax receipts of 7.9 percent of GDP. By 2014, total tax receipts had increased to 17.5 percent of GDP, and personal income tax receipts had increased to 8.1 percent of GDP.

Since 1922, the tax code has generally had more favorable tax rates for capital gains than for other forms of investment income and ordinary income as an inducement to capital investment. The only exception was in the years 1988 through 1990 when capital gains were taxed at the same rate as ordinary income as part of an overall lowering of tax rates (to a top rate of 28 percent). From 2003 to 2012, the maximum tax rate on capital gains was at a post-war low of 15 percent, and for the first time, it also applied to qualifying dividend income. The primary rationale for applying the more favorable capital gains tax treatment to dividend income was to account for the fact that these earnings had already been taxed at the corporate level prior to being distributed to shareholders in the form of dividends.

It bears pointing out that we have not one but two income-tax methodologies in the United States due to the Alternative Minimum Tax. This is an alternative tax calculation based on a nearly flat tax rate of 26 percent or 28 percent and a much higher personal exemption. In addition, taxpayers are not allowed certain deductions that are permitted when computing the regular tax, most notably deductions for local and state taxes. As a result, residents of high-tax states are more likely to owe taxes based on AMT than are residents of low-tax states. Since AMT is a parallel tax calculation, taxpayers need to compute the tax based on both the regular tax and the AMT and pay the higher amount.

Over time, more and more taxpayers have been subject to AMT as regular tax rates have declined and as the income threshold for AMT has declined in real terms due to inflating incomes. In 2008, approximately 3.9 million returns were subject to AMT, raising approximately $26 billion, up from 1.1 million returns and $6.8 billion in 2001. Far from targeting mostly the truly rich (as Mitt Romney has so helpfully demonstrated), the AMT most frequently affects taxpayers with annual incomes between $100,000 and $500,000.

As is usually the case with the US tax system, it all gets a little complicated—and unnecessarily so.

Corporate Income Taxes

The history of the corporate income tax is similar to the history of personal income taxes. Prior to World War I, the top tax rate was 1 percent, and by 1918 it had increased to 12 percent as part of the World War I funding effort. From 1919 through 1939, the top rate began a slow climb from 10 percent in 1919 to 19 percent by 1938. Again, World War II was the impetus for a dramatic increase in the corporate tax rate, to 40 percent by 1942. The top rate hit 52 percent in 1952 and remained in the high forties to low fifties until 1986, when rates began a decline to 34 percent, increasing to 35 percent in 1993 and remaining at that level through to today. Since 1951, corporate taxes as a percent of GDP have declined by nearly two-thirds, and they represented 10 percent of total federal receipts in 2013.

Despite the decline in corporate tax rates since 1986, the United States retains one of the highest corporate tax rates of any economically advanced nation in the world, particularly when state corporate income taxes are included. When the weighted-average state corporate tax rate is factored in, the total combined effective corporate income tax rate comes in at a little over 39 percent. While a couple of other advanced countries also have high corporate tax rates, notably Japan at about 37 percent, the OECD average is only about 25 percent. Ireland is at the low end at 12.5 percent, which is why a number of very profitable international companies have extensive operations (and income) in Ireland.

Even in a closed domestic economy, high corporate income taxes serve to reduce investment by increasing the cost of capital for businesses. As a result, businesses must earn a higher return on any prospective investment, which serves to reduce the number of attractive investment opportunities. However, in an open global economy, this impact is magnified. For example, if a US-based company and an Ireland-based company are looking at the same business opportunity, the Ireland-based company would have an advantage over the US-based company because its profits would be taxed at only 12.5 percent versus, say, 39 percent for the US-based company. Of course, this assumes that all other factors are equal, such as cost of labor, transportation, and so forth. While this would obviously not be the case (and such unequal factors could weigh the balances in favor of either company), the differing tax rates would strongly favor the Ireland-based company.

For multinational companies, the impact is again greater, for a US-based multinational could elect to base some of its operations in Ireland or some other low-tax country to take advantage of the lower tax rates. This is why many US-headquartered companies elect to base research activities in Ireland and lease the resulting intellectual property to their other subsidiaries (in the United States, for example). This allows them to shift income to Ireland and incur expenses in the United States. This tax planning, in addition to having a real economic impact because of the higher investment in the lower-tax countries and the lower investment in the higher-tax countries (such as the United States), shifts potential income from the United States to other countries and thus reduces taxes paid in the United States. In contrast to individuals, which are generally not as likely to move out of the United States to low-tax countries and renounce their citizenship, multinational companies have less of a problem in doing this (nor should they). In addition, since US corporations are generally required to pay US income taxes on the repatriation of overseas profits, a number of global US companies maintain very large cash holdings overseas, which totaled about $840 billion in 2012, or about 58 percent of their total cash holdings, according to Moody's Investors Service. This inefficiency is a further inducement to invest funds overseas at the expense of US investment.

Social Security and Other Taxes

One thing that has changed dramatically over the years is the increased impact of social insurance and retirement receipts (social security and Medicare), which have increased from less than 2 percent of GDP in the early 1950s to 5.7 percent of GDP in 2013. Social Security and related taxes represented 34 percent of total federal receipts in 2013. Social Security and Medicare Hospital Insurance are financed primarily from employment taxes. The current tax rate for Social Security is 6.2 percent of wages and for Medicare hospital insurance is 1.45 percent of wages, paid each by the employee and the employer. For self-employed workers, the rate is double (basically paying both the employee and the employer portion). For 2011, the social security tax rate was reduced by two percentage points for employees and self-employed persons as part of the Tax Relief, Unemployment Insurance Reauthorization, and Job Creation Act of 2010, which temporary reduction expired at the end of 2012. The social security taxes are applied to a maximum contribution and base earnings for each employee, which was $113,700 for 2013. Thus, an individual with wages equal to or larger than $113,700 would have social security taxes of $7,049.40 in 2013 (6.2 percent of $113,700), and his or her employer would also pay $7,049.40. There is currently no limit on wages subject to the 1.45 percent Medicare hospital insurance tax (both employee and employer). Per the Affordable Care Act, in 2013, an additional hospital insurance tax of 0.9 percent is assessed on earned income exceeding $200,000 for individuals and $250,000 for married couples filing jointly.

The increase in social security and Medicare taxes as a share of federal receipts has been largely offset by declines in corporate income taxes and excise taxes. Total federal receipts in 2013 were comprised of individual income taxes (47 percent), corporate income taxes (10 percent), social insurance and retirement receipts (34 percent), excise taxes (3 percent), and other (6 percent). Estate and gift taxes, which are part of the "other" component, were less than 1 percent of total federal receipts. The chart below shows the various sources of federal receipts as a percent of the total from 1934 through 2013.

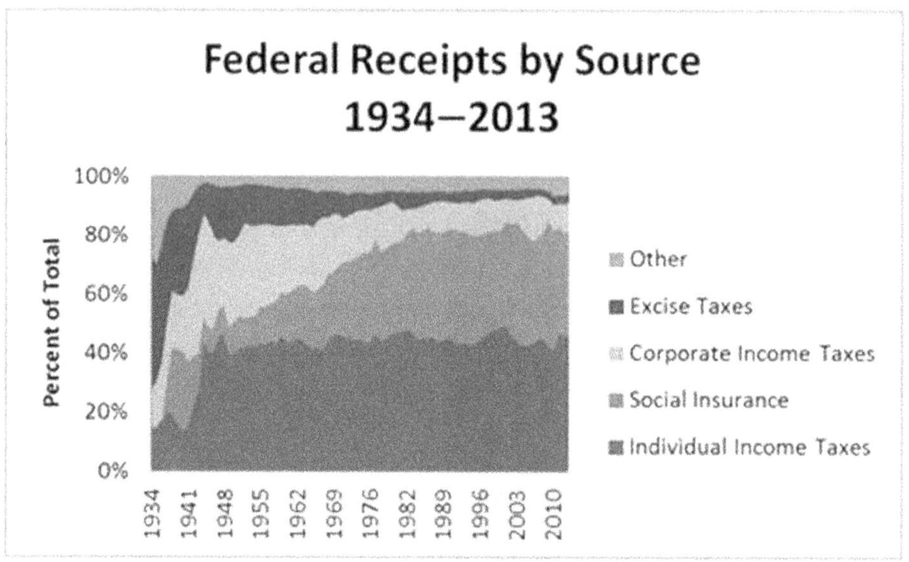

What is interesting is that despite all the changes in the tax code over the past sixty years or so, the revenues from individual income taxes and the total of all federal receipts as a share of GDP haven't changed all that much. Total federal receipts were 17 percent of GDP in 1956, 1968, 1986, 1992, 1993, 2002, and very nearly in 2013, and they ranged from 17 to 18 percent of GDP in thirty-four of the sixty-four years between 1950 and 2013. Similarly, personal income taxes were between 7 and 8 percent of GDP in forty-three of the sixty-three years between 1950 and 2013. This steadiness in total tax receipts despite varying tax rates has been referred to as Hauser's Law, named for the economist W. Kurt Hauser, who wrote, "The historical record is quite simple. No matter what the tax rates have been, in postwar America tax revenues have remained at about 19.5

percent of GDP." I guess one could quibble over the accuracy of the 19.5 percent figure, or over whether it should really be referred to as Hauser's Observation (rather than an actual law—kind of like the "Pirates' Code" in Disney's *Pirates of the Caribbean* movie, which contains more "guidelines than actual rules"), but the numbers are remarkably stable, as shown in the chart below.

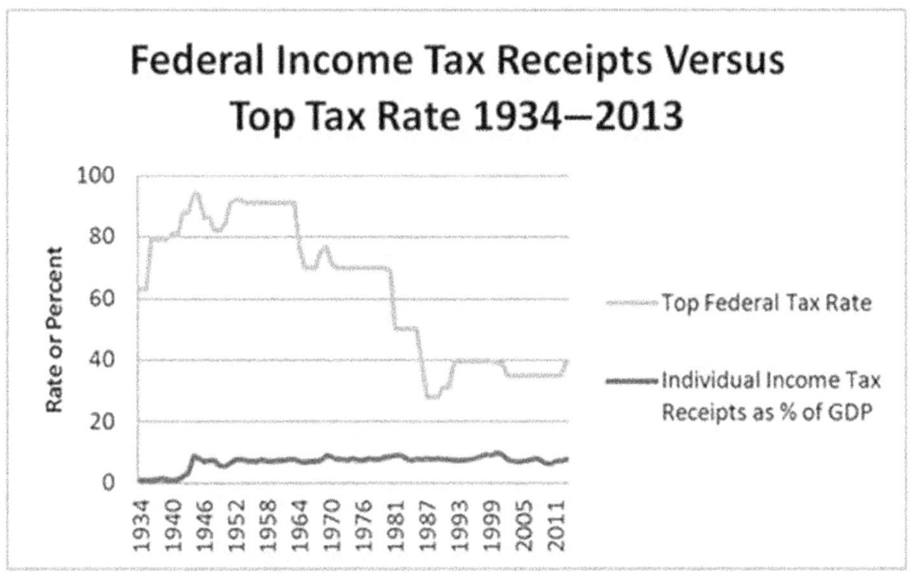

A similar concept dealing with the impact of higher marginal tax rates on total tax receipts is the Laffer Curve, named for the economist Arthur B. Laffer. An example of the Laffer Curve is depicted below.

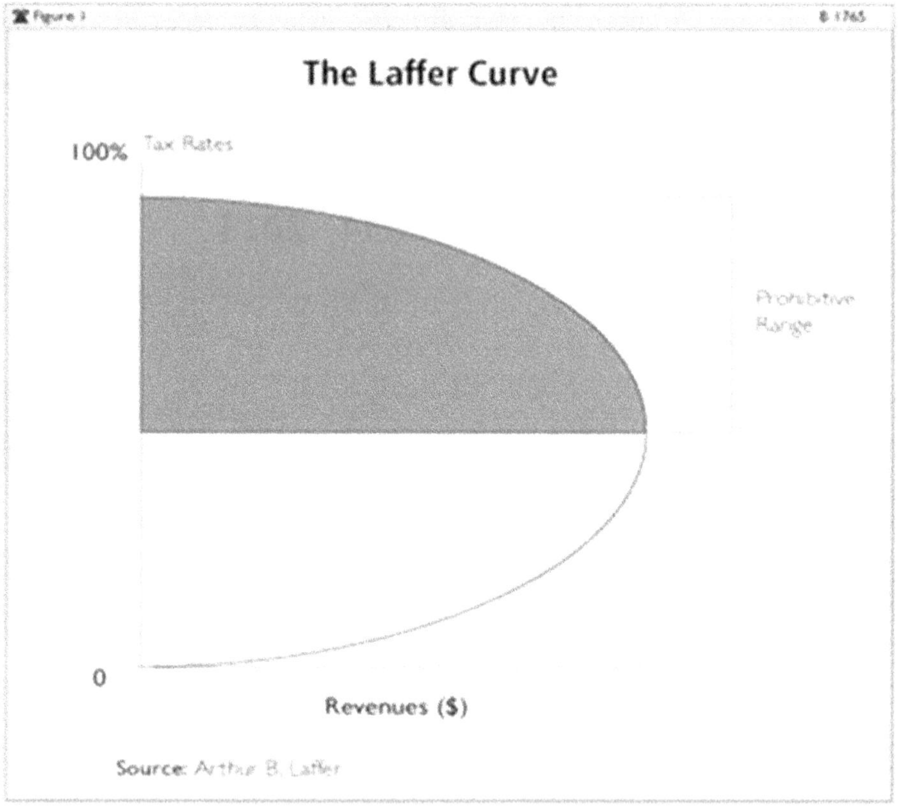

The graph shows total tax receipts as a function of tax rates. At the two extremes, tax revenues are zero. At a zero tax rate, no taxes are payable, and at a 100 percent tax rate, no income is earned (or at least reported) since there is no incentive to work (or a great incentive to not report income). In between, depending on where one is on the curve, a lower tax rate would either decrease revenues due to a lower statutory rate or possibly increase revenues due to an increase in output and income that more than offsets the impact of the lower tax rate. Presumably, if you are a fervent supply-sider, you believe we are perpetually on the top half of the graph. I have personally never seen the graph with any actual numbers displayed, perhaps to keep the mystery alive. One fears that if the revenue-maximizing tax rate were ever to be determined, that would be the rate we would have to live with.

As one might expect, Arthur Laffer is not the first one to make this observation. He reportedly drew the Laffer Curve on a napkin at a restaurant in Washington, DC, in 1974, but Dr. Laffer himself reports having no firm recollection of this. For some reason, anything sketched out on a napkin enjoys cult-like status, so the story persists. He also points out that the Laffer Curve was not invented by him, citing the Muslim philosopher Ibn Khaldun, who wrote in the fourteenth century, "It should be known that at the beginning of the dynasty, taxation yields a large revenue from small assessments. At the end of the dynasty, taxation yields a small revenue from large assessments."

What does our friend Adam Smith have to say on the subject? "High taxes, sometimes by diminishing the consumption of the taxed commodities, and sometimes by encouraging smuggling, frequently afford a smaller revenue to government than what might be drawn from more moderate taxes."

Seems insightful, if not immediately obvious. While Adam Smith is referring to excise taxes or import duties, the concept is the same as applied to income taxes. Simply raising tax rates at some point becomes counterproductive.

Other Tax Schemes

The United States has had the same basic tax system since World War II. However, several other tax schemes have been proposed, many supported by the economic profession for their relative simplicity and/or economic efficiency. Chief among these is the value-added tax ("VAT"), which is quite common in Europe. This is essentially a national sales tax, although the tax is collected at each level of production based on the "value added" and not at the final sales point. In this way, compliance is enhanced, and the ultimate tax is not as obvious to the consumer since it is imbedded in the price of the good or service being purchased. In some countries, this tax can be quite substantial. For example, in many of the European Union (EU) countries, the VAT rate is on the order of 20 percent to 25 percent. The main advantage to a value-added tax is that it can raise large amounts of revenue without as much of the distortion of the incentives to invest and work compared to a tax on income or wages. Since it does not typically apply to export goods, it is not as costly to exporters as an income or wage tax would be. Because it raises the price of goods, it does, of course, serve to reduce the level of consumption that would otherwise occur. It is still a tax, after all.

The primary objection to the VAT is that it is a regressive tax in that it applies to all consumers regardless of income level (much like sales taxes in the United States). This results in the poor paying more in VAT as a percentage of their income than higher-earning individuals, although obviously in proportion to their consumption.

Another tax concept that has been much talked about in the United States is the so-called "flat tax." While this concept can take many different forms, in its most simple form, this is really a variation of the income tax but with just one or a few (low) tax brackets. As a part of this, most if not all deductions from taxable income would be eliminated. In addition, in some forms of the proposal, all income from whatever source would be treated identically. The concept is to broaden the base of taxable income as much as possible in order to apply the lowest possible tax rate. As an example, the flat tax proposed by Steve Forbes during his Republican presidential primary run had a tax rate of 17 percent applied to all income above a standard deduction.

The ability to apply a low rate is typically based on eliminating a number of income deductions and tax credits that are endemic to the tax code. These income deductions and tax credits are commonly referred to as "tax expenditures" and total approximately $1.1 trillion per year according to the National Committee on Fiscal Responsibility and Reform ($1.2 trillion in 2012 based on information from the OMB). Hey, the deficit closed in one fell swoop just by eliminating all tax expenditures! The Office of Management and Budget lists 169 of these tax expenditures in 2012—there is quite literally something for everyone. While eliminating these deductions and credits (or loopholes, depending on your perspective) sounds good in the goal of lowering tax rates, these tax provisions include some very popular deductions. For example, the largest single tax cost item is the "exclusion of employer contributions for medical insurance premiums and medical care," which is estimated to have cost the Treasury $213 billion in reduced tax revenues in 2012. This meets the criteria of a tax expenditure because the cost of the health insurance is deductible by the employer as a legitimate business expense, but the value of the insurance to the employee is not included in the employee's taxable wages. As a result, the federal government heavily subsidizes employer-paid health care. Do the American people really want to end this favorable tax treatment? Probably not the ones who receive employer-provided health insurance. Other popular categories of tax expenditures include the net exclusion of various pension contributions and earnings, the deduction for mortgage-interest expense, deductions for charitable contributions, and the deduction of state and local taxes, among many others.

The main appeals of the flat tax are a greatly simplified tax code, eased cost of compliance, the reduced opportunity for fraud, and a much-reduced negative impact on the incentive to work, save, and invest due to the low marginal tax rate at all income levels. In addition, if all targeted deductions were truly eliminated, it would take the government out of the role of promoting favored industries or causes. Some would also say it is more fair since everyone would pay tax at the same rate (possibly after a standard deduction). The counterargument that the tax would be more regressive is somewhat offset by the elimination of deductions and other tax-planning strategies, which generally favor higher-income individuals.

Another tax scheme that has received some consideration is the so-called "FairTax," which is essentially a national sales tax that would replace all federal taxes on individual and corporate income. The federal tax system would move largely from a system of taxing income to taxing consumption. As proposed in the FairTax Act, the national sales tax rate would be set at 30 percent, although its backers prefer to reference the rate as a 23 percent "inclusive" rate to make it more comparable to an equivalent rate of tax on income. For example, if one has $100 of income that is taxed at 23 percent, then take home pay is $77 to spend on goods and services. Under the FairTax, the individual has no tax on income, so take-home pay is $100. If our consumer then buys $77 of goods or services, the tax is $23 based on a 30 percent sales-tax rate applied to the $77 cost of the item. The $23 in tax is 23 percent of the total cost of the item, *including* the associated tax. A little confusing, and mostly semantics, but hopefully you get the distinction.

In order to counter the regressive nature of the tax, the backers of the FairTax also propose a "prebate" based on family size. Each family would receive cash from the government that would essentially cover the national sales tax on a minimum level of purchases. As a result, a family near the poverty level or below would effectively not pay any tax since the prebate would be close to the tax on consumption of a near-poverty income level, while high consumers could pay something closer to the 23 percent rate. This prebate feature makes the tax more progressive on consumption while remaining regressive on income, since lower-income households typically consume much more of their income compared to high-income earners, who may save a material portion of their income. For example, in rough numbers, a family that has an income of $1,000,000 but lives on $100,000 per year (saving $900,000) would have a FairTax of $23,000 (23 percent of $100,000), less whatever the prebate is. Even before factoring in the prebate, the tax paid would only represent 2.3 percent of gross pretax income. You can see the inducement to saving as opposed to consumption.

Many of the advantages of the FairTax are similar to the advantages of the Value Added Tax. Since it is a tax on consumption rather than income, it helps to minimize the disincentives to work and save. In addition, it would help to increase US competitiveness by lowering the cost of doing business in the United States relative to the rest of the world (no employer wage tax or corporate income tax).

Of course, there are many variations or combinations of the above. For example, Arthur Laffer has proposed the repeal of the current version of the personal income tax, the corporate income tax, social security payroll taxes, and gift and estate taxes, to be replaced by a 13 percent flat tax on personal income (after some limited deductions) and a 13 percent business value-added tax (again, similar to a national sales tax). His calculations on 2007 data indicate that such a tax would raise approximately $2.4 trillion in revenue, equal to the total revenue raised by the taxes he suggests should be repealed. In this construct, revenues from personal income taxes would be roughly the same as before, while the proposed business value-added tax would raise as much as the corporate income tax, social security payroll taxes, and estate taxes combined. This is a simplification of the details of his proposal, but his overall objective is to maximize the tax base in order to minimize tax rates.

The "Fair and Flat Tax" recently proposed by Republican presidential candidate, Rand Paul, is very similar to the Laffer tax plan, with a 14.5% flat tax applied to all personal income (after some limited deductions) and a 14.5% business-activity tax on all companies.

Another variation on the theme that received much press in 2011 was the "9-9-9" plan that was proposed by Republican presidential primary candidate Herman Cain. His tax plan called for (1) a 9 percent business flat tax applied to gross income less all investments, all purchases from other businesses, and all dividends paid to shareholders; (2) an individual flat tax of 9 percent on gross income, less charitable deductions; and (3) a 9 percent national sales tax. As a part of the plan, Mr. Cain would eliminate all social security payroll taxes, end the estate tax, and have no tax on capital gains. Again, the objective is to maximize the tax base, minimize tax rates, and put more of an emphasis on taxing consumption rather that production. The objective, it is hoped, is more savings, more capital formation, and more economic growth.

One final tax scheme merits discussion, and this is the concept of a carbon tax. This can take the form of a gasoline tax—which is already prevalent in the United States and, particularly, in Europe—or other tax on carbon energy sources such as oil or coal. One could theoretically tax the commodities themselves or tax the users of the commodities for burning the oil and releasing the carbon into the atmosphere. I'll spend more time on the merits of a carbon tax in Chapter 8.

Conclusion

Financing the nearly $6 trillion of total federal, state, and local government spending is a rather large task. But hopefully you can see that at least we have options. We have seen that while taxes are high, the United States has a lower overall tax burden when compared to much of the developed world. The total tax burden at both the state and local level as well as the federal level as a percent of GDP has actually, with some modest variation, been surprisingly stable for the past sixty years. At the federal level, the vast majority of our tax revenue comes from personal income taxes and employer- and employee-paid social security and Medicare taxes. If we want to do something dramatic, the flat tax, the FairTax, the Laffer tax proposal, the Rand Paul tax proposal, and the 9-9-9 plan all have aspects that are very attractive from an economic-efficiency point of view (and some, but certainly not all, would say a fairness point of view). And there are many similar concepts floating around. They are all fairly simple and straightforward. They have particular appeal to successful conservatives since they reward effort and entrepreneurship and favor savings over consumption, thus enhancing one's ability to amass a sizable net worth. However, to some extent, they all tend to be more regressive than our current system. In addition, as I address in Chapter 8, a carbon-based tax can help to raise revenue while reducing our carbon emissions and reliance on fossil fuels. Having said all that, we also have room within our existing tax structure to increase revenues if needed. So the opportunity is certainly there to address the revenue side of the budget issue, either by working within our existing tax structure or by totally revamping how the federal government finances itself.

CHAPTER 7

Health Care Is Killing Us

I have yet to see any problem, however complicated, which, when looked at in the right way, did not become still more complicated.

POUL ANDERSON, AS QUOTED IN *LORDS OF FINANCE*, BY LIAQUAT AHAMED

NOW THAT WE HAVE REVIEWED the federal budget situation, reviewed government spending, and reviewed government taxation, you'd think I would dive right into how to balance the federal budget. Sadly, I do not. Rather the next few chapters explore some general topics that can have an impact on how we address the budget deficit. The first of these issues is health care. Once again, I don't consider myself an expert on health care, but I do know enough to recognize that the economics of the health-care system in the United States is a complete mess.

Here are some of the basic numbers. In 2013, total health-care expenditures in the United States were $2.9 trillion, averaging $9,255 per person and 17.4 percent of GDP. The Centers for Medicare and Medicaid Services (CMS) is projecting that US health-care expenditures will reach 19.3 percent of GDP by 2023. This is up from only 5 percent of GDP in 1960 and 8.9 percent of GDP as recently as 1980, so health-care expenses as a share of the economy have almost doubled in the past thirty years and have more than doubled on a real per-person basis. It makes some sense that health-care spending should increase as the wealth of a nation increases, as in some ways quality health care is a luxury we are better able to afford as our national income increases. But are we really getting our money's worth? With health-care costs at a soon-to-be 20 percent of GDP, definitely not. After all, personal spending on health care is generally not something we do because we enjoy it. Presumably there is no inherent pleasure to be derived from going to the dentist or getting a colonoscopy. The true measure of our health-care effectiveness should be based on our overall level of health and quality of life, not the actual dollar amount we spend on health-care services.

The United States spends more for health care per person than any other nation by a very wide margin. In 2012, when the United States spent 17.7 percent of its GDP on health care, the average Organization for Economic Co-operation and Development (OECD) nation spent just 9.4 percent of its GDP on health-care expenditures. For example, France spent 11.6 percent, Germany spent 11.3 percent, Canada spent 11.2 percent, the United Kingdom spent 9.4 percent, and Japan spent 9.6 percent of their respective GDP on health care. The absurdity of the US performance is shown in the chart below. Talk about an outlier.

Public and Private Expenditure on Health as a Percent of GDP
2012 or Latest Available Year

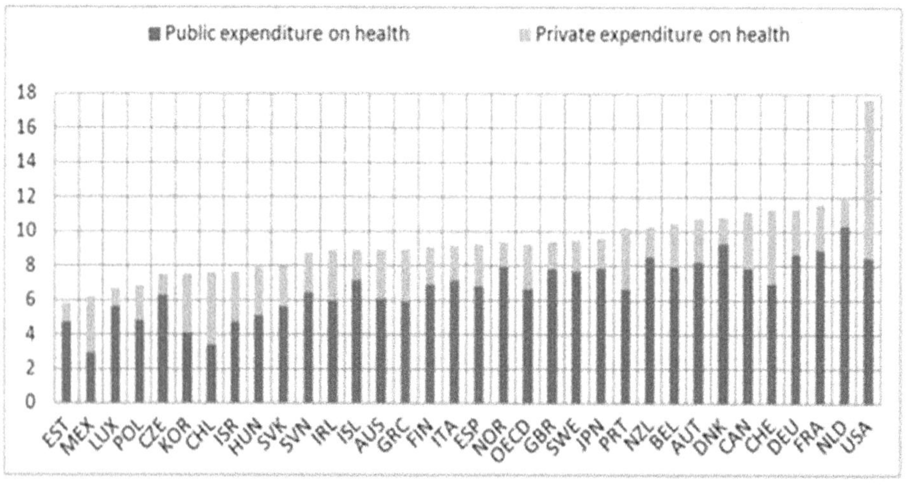

Source: OECD

If as a society we were able to bring our health-care spending in line with international norms, we would save enough money to completely balance the federal budget with money left over. And guess which nation has the lowest life expectancy of all listed in the prior paragraph? The United States is the lowest at 78.7 years, and Japan is the highest at 83 years. And the United States spends *twice* what Japan does on health care per person. Does this make any sense? On another accepted measure of the health of a nation, infant mortality, the United States again lags, with an infant mortality greater than the OECD average and more than double the best-performing nations. We may have the most technologically advanced medical care in the world, but the sad fact is that we are not getting the bang for the buck.

Some of the projections for future growth in US health-care spending are staggering. The graph below is from the CBO study *The Long-Term Outlook for Health Care Spending*, published in November 2007. Based on current law (at the time) and other assumptions that, when looked at individually, are actually quite reasonable, total health-care spending in the United States could reach 49 percent of GDP by the end of the seventy-five-year projection period.

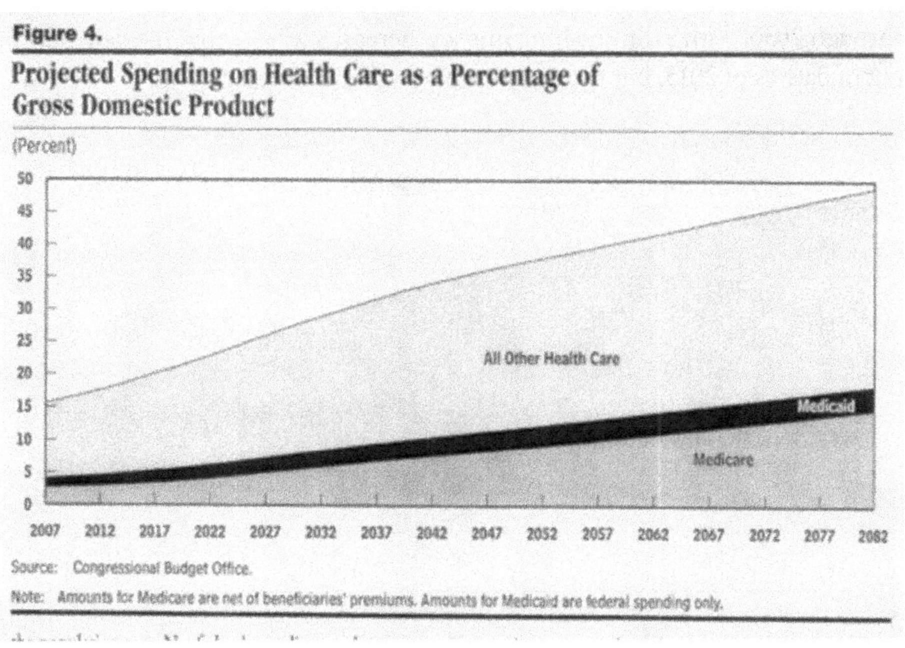

Some of the projected future growth in health-care spending in the United States is due to the aging of the population. The resulting increased national health-care expenditures are presented as inevitable. After all, average health-care spending per capita for a person in the United States over the age of sixty-five is more than double that for a person under sixty-five. However, somehow Japan manages to get by with spending about one-half what the United States spends on health care per person, and they are already beyond our future age demographic. For example, the median age in Japan is 43.5 years, compared to 36.6 years in the United States, and the percentage of the population in Japan over age sixty-five is 21.5 percent, compared to only 12.6 percent in the United States. In fact, of all the countries listed in the preceding paragraphs, the United States has the youngest population, and (I dare to repeat it) the highest level of health-care spending. While the aging of the population certainly contributes to the projected future cost of health care, and to the cost of Medicare and Medicaid in particular, it is the escalating intensity and cost of the health-care services that are the biggest factors. The chart below, from the November 2007 CBO study, shows this graphically. By itself, aging accounts for about 25 percent of the projected growth in government spending on Medicare and Medicaid through 2030, with a diminishing impact thereafter. (Note that the data may be out of date as of 2015, but the overall trend remains the same.)

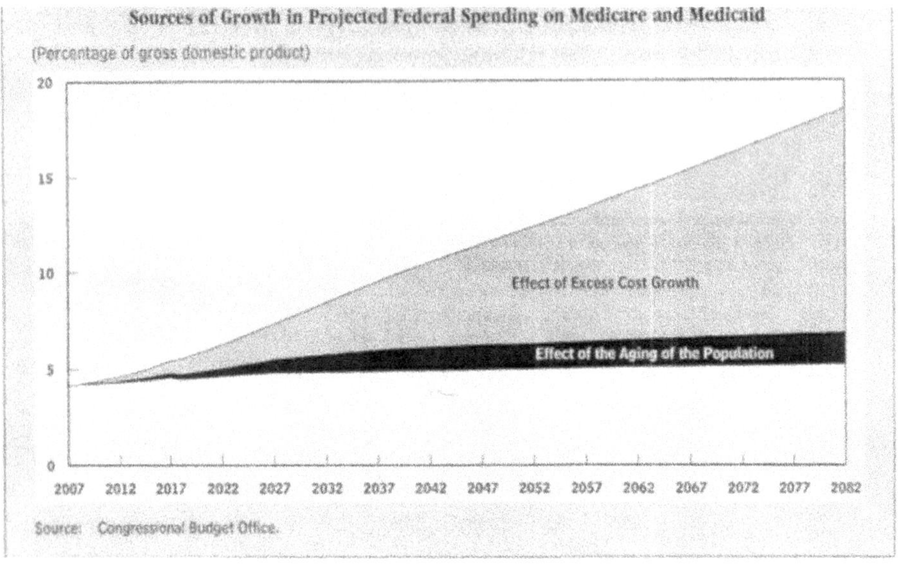

Finally, I have to include yet one more graph from the 2007 CBO study. The graph "presents projections of health-care spending under the assumption that the excess cost growth rates for spending on Medicare, Medicaid, and all other health care continue indefinitely at their average values from 1975 to 2005." Under those assumptions, total national health-care spending would reach 99 percent of GDP by 2082. Finally, all of our grandchildren will be doctors, pharmaceutical executives, or other health-care workers! Of course, this outcome is impossible, but this is literally the path on which we are on if these trends continue.

Projected Spending on Health Care Under an Assumption That Excess Cost Growth Continues at Historical Averages

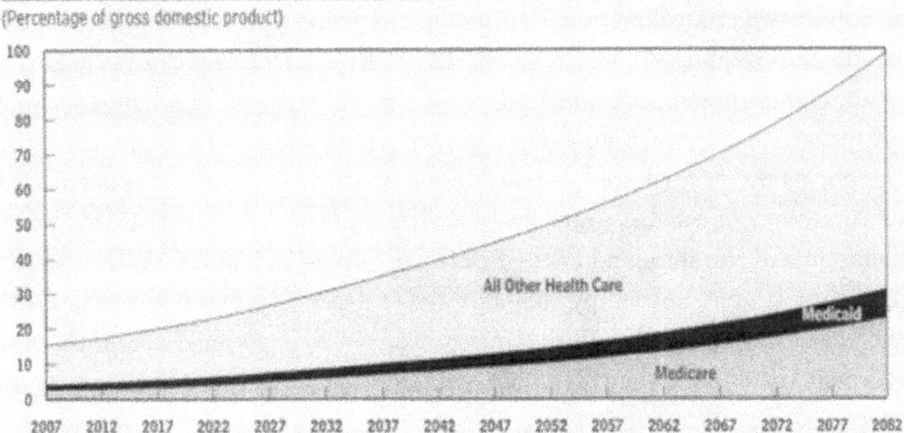

Source: Congressional Budget Office.

Notes: Excess cost growth refers to the number of percentage points by which the growth of spending on Medicare, Medicaid, or health care generally (per beneficiary or per capita) is assumed to exceed the growth of nominal gross domestic product (per capita). Amounts for Medicare are net of beneficiaries' premiums. Amounts for Medicaid are federal spending only.

Why is health care so expensive in the United States? Economically, one of the biggest factors is that the users of health-care services are infrequently the payers, at least directly. Households comprise 28 percent of health-care spending in 2013, but a portion of this represents the personal share of insurance premiums. So, while in this instance, the individual is contributing a portion of the total cost of health care, this spending is not tied to usage. Out-of-pocket payments represented only 12 percent of total spending on personal health-care expenses in 2013, and to the extent that these represent modest copay amounts, they hardly serve to moderate health-care usage. In 1970, almost 40 percent of personal health-care expenses consisted of out-of-pocket payments by individuals. It is no wonder that the United States has such a high utilization of health-care services. In what is presumably a free-market economy, the free market is not allowed to operate in one of the largest segments of the economy. As a result, the Office of Management and Budget has estimated that the United States spends as much as $700 billion a year on health care that does little or nothing to improve patients' health.

There is no question that we could make do with less expensive health care without dramatically affecting our quality of life. Examples of non-cost-effective health care abound. Take chemotherapy, for example. Citing an exhaustive study conducted in the United States and Australia, Steven D. Levitt and Stephen J. Dubner point out in *SuperFreakonomics* that in many cases, chemotherapy is *remarkably ineffective*. The study cited showed that the five-year survival rate for all cancer patients was 63 percent but that chemotherapy contributed barely 2 percent to this result. They state that for a number of cancers—including multiple myeloma, soft-tissue sarcoma, melanoma of the skin, and cancers of the pancreas, uterus, prostate, bladder, and kidney—chemotherapy had *zero* discernible effect. They further cite the example of non-small-cell lung cancer, where a typical chemotherapy regimen costs more than $40,000 but helps to extend a patient's life by an average of just two months.

And yet doctors continue to prescribe drugs for which the efficacy is limited at best. Why? In some cases, the more treatments, the greater the income for the doctor. This is particularly the case for oncology, where chemotherapy is often administered in the doctor's office (as opposed to the patient purchasing the drug from a third-party pharmacy) and is thus able to generate revenue for the oncologist. But Levitt and Dubner offer another, more benign reason: doctors and patients just want to try something. Even if the chance of any success is only 10 percent (or even 2 percent), at least that is better than nothing. This is particularly true if the patient doesn't have to pay for it directly. However, as a society, we of course do pay for it, and it can be very expensive. Should we? Does it make a difference if the patient is an otherwise healthy forty-five-year-old mother of two with private health insurance or an eighty-five-year-old man with government-funded health care and with other life-threatening health issues? I don't know the answer to this question (although I have my opinion), but I do know that the question should be asked. The budget is not unlimited, or at least it *shouldn't* be unlimited. Clearly, if an individual or his or her family wants to pay for expensive, risky, and unproven treatment, that is their absolute right and their decision to make. But what if taxpayers have to foot the bill? Life is certainly precious, but after all, we are not going to live forever.

Here is another example I saw recently. Apparently, pancreatic cancer is a particularly deadly form of cancer with a five-year survival rate of approximately 6 percent. Basically, there is no cure. In May 2011, *The New England Journal of Medicine* reported a study that showed that a combination of four chemotherapy drugs known as FOLFIRINOX resulted in an 11.1-month mean survival rate as compared to a 6.8-month mean survival rate for patients treated with another chemotherapy drug, gemcitabine. (I don't know what the mean survival rate would be for an untreated group, presumably something less than six months.) The general press picked this up as great progress against pancreatic cancer, and maybe it is. But it is hardly a cure. After eighteen months, more than 80 percent of the patients on FOLFIRINOX had died, and only 3 percent had progression-free survival. And patients on FOLFIRINOX experienced more severe side effects than patients on the alternative drug. Is this progress? Maybe. Is this soon to become the standard treatment protocol? Probably. Is it worth the cost (about $40,000 versus about $30,000 for the alternative treatment)? I am not so sure. Steve Jobs, who died of pancreatic cancer in 2011, could afford any experimental treatment he wanted. But if the rest of us are paying for treatment of only marginal efficacy, the system as a whole cannot foot the bill.

In many cases, alternative treatment options are vastly less expensive than others and yet just about as effective. Again, a study was published in May 2011 in *The New England Journal of Medicine* that showed that the use of Avastin (bevacizumab), a drug developed to treat cancer, was just as effective as Lucentis (ranibizumab) in the treatment of age-related macular degeneration (AMD). The efficacy of Lucentis in the treatment of AMD was established in 2005 and was approved for this use by the FDA in June 2006. In the interim, doctors began treating AMD with Avastin, which has a similar therapeutic effect on the body. (Doctors can and do prescribe approved drugs for other than their approved use, in so-called "off-label" usage.) Both drugs were developed by Genentech, and while both have now been shown to be equally effective in the treatment of AMD, a single dose of Lucentis costs forty times as much as a single dose of Avastin. According to the *New York Times*, in 2008, Medicare paid for 480,000 injections of Avastin to treat AMD at a cost of $20 million—and paid for 337,000 injections of Lucentis at a cost of $537 million. As the *NYT* concludes, "Medicare could save hundreds of millions of dollars annually if doctors used Avastin. But, as the system now works, Medicare cannot push doctors to switch. That means that taxpayers will likely continue to pay a lot more for a treatment that is no more effective. That makes no sense for anybody, except the drug maker." The Office of the Inspector General of the Department of Health and Human Services calculated that Medicare could have saved $1.1 billion and patients could have saved approximately $275 million in copayments if all Medicare patients treated with Avastin or Lucentis for AMD had been paid at the Avastin rate during calendar years 2008 and 2009. As an interesting side note, in 2011, the FDA rescinded the approval of Avastin for treating breast cancer (Avastin is still approved for other cancers), concluding that the side effects outweighed its effectiveness in slowing tumor growth. In the case of breast cancer, treating a patient with Avastin costs about $90,000 per year, according to Frederick C. Tucker, an oncologist writing in the *New York Times*.

The headline on the October 28, 2013, issue of *New York* magazine read "The Cancer Drug Racket." In the article titled "The Cost of Living," the author, Stephen S. Hall, recounted how even some doctors are rebelling against the high cost of certain cancer drugs that in many cases are only marginally effective. The primary example cited (Zaltrap) was statistically shown to extend life for forty-two days at a monthly cost of $11,000, or a total of about $75,000 for the seven-month treatment period, which was the case in the clinical trials. Other examples of costly cancer drugs cited include Yervoy at $39,000 per month, Provenge at $93,000 over the course of treatment, Gleevec at $92,000 per year, Tasigna at $115,000 per year, and Sprycel at $123,000 per year. In some cases, the drug merely extends life for a matter of months, while in other cases, the drug is more effective against the targeted disease, which raises an interesting question. Is it better to extend a patient's life by a couple of months (statistically) at a cost of $75,000, or to extend a patient's life indefinitely (through a treatment that is actually known to work) at a cost of $100,000 a year, every year? I would guess the latter, but in each case, the cost is obviously very high. And the author cites a study in the *New England Journal of Medicine* that showed that 81 percent of patients with advanced colon cancer did not understand that the drugs being used would not cure them, so it sounds as if either the doctors are not adequately communicating the limited effectiveness of the treatment being prescribed, or the patients are only hearing what they want to hear.

There are many other examples one could cite, from medically questionable back surgeries, to unneeded tests, to something as mundane as the over prescription of antibiotics, which can be not only medically useless (if one has, say, a viral infection as opposed to a bacterial infection) but can actually breed more-resistant bacteria strains, ultimately reducing the effectiveness of the antibiotic. Or how about the 2009 recommendation of the US Preventative Services Task Force against routine breast-cancer screening in women aged forty to forty-nine, and the recommendation to reduce the frequency of breast scans in women fifty to seventy-four to biennially—rather than every one to two years for all ages, as had been the prior generally accepted practice? This recommendation was *made without regard to monetary cost* but by weighing the medical benefits as well as the medical downsides of screening. While mammography is generally considered safe, nonsymptomatic screening can result in unnecessary biopsies and inconvenience due to inconclusive results or false-positives (a screen indicating the presence of cancer, when in fact none exists). When this recommendation was released in 2009, there was, of course, the outrage of many claiming that early and frequent testing saves lives, which may be true in some individual cases but statistically has not been shown to be the case.

In the interest of gender fairness, I point out that Richard J. Ablin, a discoverer of the prostate-specific antigen (PSA) in 1970, wrote an op-ed in the

New York Times on March 10, 2010, decrying the overuse of PSA screening for detecting prostate cancer in men, at an annual cost of at least $3 billion. He pointed out that American men have a 16 percent lifetime chance of receiving a diagnosis of prostate cancer but only a 3 percent chance of dying from it. Many more men eventually die *with* prostate cancer than die *from* it. Again, in many cases, elevated levels of PSA led to unnecessary biopsies or surgery. After reviewing the results of some large clinical trials, in 2012, the US Preventive Services Task Force came out with a recommendation *against* PSA-based screening for prostate cancer. While the data indicates that PSA screening may help 1 man in 1,000 avoid death from prostate cancer (and most likely less than that), about 100 to 120 of every 1,000 men screened receive a false-positive test, leading to unnecessary biopsies. In addition, those who were found to have cancer tend to over treat, leading to side effects including erectile dysfunction (29 men affected per 1,000 screened), urinary incontinence (18 men affected per 1,000 screened), and even a small risk of death. In short, the task force concluded that "the potential benefit does not outweigh the expected harms." Again, this recommendation was made without even weighing the cost of this screening and resultant (mostly excessive) treatment.

There are many more examples. In 2013, the *New York Times* ran a series of articles on the high costs of common medical care and how they contribute to health-care spending in the United States. According to the *New York Times*, childbirth is the largest single category of hospital payouts for most commercial insurers and Medicaid programs. Citing data developed by Truven Analytics and the International Federation of Health Plans, the author, Elizabeth Rosenthal, found that the average total-billed price for pregnancy and newborn care was $30,000 for a vaginal delivery and $50,000 for a caesarean delivery. Of course, the billed amount and the paid amount in the US health-care system frequently bear little resemblance to each other, which is a contributing factor to why the system is broken. Generally, the consumers don't know beforehand how much a medical procedure should or will cost. In any case, the average 2012 amount actually paid for childbirth in the United States was $9,775 for a conventional delivery and $15,041 for a caesarean delivery. In Switzerland, the comparable costs were $4,039 and

$5,186, respectively, while in Britain, the costs were $2,641 and $4,435, respectively. The article points out that even Medicaid, which pays for more than 40 percent of all births nationally (which in itself says something), pays only slightly less than the national average. Once again, the United States has the highest-cost care system in the world and yet "has one of the highest rates of both infant and maternal death among the industrialized world."

Yet another example from the *New York Times* series looked at the cost of hip-replacement surgery. The specific individual highlighted in the article was a sixty-year-old male who required a hip-replacement surgery due to arthritis arising from an old sports injury. The procedure was not covered by the patient's insurance because this was considered a preexisting condition. As such, he cared about the cost since he would have to pay for it out of his own pocket. His estimated cost in the United States was over $78,000, which included $13,000 for the artificial hip (which costs about $350 to manufacture in the United States) and another $65,000 in hospital charges, not including the surgeon's fee. He ultimately chose to have the replacement done in Brussels, Belgium, for $13,660, including the price of the artificial hip, which was made by US-based Zimmer Holdings, as well as all doctors' fees, operating-room charges, and cost of five days in the hospital, a week in rehab, and a round-trip plane ticket from the United States. According to the author, the Belgian hospital paid about $4,000 for the high-end Zimmer implant at a time when American hospitals were paying about $8,000 for the same hip. Other specific patient examples cited by the author included a $37,000 implant as part of a total approximately $100,000 bill, an artificial knee billed at $26,000 as part of an approximately $112,000 bill, and an artificial hip billed at over $30,000 as part of an over $50,000 bill. As the *New York Times* article points out, insurers negotiate discounts on those charges, but still the negotiated cost can be huge. In the case of the $100,000 bill referenced above, the insurer paid close to $70,000.

Finally, here is a personal experience with my daughter, who had her appendix removed in 2013. One would think that removing an appendix is not an example of high-cost miracle medicine. However, one year later, I am still trying to figure out the bill from all of the various health-care providers. Just the hospital bill, *excluding* the surgeon and the anesthesiologist, came out to

$33,699.43, including almost $5,000 for a CAT scan, over $6,500 for a semi-private room (she was in the room for about twelve hours), and $11,603.23 for the operating room. Presumably, the amounts will be reduced by the contract insurance rates, but the system as it exists is just crazy. Maybe consumer protection is where the government should address their attention as it relates to health-care reform, not spending more federal money on care.

And this litany does not even include medical fraud, which the National Health Care Anti-Fraud Association estimates conservatively at 3 percent of all health-care spending, or about $75 billion at today's spending rate. Other estimates of medical fraud range as high as 10 percent of the country's health-care spending, or $250 billion. Examples of medical fraud include billing for services that were never rendered, "upcoding" (billing for more expensive services than were actually required given the patient's true condition), falsifying a diagnosis to justify tests or other procedures that are not medically necessary, and so forth.

I am sure that many more examples of such costly, or even medically ineffective, treatments exist. I merely cite examples I have found by reading the popular press. The point is that the cost of the treatment is not part of the decision-making process in the United States. And why shouldn't it be? Cost considerations are a factor in almost every other decision we make in daily life. With all of the innovation in this country, what would happen if the health-care sector were incentivized to develop *cost-effective* medical care? I bet we would be very positively surprised.

Our Unhealthy Selves

What about personal lifestyle? There is no question that unhealthy lifestyles have a big impact on national health-care costs. For example, the United States is about the most obese major nation in the world. Former Senator Phil Gramm was criticized for making the statement, "We are the only nation in the world where all our poor people are fat." At the time he said that in 1981, maybe a little over 50 percent of the US population was either obese (defined as a body mass index (BMI) of 30 kilograms/meter or greater) or "overweight" (defined as a BMI of 25 kilograms/meter or greater).

Today, the figure has risen to more than 65 percent—over one-third of the US population is obese and another one-third is overweight but not obese. Senator Gramm should have said that all of our people are fat, *including* our poor people, for then he would have been mostly right; obesity is relatively constant across lower- and middle-income levels: 67.8 percent of Americans twenty years and older and below the poverty line are overweight or obese, and 68.5 percent of Americans aged twenty or older and with an income of 400 percent of the poverty level or higher are overweight or obese. Based on my own anecdotal observations, the level of obesity among very high-income earners is materially less than the national average, but there's no science in that observation. I presume that Mitt Romney and President Obama are more representative of high achievers than Chris Christie when it comes to body mass index.

The obesity trend among our children is even more alarming. Today, almost 19 percent of our youth aged six to eleven are classified as obese, from a level closer to 5 percent during the sixties and seventies. For children, there is a clear correlation between income and obesity, with the obesity rate near the poverty level nearly double that of the upper-middle-income population. This is not a good trend. Compared to the rest of the world, we have few rivals in the fat department. In Japan, for example, only 3.5 percent of the population is obese and approximately 25 percent of the population is obese or overweight. Mexico, on the other hand, is a close neighbor in more ways that just geographically: 30 percent of its population is obese and 69.5 percent are classified as obese or overweight, so right in line with the United States.

There are many health issues associated with obesity. Obese people are more likely to suffer from heart disease, stroke, diabetes, cancer, and many other medical conditions. In particular, diabetes has become almost an epidemic in the United States, currently affecting 8.3 percent of the total population and over 25 percent of the population over the age of sixty-five. Diabetes is a major cause of heart disease and stroke and is the leading cause of kidney failure, nontraumatic lower-limb amputations, and new cases of blindness among adults in the United States. Studies have shown that lifestyle intervention to lose weight and increase physical activity can reduce the development of type 2 diabetes (the most prevalent type) by over 50 percent—and by more than 70 percent among adults aged sixty years or older. *This is free treatment and known to be effective.* Compare this to some of the prior statistics cited on the relative effectiveness and cost of some chemotherapy regimens. Direct medical costs in the United States related to diabetes are estimated at $116 billion. For obesity generally, the OMB estimates that we spend $150 billion a year treating obesity-related diseases.

I expect that the cost of obesity will continue to grow. For example, a recent article in the *New York Times* reported on the rapid increase in nonalcoholic fatty liver disease, which is quickly becoming one of the leading causes of liver transplants. One of the doctors quoted in the article likened the condition to foie gras, which is fatty liver obtained by force-feeding ducks. By the way, the State of California banned the force-feeding of ducks in 2012 because it is considered cruel and inhumane, but apparently humans are able to develop the condition without being forced. According to the article, approximately 10 to 20 percent of people with nonalcoholic fatty liver develop the more progressive form of the disease, known as nonalcoholic steatohepatitis, or NASH. At the UCLA Medical Center, 25 percent of all liver transplants are the result of NASH. And liver transplants can cost over $500,000 and more once all of the long-term costs are factored in. One of the doctors quoted in the article suggested that five million people with NASH will need new livers by 2025 if effective treatments are not found (other than not being obese, which would work just fine). That would be a big health-care ticket.

Smoking is another lifestyle factor affecting cost in the US health-care system. In 2012, an estimated 18 percent of US adults were smokers. In contrast to the problem of obesity, at least the incidence of smoking has generally been declining in the United States, falling by about one-half since 1965. In the case of smoking, there is more incidence of smoking at lower income levels. Between 2009 through 2011, 33.2 percent of males below the poverty line were smokers, compared to 15.1 percent of males at 400 percent or more above the poverty level. Smoking would seem to be an expensive habit if one is below the poverty line, but there you have it. Presumably the incidence of smoking is even lower at higher income levels since the incidence of smoking among holders of an undergraduate degree is 9.1 percent and only 5.9 percent among holders of a graduate degree.

Compared to the rest of the world, the United States is about in the middle of the pack in terms of smoking. Many countries in Asia have much higher smoking rates, particularly among men. For example, in China approximately 51 percent of men smoke, and in our otherwise healthy country of Japan, approximately 37 percent of men and 10 percent of women smoke (compared to 22 and 17 percent of American men and women, respectively).

Smokers have a higher risk of cancer, heart disease, stroke, and chronic disease. According to a major report prepared by the US Department of Health and Human Services (HHS), "Since the 1964 Surgeon General's report, cigarette smoking has been causally linked to diseases of nearly all organs of the body, to diminished health status, and to harm to the fetus." HHS further estimates that smoking-attributable economic costs for the years 2009–2012 were between $289 billion and $332.5 billion per year, including between $132.5 billion to $175.9 billion in annual direct medical costs for adults. At least cigarette smokers do pay for some of their sins in the form of taxes—when last I looked, $4.35 per pack in the state of New York and a combined $5.85 per pack in the city of New York. Almost makes one want to quit just for financial reasons. And yet, over 30 percent of males below the poverty level are smokers.

Should the government (read "we") pay for health-care costs related to smoking or obesity? Maybe the government should charge a premium to obese persons or smokers. In May 2011, it was reported that Arizona had proposed imposing a $50 fee on childless adults on Medicaid who are either obese or smokers. In Arizona, almost half of all Medicaid recipients smoke, and while the number of obese people receiving Medicaid is unclear, generally over 25 percent of the population in Arizona is obese (probably over 30 percent since the 25 percent statewide estimate is based on *self*-reported data as opposed to the national data, which are based on actual measurements—we would all like to think we are a little slimmer than we actually are). I actually think this is a good idea, but it probably won't happen. Of course, I would phrase it in the positive—charge everybody on Medicaid a fee of $50 (or something) but waive it for people who don't smoke and are not obese.

Is that not fair? It's basically a $50 bonus for doing your bit to help out, plus it's good for you. Recently, other states, such as Michigan, have incorporated lower premiums and cost sharing into their Medicaid programs based on developing healthy living habits. Hopefully, this will have its desired effect.

Apparently this approach is becoming more popular in the private sector. A 2011 article in the *New York Times* referenced a study that showed that company policies that imposed financial penalties on employees for unhealthy lifestyles, such as smoking or obesity, had doubled in the prior two years to 19 percent of 248 major American employers. Major companies mentioned with financial incentives for "healthy living" include Home Depot, PepsiCo, Safeway, Lowe's, General Mills, and Wal-Mart. The annual discounts mentioned ranged from $240 to up to $2,000. Whether you consider it cost sharing by the employer or a financial incentive for good health, either way, I don't see how one could consider it unfair.

The Government and Health Care

I had always heard that the more enlightened countries of the world paid for the health care of their citizens, while the less generous US government did not, but here is a surprising fact (at least it was surprising to me). Despite the general impression that Canada, Japan, and most European nations spend more public money on health care than the United States, this is in fact not true. Government-funded health-care expenditures in the United States totaled 8.5 percent of GDP in 2012, compared to 7.8 percent in Canada, 7.8 percent in the United Kingdom, and 7.9 percent in Japan. France and Germany were slightly higher than the United States, with government expenditures on health care of 8.9 percent and 8.7 percent, respectively. As one would expect, the US private health-care expenditures are much higher than any of the other OECD countries. But still, about 48 percent of total health-care expenditures in the United States are funded by government in one form or another.

The US government got into health care in a big way when both Medicare and Medicaid were enacted as Title XVIII and Title XIX of the Social Security Act, signed into law by President Lyndon B. Johnson on July

30, 1965. Former President Harry S. Truman was ceremonially enrolled as the first Medicare beneficiary and his wife, Bess, as the second. Medicare generally provides hospital and medical insurance for all persons over the age of sixty-five who have been legal residents of the United States for at least five years. Broader prescription-drug coverage was added on January 1, 2006. Since Medicare's inception in 1965, annual expenditures have increased dramatically, reaching $583 billion in 2013.

Medicare is financed by payroll taxes totaling 2.9 percent of wages. In the case of employees, one-half is withheld from the worker, and one-half is paid by the employer. Self-employed individuals are responsible for the entire 2.9 percent tax. Beginning in 2013, high-income workers pay an additional 0.9 percent tax on their earnings above $200,000 for single taxpayers and above $250,000 for married couples. Since these thresholds are not indexed to inflation, more and more taxpayers will be subject to this higher tax over time. When Medicare Part D (prescription-drug coverage) went into effect in 2006, no provision was made to pay for it, and the government portion is funded from general federal-government revenues. This was a Republican initiative, proving that despite the tough talk, both major political parties can jump on the something-for-nothing bandwagon. Part D expenditures by the federal government were $67 billion in 2012 and are projected to exceed $100 billion by 2017. Total Medicare spending is projected to exceed $1 trillion by 2022.

The *Medicaid* program was enacted to provide health-care services to low-income children deprived of parental support, their caretaker relatives, and the elderly, the blind, and individuals with disabilities. It is essentially the government-funded medical program for people with low incomes and resources (now joined by the Affordable Care Act). The program is jointly funded by the federal government and the states and administered by the states. Total Medicaid expenditures in 2012 were $414 billion, of which the federal government funded $238 billion and the states funded $127 billion. Total CMS program outlays, including both Medicare and Medicaid, were nearly $1 trillion, of which the federal share was $799 billion.

Medicaid expenditures have grown to become one of the biggest budget items of many states. In my home state of New York, total Medicaid expenditures for fiscal 2012 were projected at $52.6 billion (including the local contribution). This represents a little over 35 percent of the New York State "all funds budget" (which includes federal grants) and is by far the largest single component of state spending. On a state-funds-only basis (excluding the federally funded portion of Medicaid), the New York State share of Medicaid disbursements of $17.7 billion in fiscal 2011 represented over 20 percent of the state operating budget. Public pensions may be getting all the press, but escalating Medicaid expenses pose the biggest budget burden to the states.

This is also a burden for the counties. My home county of Westchester, New York, has a 2014 budget of $1.7 billion (it's a populated county, with about the highest property taxes in the nation), of which $214 million is unfunded Medicaid mandates (not met by federal or state funding). This is the largest single unfunded line item in the budget, representing 12 percent of the total county budget and 17 percent of nonaid revenue. It is equal to nearly 40 percent of the total Westchester county property taxes, which gives you an idea of its impact on at least one form of taxes, the level of which is frequently targeted for complaint.

The federal government involvement in health care took a big step forward when The Patient Protection and Affordable Care Act (also known as the Affordable Care Act (ACA) or "Obamacare") was signed into law by President Barack Obama on March 23, 2010. According to healthcare.gov, a federal-government website managed by the US Department of Health and Human Services, the act will provide for new consumer protections, improve the quality and lower the cost of health care, increase access to affordable care, and hold insurance companies accountable. That sounds pretty good, but whether it will actually do any of these things is questionable. I considered reading the official Compilation of Patient Protection and Affordable Care Act, but it is 974 pages long, and as one might expect, it's not an easy read. It seems as if the act was written by committee, and in fact, it was probably written by several committees. The act has been controversial to say the least. It seems as if people are either vehemently in favor of it or vehemently against it, but of course very few people are familiar with the details.

So here are a couple of the highlights. In terms of coverage, the law puts a number of requirements on health-insurance policies. These include preventing insurers from denying coverage for preexisting conditions, allowing young adults to stay on their parents' health insurance until age twenty-six, ending annual and lifetime limits for most types of benefits, requiring free preventative care without copayments, and many other new regulations. Most of these provisions are designed to benefit the consumer, although they must obviously come at a cost, since all benefits are ultimately paid out of insurance premiums. In particular, if a healthy consumer lives in a state that allowed health rating of policy holders, then they would expect to pay much higher prices under the Affordable Care Act since they could no longer gain favorable pricing due to their good health (or perhaps accept more limited coverage). This is a part of the flack that President Obama faced in 2013 due to his prior statement that "if you like your health-care plan, you'll be able to keep your health-care plan." In many cases, this is just not true.

The real focus of the Affordable Care Act, though, is to expand insurance coverage to more currently uninsured Americans. It does this with three basic mechanisms. First are the incentives for individuals to purchase insurance through the much-publicized state or federal insurance exchanges. To make the premiums affordable to middle-income families, the law provides for tax credits for people with incomes between 100 percent and 400 percent of the poverty line (up to over $90,000 for a family of four) who are not eligible for other affordable coverage. The tax credit is advanceable monthly and is refundable whether or not the recipient owes any federal tax. This is the carrot.

To further induce Americans to participate (including the highly sought-after younger and healthier Americans), the law includes the much-maligned "individual mandate" which requires individuals to purchase insurance or else face a tax penalty. The penalty for 2014 is the greater of $95 per adult and $47.59 per child, or 1 percent of taxable income, growing to 2.5 percent of taxable income in 2016. This is the stick.

The ACA also includes an employer mandate that requires employers with more than fifty full-time-equivalent employees to offer health insurance to their full-time employees or pay a penalty, but as of 2014, this had been delayed. As of the end of the second open-enrollment period on February 15, 2015 (including the additional special-enrollment-period activity reported through February 22, 2015), nearly 11.7 million Americans had signed up for private health coverage through the Health Insurance Marketplaces. However, many surveys suggest that maybe only a quarter of enrollees were previously uninsured. Also, 86 percent of the persons who have selected a plan did so with financial assistance (the tax credits described above).

The other expansion of insurance coverage came through the expansion of Medicaid eligibility to individuals under the age of sixty-five and with incomes up to 133 percent of the federal poverty level. Coverage for newly eligible adults will be fully funded by the federal government for three years, phasing down to 90 percent by 2020. Despite the very large funding share being borne by the federal government, a number of states have rejected the expansion of Medicaid, proving that politics often trumps practical benefits for constituents. The Department of Health and Human Services reports that Medicaid enrollment has grown from 57.8 million enrollees in the July-to-September-2013 baseline period to 70 million enrollees in January 2015. Enrollees in states that have expanded Medicaid coverage increased by 26 percent, while enrollees in states that have not expanded coverage increased by 8 percent.

All in, the Department of Health and Human Services reports that from October, 2013, through March 4, 2015, 14.1 million adults gained health-insurance coverage, and the uninsured rate dropped from 20.3 percent to 13.2 percent. So from the perspective of increasing access to health insurance, the ACA largely does what it was designed to do. This, of course, is no surprise since people are rational enough to take advantage of a benefit that is largely paid for by the federal government.

There is no question that some form of health-care reform is needed. After all, the United States spends about 50 percent more than other rich countries on health care, but our population isn't any healthier. So I am all for health-care reform. But here is the rub. It shouldn't cost us taxpayers a dime more than the government currently pays for health care. As stated earlier, governments in the United States already pay more for public health care than the supposedly more generous social-medicine countries of

Canada, the United Kingdom, and Japan. Despite this, the Affordable Care Act is designed to *increase* government spending on health care and to generate increased tax revenues to help pay for it.

In May 2013, the CBO estimated that the insurance coverage provisions in the ACA would cost the federal government $1.8 trillion gross over the next ten years (2014–2023) and almost $1.4 trillion net after accounting for the various penalty payments, excise taxes on high-premium insurance plans, and other effects on tax revenues and outlays, which partly offsets the increased cost. So this is an expensive expansion of health care in the United States. The government is paying for this by reducing spending on other federal health-care programs by about $700 billion over ten years, primarily for Medicare, and by raising taxes and revenues by about $600 billion over ten years. Over half of this extra revenue is to come from increasing the Medicare tax base for high-income taxpayers. In 2013, the Medicare Hospital Insurance tax on both employees' wages and self-employed individuals' earnings is being increased by 0.9 percent on amounts exceeding $200,000 for single filers and $250,000 for those filing a joint return. In addition, a new Medicare tax of 3.8 percent will be assessed on unearned income of high-income households. Unearned income consists of earnings from interest (other than tax-exempt interest), dividends, capital gains, annuities, royalties, and rents.

So here is the bottom line: while the Affordable Care Act is fully funded through other cost reductions and new revenue sources (taxes), it is hugely expensive at $1.8 trillion over the next ten years, or an average of $180 billion per year. Now in my opinion, the jury is out on the merits of many of the provisions of the Affordable Care Act. There must be some good stuff in those 974 pages. But what the ACA mostly does is simply provide more people access to the country's bloated and inefficient health-care system at government expense. And did I previously mention that the United States spends more public money on health care as a share of GDP than Canada, the United Kingdom, and Japan? This is true despite the fact that 64 percent of our citizenry is covered by *private* health insurance, so we are spending roughly twice the level on a per-beneficiary basis. So here is the challenge to the politicians—reform health care without spending more. It shouldn't be that hard given our current very high level of spending.

Government Distortion of the Health-Care Market

Here is an example of how government intervention in health care can distort the market, and it is a warning on the possible unintended adverse impacts of the ACA. As I've said before, I am blessed to live in the state of New York. As such, I am afforded the protection of the health-insurance laws of New York. The insurance industry is highly regulated in New York, and that is why in 2011, very few insurance companies were willing to offer individual (nongroup) health-insurance policies in the state. New York law says that no one can be denied coverage due to preexisting conditions and that insurance companies have to charge everyone the same rates without regard to their health (similar to the requirements of the ACA). As a result, individual health insurance in New York was very expensive in 2011.

When I looked in 2011, the state of New York website listed pricing from six insurance providers. For coverage for a family of four, the options for HMO coverage ranged from monthly premiums of $1,939.32 to $7,052.27, and for a traditional indemnity plan, the monthly rates ranged from $4,283.84 to $8,462.86. So the cheapest option for family coverage was over $23,000, per year and the most expensive option was over $100,000 per year! To take one example somewhat in the middle, the traditional indemnity plan offered by BlueCross BlueShield was almost $5,000 per month, or almost $60,000 per year. That is 20 percent *more* than the median US annual household income.

How is this a viable situation? Why would anyone buy individual health insurance in New York unless one is already very ill? In fact, that is probably exactly what happened. Relatively healthy people without access to employer-provided group coverage roll the dice and pay for health-care expenses out of pocket. Individuals with expensive health problems buy insurance (if they can afford the premiums), knowing that they will be submitting large health-care claims. The whole program is designed to force what is called "adverse selection," or a program in which, by and large, only sick people participate. And to be rational, *only* sick people should participate. As a result, according to a 2013 article in the *New York Times*, only seventeen thousand New Yorkers bought insurance on their own, while 2.6 million were uninsured. The Affordable Care Act deals with the problem of adverse selection by providing subsidies based on income and by requiring all citizens to purchase health insurance under penalty of fines for noncompliance (the so-called "individual mandate"). The theory is that by forcing enough healthy people to purchase health insurance, the price would come down enough to make individual insurance economically feasible. While this may be true to some extent, it still means that healthy people, or lower users of health-care services, will be subsidizing heavy users of health-care services.

To find a contrast to New York, I checked online for insurance plans available in the state of Florida in 2011. The eHealthInsurance website showed 114 different plans offered by ten different insurance companies for a resident of Boca Raton. The cheapest plans were less than $400 per month. The most expensive plans were still under $2,000 per month. Deductible options ranged from no deductible to a $10,000 annual deductible. The high-deductible plans are my personal preference since I would prefer to pay for "insurance" against unusually high medical expenses and pay the routine expenses out of pocket, rather than purchase a low-deductible plan that pays for all claims (and that by definition would have to cost more). Under a high-deductible plan, the insurance cost is less, but the patient is responsible for a higher deductible. For example, Florida BlueCross BlueShield offered a preferred-provider plan with a $5,000 deductible for $559 per month, or $6,708 per year. The plan generally covered most expenses once the deductible had been reached. Some services are excluded, and some coverages are extra (such as maternity care). The point is that there is some real consumer choice, and an individual can select the type of coverage appropriate for his or her situation. Please sign me up. However, by law I couldn't buy this policy in 2011 since I am a resident of New York.

Maybe the ACA will help to mitigate the prior problem in New York. At the time of this writing, at least, it appears it may be having the desired effect. For example, based on plans offered on the New York State Official Health Plan Marketplace, the annual premiums for a family health plan range from $11,000 to $19,000 for a "bronze" plan, $13,000 to $23,000 for a "silver" plan, and $15,000 to $28,000 for a "gold" plan (before any subsidies), dramatic reductions from the cost of individually purchased insurance in previous years.

Presumably this improved insurance market is a result of the increased demand for individual policies due to the individual mandate and the availability of subsidies for lower- and middle-income New Yorkers, as well as increased competition from insurers to profit from the new demand. According to the US Department of Health and Human Services, as of February 22, 2015, over four hundred thousand New Yorkers had selected a private insurance plan on the New York exchange. So maybe some aspects of the ACA are working. At least for 2014 and 2015, many more New Yorkers were able to purchase private insurance and at much lower costs than previously. However, we shall see how this plays out over time as the market settles down and insurers are able to determine the composition of their new insureds. According to the *Wall Street Journal* (and others) in June 2015, many insurers were seeking substantial premium increases for the following year, and the *Journal News*, for one, reported that New York insurers were seeking a 13.5 percent rate increase in 2016. So, as I said, we shall see.

What Can Be Done about Health Care?

It is not a question of *should* we do something about controlling health-care costs, for that is clear. It is a question of *what* should be done. The details may not be so simple, but the approach is straightforward: make the cost of health care relevant to the users, both in the private sector and the public sector.

While people like to have access to more-or-less free health care, everyone has to realize that, as with everything else, there is no free lunch. We are receiving health-care services in the form of "invisible" compensation or higher taxes. In regards to employer-provided health care, would we rather receive higher cash compensation and have an incentive to reduce our overuse of health-care services? For government-funded health care, we simply cannot afford to continue on the same path as we are now on. Something has to give.

There are many options available. In December 2008, the Congressional Budget Office released a publication called *Budget Options, Volume I: Health Care*, which lays out 115 options for altering laws, regulations, or programs affecting health care in the United States. Some reduce the overall cost of health care, some reduce the federal budget cost (either through revenue enhancements or reduced benefit payments), and some increase the cost to the federal government (through increased eligibility, for example). A number of proposals attempt to limit the current tax benefit that many employees receive due to the fact that employer paid insurance premiums are part of many employees' total compensation, but those premiums are not subject to individual income or payroll taxes. In addition, the cost of this invisible compensation is not evident to the employee. The increased revenue to be realized from changing this (but not eliminating it) ranges from $40 billion to over $60 billion per year, depending on what change is made. Yes, I know this is a tax increase, but let's add it to the maybe list anyway.

Other options that have been the topic of discussion lately include converting Medicare to a premium support system (saving about $20 billion per year) and converting the federal share of Medicaid's payments for acute-care services into an allotment (saving over $50 billion per year). The combination of altering the tax-free nature of employer health care and changing the payment system of Medicare and Medicaid can easily reduce the federal budget deficit by over $100 billion per year. But there are many other opportunities for cost reduction.

Personally, I don't really care too much how specifically we fix the problem. I just think we should set a budget and stick with it. Let the free market work! Suppose, for example, that we limit all future growth in Medicare spending per participant to current levels plus the overall inflation rate (not the current health-care inflation rate). For example, we could set the copay amount for basic Medicare services (currently 20 percent) at whatever level meets the annual budget. As projected total expenditures increase, the copay would increase. As the copay increases, then maybe some services are consumed on a more cost-sensitive basis. This would tend to reduce total health-care expenses of the system. The actual details may be complicated, but we've got many smart people available to work on the problem. At some point, the power of the market would come into play, because it has to.

CHAPTER 8

Let's Capitalize on Global Warming

Preservation of our environment is not a liberal or a conservative challenge, it's common sense.

RONALD REAGAN

THE TOPIC OF GLOBAL WARMING may seem to be a little out of place in this book. After all, we are focused largely on economic issues and the government's fiscal situation. However, I include it for a couple of reasons. For one, I believe it to be an important topic, just as the environment in general is an important topic. Even if you don't believe in global warming or that global warming is a man-made phenomenon, you can't deny that the topic is relevant; you can only claim that the global warming alarmists have it all wrong. Personally, I believe that global warming is an issue, but I am not sure of how material the problem might be. In any case, I doubt if I am going to see a huge impact in the rest of my lifetime. But who knows? And in any case, the remaining life span of a fifty-five-year-old is probably not the right time frame to be considering.

Here are a couple of global warming findings per the *Working Group I Contribution to the Fifth Assessment Report of the Intergovernmental Panel on Climate Change (IPCC)*. The IPCC's *Fifth Assessment Report (AR5)* contains contributions from three Working Groups. Working Group I assesses the physical-science basis of climate change. Working Group II assesses impacts, adaptation, and vulnerability, while Working Group III assesses the mitigation of climate change. The Synthesis Report, which was approved on November 1, 2014, draws on the assessments made by all three Working Groups. According to the IPCC's website, a total of 209 lead authors and 50 review editors from 39 countries and more than 600 contributing authors from 32 countries contributed to the preparation of Working Group I AR5. The IPCC doesn't conduct its own research but rather considers evidence of climate change based on independent studies. The United Nations Environment Programme (UNEP) and the World Meteorological Organization (WMO) established the IPCC in 1988 to provide the world with a clear scientific view on the current state of knowledge in climate change and its potential environmental and socioeconomic impacts. The IPCC summaries are considered the definitive assessment of the risks of climate change. Of course, others may disagree, but it seems to me that this is the most comprehensive review of the subject matter available.

Anyway, here are some of the key findings from *Working Group I Contribution to the IPCC Fifth Assessment Report, Climate Change 2013: The Physical Basis, Summary for Policymakers*, September 27, 2013:

"Warming of the climate system is unequivocal, and since the 1950s, many of the observed changes are unprecedented over decades to millennia. The atmosphere and ocean have warmed, the amounts of snow and ice have diminished, sea level has risen, and the concentrations of greenhouse gases have increased."

"Each of the last three decades has been successively warmer at the Earth's surface than any preceding decade since 1850."

"Over the last two decades, the Greenland and Antarctic ice sheets have been losing mass, glaciers have continued to shrink almost worldwide, and Arctic sea ice and Northern Hemisphere spring snow cover have continued to decrease in extent (high confidence)."

"The rate of sea level rise since the mid-19th century has been larger than the mean rate during the previous two millennia (high confidence). Over the period 1901–2010, global mean sea level rose by .19 meters [0.17 to 0.21]."

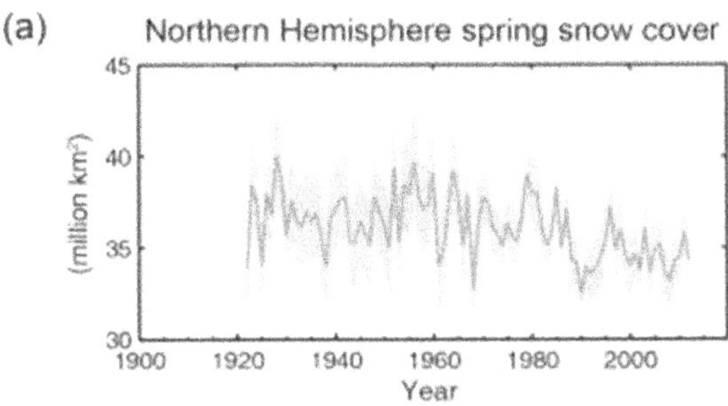

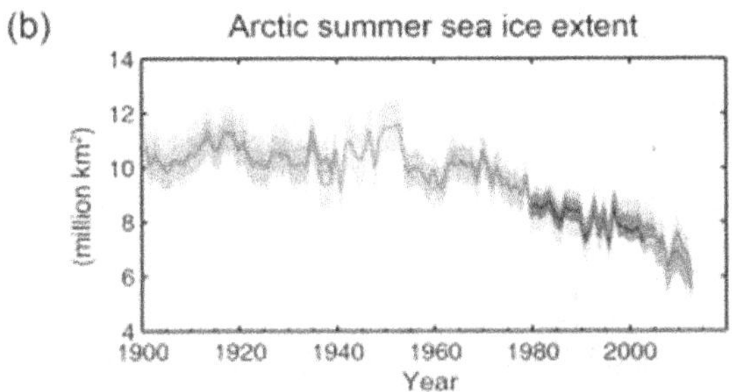

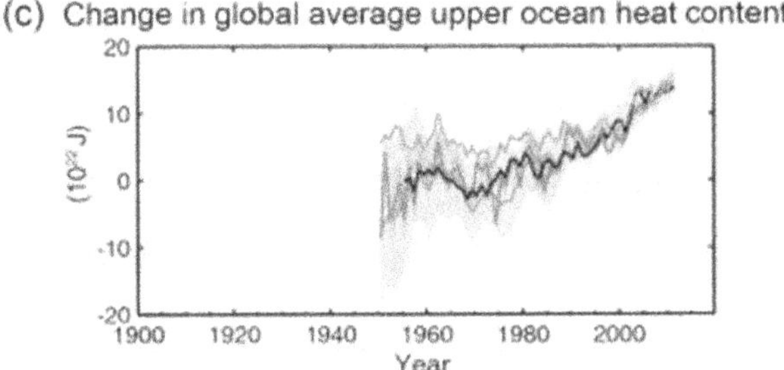

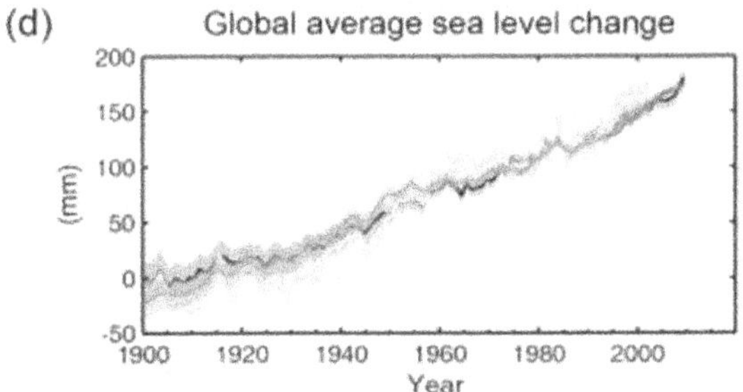

Graph Source: *Working Group I Contribution to the IPCC Fifth Assessment Report, Climate Change 2013: The Physical Science Basis, Summary for Policy Makers*, September 27, 2013

The report continues:

> The atmospheric concentrations of carbon dioxide (CO2), methane, and nitrous oxide have increased to levels unprecedented in at least the last 800,000 years. CO2 concentrations have increased by 40 percent since pre-industrial times, primarily from fossil fuel emissions and secondarily from net land use change emissions. The ocean has absorbed about 30 percent of the emitted anthropogenic carbon dioxide, causing ocean acidification.

The above are mostly observed and measured facts. Now here are some perhaps more subjective conclusions:

"Human influence has been detected in warming of the atmosphere and the ocean, in changes in the global water cycle, in reductions in snow and ice, in global mean sea level rise, and in changes in some climate extremes. This evidence for human influence has grown since AR4 [in 2007]. It is extremely likely that human influence has been the dominant cause of this observed warming since the mid-20th century."

"Continued emissions of greenhouse gases will cause further warming and changes in all components of the climate system. Limiting climate change will require substantial and sustained reductions of greenhouse gas emissions."

"Global surface temperature change for the end of the 21st century is likely to exceed 1.5°C relative to 1850 to 1900...The global mean surface temperature change for the period 2016-2035 relative to 1986-2005 will likely be in the range of 0.3° C to 0.7° C."

"Changes in the global water cycle in response to the warming over the 21st century will not be uniform. The contrast in precipitation between wet and dry regions and between wet and dry seasons will increase, although there may be regional exceptions."

"It is very likely that the Arctic sea ice cover will continue to shrink and thin and that Northern Hemisphere spring snow cover will decrease during the 21st century as global mean surface temperature rises. Global glacier volume will further decrease."

"Global mean sea level will continue to rise during the 21st century. Under all RCP scenarios the rate of sea level rise will very likely exceed that observed during 1971-2010 due to increased ocean warming and increased loss of mass from glaciers and ice sheets."

"Climate change will affect carbon processes in a way that will exacerbate the increase of CO2 in the atmosphere (high confidence). Further uptake of carbon by the ocean will increase ocean acidification."

"Cumulative emissions of CO2 largely determine global mean surface warming by the late 21st century and beyond. Most aspects of climate change will persist for many centuries and beyond even if emissions of CO2 are stopped. This represents a substantial multi-century climate change commitment created by past, present and future emissions of CO2."

"It is virtually certain that global mean sea level rise will continue beyond 2100, with sea level rise due to thermal expansion to continue for many centuries."

That last part doesn't sound too good to me. Sounds like the seas are going to rise no matter what we do about CO2 in the short term. Of course, nothing is certain, since climate prediction, like the weather, is an inexact science. However, the overall trends do seem fairly obvious. While there are dissenting critics of the IPCC, some critics have also contended that the IPCC reports are too conservative. So it goes both ways.

In fact, most scientists are in agreement that global warming is a fact and that human activity is the primary cause. A 2013 survey of scientific views found that of 11,944 scientific abstracts dealing with global warming, 66.4 percent expressed no position on anthropogenic global warming (AGW, or man-made global warming), 32.6 percent endorsed AGW, while only 0.7 percent rejected AGW and 0.3 percent were uncertain on the cause of global warming. Those classified as expressing no position simply did not address or mention the cause of global warming, rather than remaining uncertain or being unable to reach a conclusion. Of the abstracts that take a position, 97 percent endorsed the position that human activity is the primary cause of global warming. Despite this apparent scientific consensus, a 2012 poll by the Pew Research Center found that only 45 percent of US adults say that scientists agree the earth is getting warmer because of human activity, while

43 percent say that scientists disagree. That poll also found that 67 percent say the earth is warming and 42 percent believed that global warming is caused mostly by human activity, so the American public is a little out of sync with most of the scientific community.

Of course a modest rise in temperature and sea level might not be that bad. If that happened gradually, people would probably be able to adapt. But even a modest increase can have harmful impacts on humans. This would include changes in food productivity depending on the extent of warming and the local area in question (increases in some higher latitudes and decreases in lower latitudes), hundreds of millions of people exposed to increased water stress, increased damage from floods and storms, increased malnutrition, increased health issues and mortality from heat waves, and increased floods and droughts (although fewer deaths from cold exposure, so we got that going for us). Any more extreme increase in temperature and sea level could have catastrophic consequences for low-lying areas of the world. Katrina was a disaster for New Orleans, and just consider how much worse the recent extensive damage from hurricane Sandy could have been in New York and New Jersey if sea levels were higher than they are now.

But again, I am not an alarmist. I am not suggesting that we all start riding our bicycles to work, although that wouldn't be so bad for other reasons (we could certainly use the exercise). I am not suggesting that we ban the burning of coal to generate electricity. I am not suggesting that we spend billions of dollars on green energy. I am not suggesting that we start spending money on various carbon-capture technologies.

I am not even suggesting a limit on carbon through a cap-and-trade scheme, which is favored by many politicians. In this form of limiting CO2, the government would set an overall limit on carbon emissions and then allocate or sell the carbon credits to firms, allowing them to emit carbon. Firms would then be allowed to sell the carbon credits to other carbon emitters that require them. If the government sells the initial (or future) credits, this can be a large revenue source. If the initial credits are allocated based on current emissions, then obviously no revenue is raised. Not surprisingly, many governments would prefer to sell the initial credits. For example, assume total carbon emissions in the United States are 100 million tons (not tied to reality!), and the government wants to reduce emissions to 90 million tons—then the government would sell permits to emit 90 million tons of carbon. Since current emissions are 100 million tons, the carbon credits would have value. Some carbon emitters would be able to reduce emissions without too much cost and so would require credits less than their current emissions, while perhaps others would have difficulty reducing their emissions and would have to purchase credits for their current emissions. Over time, a market for credits would develop such that companies that need more credits could purchase them from companies that don't need as many credits. In this way, a cap-and-trade scheme is a more efficient way to reduce the carbon emitted because companies that have the best opportunity to reduce emissions have an economic incentive to do so since their excess credits can be sold.

But again, I am not suggesting a cap-and-trade scheme. What I am suggesting is that the United States institutes a tax on carbon as a part of the solution to the fiscal mess. We tax cigarettes, which are bad for your health, and we tax whiskey, which at least in large quantities is bad for your health (but a wee dram, not so bad). We also tax work and investment, which are *good* for the economy. Why not tax carbon, which perhaps is bad for the earth and all of humankind?

Why do I support this? Again, I don't *like* any taxes, but I *prefer* this tax because it addresses a number of issues. First of all, it raises significant revenues from a very broad base of the population, so it actually helps solve the fiscal problem at hand.

Second, to the extent that it reduces our energy usage, it reduces our dependence on foreign oil (I recognize that a carbon tax also affects coal and natural gas, which are primarily domestically sourced fuels). This helps our balance of payments and reduces our need for oil from less-than-friendly nations. It seems as if everyone is for energy conservation in the abstract, but no one actually wants to do anything about it. Increased fuel and carbon taxes would give some economic teeth to the current CAFE regulations, which call for dramatic increases in automobile fuel mileage. Perhaps increased taxes on carbon and fuel would incentivize people to desire the automobiles that the manufacturers will be obligated to produce.

Third, a carbon tax could reduce our carbon emissions, helping in the "fight" against global warming. Honestly, I don't even know for certain if global warming is real; if it is real, that it is caused by human activities; and if it is caused by human activities, just how bad that is. Clearly, if you live on a Pacific atoll three feet above sea level, global warming could be bad, but if you are a farmer in Canada, maybe not as much. In addition, I recently read that if not for the increased carbon emissions, we could have been heading to another ice age. On the other hand, I also read somewhere that by 2017, it will already be too late to do anything about it. So if we don't address carbon emissions in the next few years, the earth (or at least human life) may be doomed. That doesn't sound too good either.

In any case, according to the Intergovernmental Panel on Climate Change and most experts, the science on global warming is compelling, so what the heck. One thing I do know is that if it is a problem, starting earlier rather than later is better (just like the federal deficit!). And, if we can efficiently raise public revenue in the process, why not do so?

CHAPTER 9

I Love Rich People

Private people who want to make a fortune, never think of retiring to the remote and poor provinces of the country, but resort either to the capital, or to some of the great commercial towns. They know, that, where little wealth circulates, there is little to be got, but that where a great deal is in motion, some shares of it may fall to them.

ADAM SMITH, *THE WEALTH OF NATIONS*, 1776

I LOVE RICH PEOPLE. NOT all rich people, of course. Some of them can be real jerks. But thank goodness for ambitious, successful, and (frequently) rich people, for they are the dynamic forces that drive our economic growth.

And I don't want to imply that all successful people are rich or that all rich people are successful. Many successful people choose relatively low- or average-paying but potentially high-impact jobs in areas such as education, social services, public service, and the like. Many people, such as Tim Berners-Lee, inventor of the World Wide Web, may choose not to commercialize their invention but leave it in the public domain, available to all free of charge. Many moderately successful small-business owners may earn a comfortable living but not be rich, and the economy as a whole definitely benefits from the collective efforts of their entrepreneurship. In contrast, there are many who are rich but not "successful." There are those who have simply lived off of their inherited wealth, and those who have obtained their wealth through theft, fraud, or other similarly nefarious methods.

But let's start with the premise that successful people are generally financially rewarded for their efforts. I believe that to be the case. Or perhaps more accurately stated, successful people who *want* to make money can be financially well rewarded. That is why Ace Greenberg—the former CEO of Bear, Stearns—reportedly looked to hire people with PSD degrees: "poor, smart, and determined to get rich." I add this caveat because there are measures of success other than just money. For example, public recognition, political power, the respect of your peers, and just plain old personal satisfaction in one's job and accomplishments are all measures of success. As a result, there are many successful business people, professionals, educators, public servants, scientists, technicians, and the like who enjoy financially comfortable lives but are not typically rich.

But what about the truly rich? What do they do for us, and do they deserve their substantial rewards? How much does it take to be a high-income earner? According to the US Census Bureau, the amount of annual income required to make it to the top 20 percent of US households was about $104,000 in 2012. That is probably enough to provide you with a comfortable lifestyle, but I certainly wouldn't say you'd be rich. A household income of $146,000 gets you to the top 10 percent of households, and a household income of $191,000 gets you to the top 5 percent of households. Maybe we are now at the level of the "mass affluent," but, at least in my perhaps distorted opinion, I wouldn't say you're rich just yet. We probably need to be looking at about the top 1 percent of households to be really talking about the rich. According to an analysis of IRS statistics done by Emmanuel Saez at UC Berkeley, the income level required to make it to the top 1 percent in 2012 was approximately $394,000. At an income at that level, presumably a family can pay their taxes, live a somewhat affluent lifestyle, and still accumulate some wealth over time, assuming they can remain at that income level for an extended period of time.

Now, let's look at who comprise the top 1 percent of income earners in the United States, the one-percenters, as we have come to call them. A study of statistics from individual income tax return data at the US Department of the Treasury tabulated the share of top income earners by occupation over selected years from 1979 to 2005. Not surprisingly, the data shows that nonfinance executives and managers, those in the medical profession, and financial professionals comprised the largest categories of the top 1 percent of income earners (excluding capital gains) in 2005 at 31 percent, 16.7 percent, and 13.9 percent respectively, or 61.6 percent of all taxpayers in the top 1 percent of income.

Next down the list are lawyers, computer or technical professionals, and those not working or deceased. The overall results are similar if capital gains are included in the definition of income, although the not-working-or-deceased category moves up slightly, presumably because a number of wealthy nonworkers (and dead people?) earn a considerable portion of their income from capital gains.

Arts, media, and sports, where there are a number of high-profile high earners, comprise only 1.6 percent of the top 1 percent of earners. I've always rationalized (to myself anyway) that it is better financially to be the thousandth-best investment banker or lawyer in the country rather than the thousandth-best golfer in the country. Tiger Woods, the top PGA moneymaker in 2013, had over $8 million in winnings on the PGA Tour (plus a $3 million bonus for coming in second in the FedEx Cup), but number two hundred on the PGA money list won "only" $110,000 in 2013. Not bad, but not enough to make it to the top 10 percent of income earners in the United States, let alone the top 1 percent. Number one hundred on the Ladies PGA tour won $53,000, and number fifty on the Web.com Tour (kind of the golf minor leagues) in 2013 earned $95,000. Now I understand that touring pros can make substantial income in endorsements and the like, but they also have expenses, and I venture to say that the net income is very much concentrated at the top of the leader board. I suspect that a moderately successful investment banker or lawyer makes much more than a journeyman professional golfer. And he or she does this, quite honestly, with much less talent.

If we look at the top 0.1 percent of income earners, the share comprised by executives and managers (nonfinance) and financial professionals increases to 42.5 percent and 18 percent, respectively, while the share in the medical profession falls to 5.9 percent, behind lawyers at 7.3 percent. Arts, media, and sports increases to 3 percent of those earning in the top 0.1 percent of income. All of this is again not unexpected, for while those in the medical profession are very well compensated, it is difficult to earn truly outsized income in the medical profession compared to the pay opportunities available in finance, corporate America, or for the very successful actors and athletes. Based on my review of the IRS data for 2011, I estimate that one would require about $1.5 million of adjusted gross income to make it to the top 0.1 percent of households, so now we are talking about some real money.

And it makes complete sense that the top earners are in business management, finance, the medical profession, the legal profession, and arts, media, and sports. After all, as Willie Sutton supposedly said, "That's where the money is." If one is a senior manager at a company with almost $500 billion in sales and $45 billion in income (Exxon Mobil), it is not surprising that one would be well compensated. The same would be true for finance professionals at a money manager with $4 trillion under management (BlackRock, Inc.), highly specialized medical professions, lawyers, or highly successful professional athletes or entertainers. And these people typically work extremely hard for their money, with years of academic or other training, eighty-hour workweeks, and huge job stress, in addition to plain old talent. Michael Milken, the Drexel Burnham Lambert junk-bond king, was famous for his 5:00 a.m. meetings, which kind of sounds crazy if one doesn't even need to work. But many of these people are driven to succeed and do work very hard. So at least on one level, we can't begrudge their success.

Another way to categorize the wealthy is by net worth rather than income. Using this measure gives a different look at the wealthy and, at the high end, gives more weight to those who have started their own firms or businesses. For example, Bill Gates, who was number one on the 2012 *Forbes* 400 list of the wealthiest Americans with a net worth of $66 billion, retired as an employee of Microsoft Corporation effective July 1, 2008, but remained chairman of the board of directors of the company. In that capacity, he earned a total of $225,000 from Microsoft in fiscal 2011. According to *Forbes*, Mr. Gates has already given away more than $28 billion, so if he kept it all for himself, he could have been worth almost $100 billion. That would have been pretty impressive. Of course, I assume he is doing just fine with his remaining $66 billion, and as a practical matter, he may not even miss the other $28 billion.

The more recent chief executive officer of Microsoft, Steve Ballmer (Microsoft employee number thirty), was number nineteen on the 2012 *Forbes* list with a net worth of $15.9 billion. He earned $1.4 million in compensation at Microsoft in 2011. Number two on the *Forbes* list was Gates's friend and confidant Warren Buffet, with a net worth of $46 billion. Warren Buffet serves as chief executive officer and chairman of the board of Berkshire Hathaway, Inc., for which he received a total of $500,000 in compensation in 2011. Obviously these gentlemen didn't get mega rich from their annual compensations but from the increases in value over time from the stock of the companies that they founded or run. If you don't sell your shares and report a gain, you don't report any income, and thus this increase in net worth doesn't show up in the IRS income statistics.

A look at the rest of the *Forbes* 400 (September 2012) reveals that many of the ultrarich either started their own businesses (Bill Gates—Microsoft, Sergey Brin and Larry Page—Google, Mark Zuckerberg—Facebook), inherited wealth that was generated by someone who started their own business (the Walton family—Wal-Mart), made money in real estate (Stephen Ross—Related Companies, Donald Trump—the Trump Organization) or in investments (Warren Buffet—Berkshire Hathaway, George Soros—hedge funds). Most of those who didn't inherit their wealth were entrepreneurial in some form. *Forbes* reports that 279 members of the *Forbes* 400 in 2012 were "self-made" and that 100 members made their money in investments, 47 made their money in technology, 35 made their money in media, 34 made their money in energy, and 30 made their money in food and beverage.

The benefits to us as consumers of PC software, Apple products, Google search capabilities, and the product availability and pricing at Walmart are substantial. Not to mention the large number of jobs created in the United States and around the world by these entrepreneurs. By definition, this wealth is earned since it was awarded by the market. Even investors, who can be criticized as merely rearranging the deck chairs rather than actually creating value, have had their wealth awarded by the markets. Obviously companies, and startups in particular, need financing, and investors who back the winners share in the value created, which can sometimes be substantial.

So I don't begrudge those who earn outsized income, with some obvious exceptions such as fraud. Is luck involved? Absolutely it is, although many people make their own luck. Is it deserved? Often it is but not always. There are many examples of overcompensated CEOs who do little to increase the value of the companies they run. For example, in April 2008, *Forbes* reported that Richard Fuld, the CEO of Lehman Brothers, earned total compensation of $71.9 million in the prior fiscal year and had total compensation of $354 million over the prior five years. Angelo Mozilo, the CEO and founder of Countrywide Financial, had total compensation of over $100 million for the year. Stock gains account for a large share of this compensation, but salaries and bonuses in each of these cases were substantial as well. Lehman Brothers filed for bankruptcy protection in September 2008, and Countrywide Financial was acquired by Bank of America in 2008 in a distressed sale. Of course, Bank of America itself required a government bailout soon thereafter (and its CEO was replaced). That's pretty impressive compensation for presiding over the decline of, and in Lehman's case, the liquidation of your company.

Are these high levels of compensation fair? For the top 20 percent of income earners, excluding the top 1 percent (so the eightieth percentile to the ninety-ninth percentile), I would mostly say that it is. This includes household income of roughly $100,000 to $400,000 and comprises the broad upper class of generally successful people to which many of us aspire. I don't view this level of compensation to be out of line with their economic contributions to society. Once you get to the top 1 percent—and in particular, the top 0.1 percent—to some extent, it really depends on how you look at it. If someone starts her own business and is able to make it a financial success, it is kind of hard to argue with whatever income she is able to earn. She is effectively paying herself.

For very highly paid corporate executives, maybe it is a little different. Is it fair that the CEO of Exxon Mobil, for example, made five hundred times the minimum wage, or two hundred times the wage of an average American worker in 2012? (And the CEO of Exxon Mobil, while very well paid, made much less than many other corporate CEOs.) In the abstract, perhaps it is not. But in the context of managing a $500 billion company, maybe it is.

Presumably, the shareholders and the board of directors think he is worth the money. If a money manager is talented enough to raise billions of dollars for investment and then generate an above-market return, good for him or her. If a salesperson can bring in large amounts of revenue for his or her employer, then good for him or her. If Tiger Woods can increase attendance and television viewership of golf events, then good for him. Obviously someone is willing to pay for it, so from that perspective, they deserve what they earn.

In addition, hopefully the rich *do* something with their wealth—such as invest it in productive enterprises. The vast majority of Warren Buffet's wealth is in the form of Berkshire Hathaway stock. As such, it is all invested, as are all of the earnings that accrue from it since Berkshire Hathaway does not pay a cash dividend. Granted, a substantial use of funds for Berkshire Hathaway's free cash flow is to acquire other businesses, which economically does not represent new investment. However, the shareholders of the acquired businesses would then have cash that could then be invested in other companies or endeavors. It is all a big cycle.

Or perhaps they could just spend it. As Bernard Mandeville's poem from *The Fable of the Bees* implies, some of the classic vices—prodigality, pride, vanity, and fickleness—drive economic activity. Mandeville says, as to the prodigal, "For as the avaricious does no good to himself, and is injurious to all the world besides, except his heir, so the prodigal is a blessing to the whole society, and injures nobody but himself." As to pride, he says, "We are possessed of no other quality so beneficial to society, and so necessary to render it wealthy and flourishing as this, yet it is that which is most generally detested." Consider the following:

The Root of Evil, Avarice,
That damn'd ill-natur'd baneful Vice,
Was Slave to Prodigality,
That noble Sin; whilst Luxury
Employ'd a Million of the Poor,
And odious Pride a million more:
Envy it self, and Vanity,

Were Ministers of Industry;
Their darling Folly, Fickleness,
On Diet, Furniture and Dress,
That strange ridic'lous Vice, was made
The very Wheel that turn'd the Trade.
Their Laws and Clothes were equally
Objects of Mutability;
For, what was well done for a time,
In half a Year became a Crime;
Yet while they alter'd thus their Laws,
Still finding and correcting Flaws,
They mended by Inconstancy
Faults, which no Prudence could foresee.

Thus Vice nurs'd Ingenuity,
Which join'd with Time and Industry,
Had carry'd Life's conveniencies,
It's real Pleasures, Comforts, Ease,
To such a Height, the very Poor
Liv'd better than the Rich before,
And nothing could be added more.

(Bernard Mandeville, a selection from "The Grumbling Hive, or Knaves Turn'd Honest" from *The Fable of the Bees: or, Private Vices, Public Benefits*, vol. 1, 1705, 1723.)

But enough of trickle-down economics from the early 1700s. Let's go to more current events. In August 2011, Leon Black, the founder of Apollo Global Management, celebrated his sixtieth birthday party with a big bash at his oceanfront estate in Southampton, New York. As reported by the *New York Times*, "Mr. Black had his backyard transformed into a faux nightclub setting, constructing a wooden deck over his swimming pool and building a tent for Mr. [Elton] John's concert. After a buffet of crab cakes and steak, partygoers sat on couches with big puffy pillows…Mr. John then took the stage and performed many of his hits including 'Your Song,' 'Benny and the Jets' and 'Candle in the Wind.'" Elton John was reportedly paid at least $1 million for his performance.

Now the party sounds extravagant, and surely it was. The *New York Times* reported a quote from Michael M. Thomas, "It displays a kind of moral bad taste given the vast economic problems in the country." Maybe that is true, but really, why should we care? Yes, he could have given the money to charity (and Leon Black does give much to charity), but let's look at it this way. First, as to the (let's say) $1 million paid to Elton John, presumably Elton John paid New York State and US federal income taxes on those earnings since it was earned in the state of New York. Let's call it roughly $400,000, all in, to the state and federal government. That certainly helps the fiscal situation, so thank you, Leon Black and Elton John.

Then what did Elton John do with the remaining $600,000? Hopefully he did something productive. Maybe he donated it to charity or invested it or spent it. Then there are the other expenses of the party, the food, the decorations, the tent rental, the parking (I assume one has valet parking for a function such as this). These expenses represent payments to the food caterers, the food distributors, the farmers, the waiters, the parking attendants, the tent-rental company, and the tent-setup people—all of whom probably consider themselves fortunate to have the business and the opportunity to earn a wage.

And presumably they pay social security and income taxes as well as use their after-tax earnings to purchase goods and services for themselves and their families. When you think about it, Leon Black was just doing his patriotic duty by throwing such a lavish party and "wasting" a couple of million dollars or so. Maybe he read *The Fable of the Bees* and is just doing his best to help during difficult economic times.

And Leon Black is not the only financial executive doing his part. In 2007, Stephen Schwarzman, the chairman of Blackstone, had a sixtieth birthday party featuring a performance by Rod Stewart; in 2012, David Bonderman, the founder of TPG (Texas Pacific Group), had a seventieth birthday party for seven hundred guests featuring performances by Paul McCartney, Robin Williams, and John Fogerty (Mr. Bonderman had the Rolling Stones and

John Mellencamp perform at his sixtieth birthday party—I am guessing that he likes rock and roll music); and in 2013, Thomas Kempner, manager of Davidson Kempner Capital Management, had a sixtieth birthday party featuring a concert by Billy Joel. Really, we just need these guys to stop being so stingy and celebrate their birthdays *every* year. The country could use the economic stimulus.

The Rich Pay the Taxes

A common refrain I hear today, particularly from the Democratic side of the aisle, is that "rich" people are not paying their "fair share" of taxes. Is this true? I am not sure of what "fair share" even means, but let's look at some facts, first as it relates to federal income taxes.

First off, as has been widely reported, *nearly 50 percent of American households currently pay no federal income tax*. By and large, these are low- or modest-income households, many of which are elderly or are families with children. In fact, the bottom 40 percent of households by income have, on average, a *negative* federal income tax rate. For example, in 2011, the lowest quintile (bottom 20 percent) of households by income had an average individual federal income tax rate of -7.5 percent, meaning, on average, they received a check from the government equal to 7.5 percent of their pretax income. This is largely the result of a combination of low taxable income and various tax credits, which in some cases are "refundable" even if the "taxpayer" otherwise owes no income tax. These credits include the Child Tax Credit and the Earned Income Tax Credit, among others, many of which are targeted to low-income families with children. These types of credits have tended to grow over both Republican and Democratic administrations as an incentive for lower-income people to work (since one must have income to receive the credits). Also, to some extent, they can be viewed as a refund of the social security taxes paid by low-income households as opposed to negative taxes, as the average payroll tax rate for the bottom quintile of households by income in 2011 was 7.1 percent. I'm not sure if that sounds any better since these individuals will be receiving social security payments in the future based on their social security taxes paid, but maybe this rationalization helps for some people.

For the second-lowest quintile (the 20 to 40 percent range), the average individual income tax rate was -1.3 percent. The middle income quintile (40 percent to 60 percent range) paid, on average, federal income tax at a rate of 2.4 percent on income, so we are finally in the marginally positive tax rate category. In fact, in an analysis by Deloitte Tax cited by the Associated Press, a family of four with an annual income of $50,000 in 2009 (the approximate median household income in the United States) would owe no tax due to the basic provisions of the tax code and the use of the standard deduction. The "typical" American family has very little or even no federal income tax liability.

Of course, this does not mean that all households in the bottom 40 percent of households by income pay no federal tax, but the vast majority of such households do not pay income tax. For example, based on a study by the Tax Policy Center, almost 90 percent of households with cash income less than $20,000 per year pay no income tax or receive a cash tax credit, but 10 percent do pay some income tax. Also, some higher-income households pay no income tax. The Tax Policy Center estimates that a little less than 2 percent of households with cash income of more than $100,000 paid no tax in 2011. Most of these higher-income nonpayers have no tax liability because of the favorable tax treatment on dividends and capital gains and the tax-exempt nature of interest on municipal bonds, combined with the impact of itemized deductions and other deductions that reduce taxable income (for example, the deductions for state and local income taxes and charitable donations). (The Tax Policy Center uses the term "tax units," but I use the term "households" as a convenience.) Maybe they give a very large share of their income to charity, thus drastically reducing their taxable income. Still, the average income tax rate for the top 20 percent of households by income was 14.2 percent in 2011, and the average rate for the top 1 percent of households was 20.3 percent. The graph below shows the average income tax rate by income quintile over the period from 1979 through 2011.

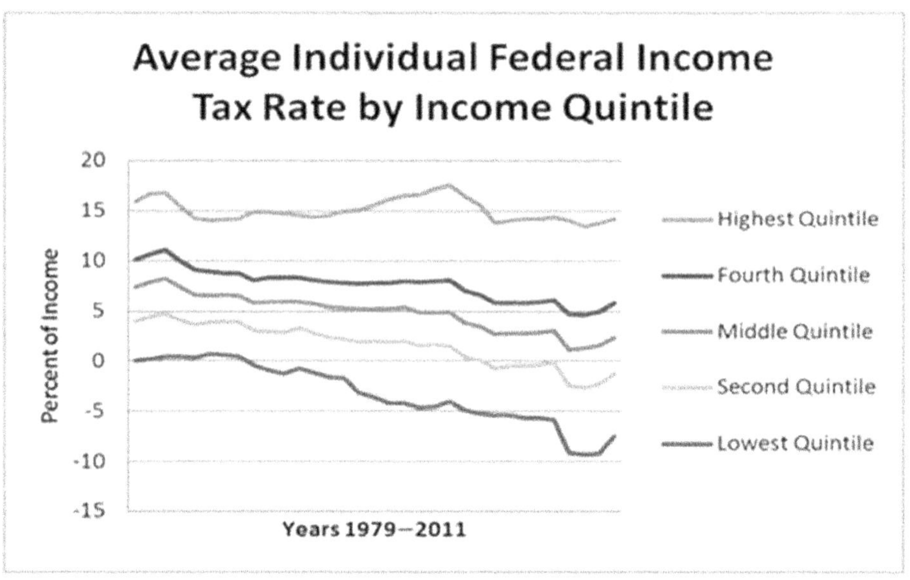

As the graph indicates, the average federal income tax rate has generally been declining for the bottom 80 percent of households since 1981 to a low in 2008 when the middle quintile, for example, had an average federal income tax rate of 1.2 percent, compared to a rate of 8.2 percent in 1981. Average rates for lower- and middle-income Americans declined significantly in 2008 due to the enactment of various tax breaks targeted toward moderate-income taxpayers. The average rate for the highest income quintile declined after the Reagan tax cuts, increased during the Clinton years, and then declined again after the Bush tax cuts in 2001 and 2003, reaching a low of 13.4 percent of income in 2009, before ticking up a bit in 2010 and 2011.

The graph that follows below shows the total share of federal income tax paid by income quintile. In terms of the share of individual income tax liabilities, higher-income households certainly pay their "fair share." For example, as a group, the bottom 60 percent of US households didn't even make it into the positive contribution category in 2011, with the top 40 percent of households accounting for 102.2 percent of all federal income taxes. So I am not sure that the bottom 60 percent paid their fair share of federal income taxes. The top 20 percent of households paid 88 percent of income taxes (the 80/20 rule in action, supercharged), and the top 1 percent paid 35.4 percent of all income taxes. How can one say that the rich don't pay their fair share when in fact they pay a hugely disproportionate share of total income taxes?

This is a big change from 1981, when the top 20 percent of households paid 64 percent of total income taxes, and the top 1 percent paid 16.3 percent of all income taxes. Since that time, tax rates have declined across the board but more so at lower income levels. Now it is true that the increase in the share of taxes paid by higher-income levels has also been driven by an increase in incomes for higher-income households. While this income shift merits discussion in its own right, it does not change the fact that the rich pay their fair share of taxes, particularly when it comes to federal income taxes.

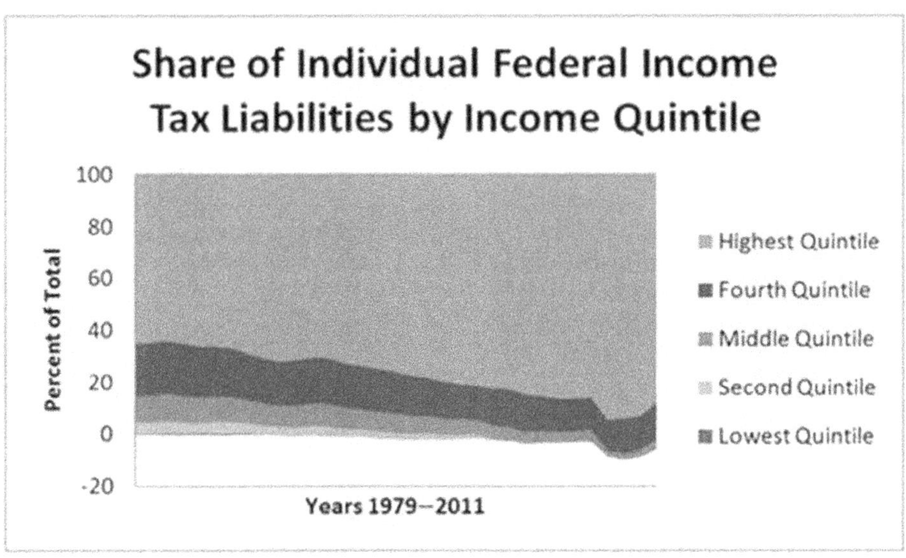

Of course, income taxes are only a part of federal taxes. If we look at total federal taxes, including social security taxes (which, of course, are substantial), excise taxes (such as the federal gasoline tax), and attributable corporate income taxes, the numbers are bigger and not quite so skewed toward high-income households. On this measure, the lowest quintile paid all federal taxes at an average rate of 1.9 percent of income in 2011, the middle quintile paid federal taxes at an average rate of 11.9 percent of income, the highest quintile paid federal taxes at an average rate of 23.4 percent of income, and the top 1 percent paid federal taxes at an average rate of 29.4 percent. To me at least, that all sounds kind of fair in the abstract, maybe more than fair given that these tax rates do not include any state or local taxes, so the total tax burden on all of us is much higher.

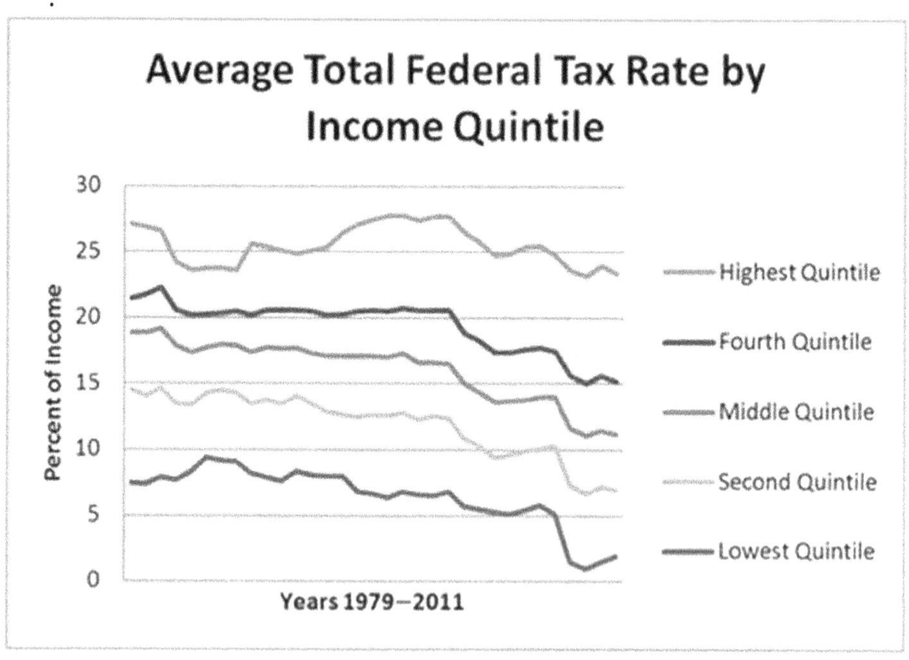

In addition, all of these effective average rates will be higher in 2013 and beyond as the tax increases relative to 2011 law in the American Taxpayer Relief Act of 2012 take effect. For example, the CBO estimates that overall federal tax rates will increase by a little more than 1 percentage point for most income quintiles and by about 2.1 percentage points for the top quintile of households by income. The average total federal tax rate for the top 1 percent of households is projected to increase by about 4.3 percentage points to an average rate of 33.3 percent, the highest it has been since 1997 and about the same as it was in 1980 before the Reagan tax cuts.

As a share of total federal tax liabilities (graph below), the numbers shake out as follows. The bottom 60 percent of households by income pay 13.3 percent of all federal taxes, and the top 40 percent of households pay 86.3 percent of all federal taxes (I guess a little rounding there). While one could always say that the rich could afford to pay more in taxes, it is hard to say that they don't pay their fair share, largely because the average- and lower-income households pay so little.

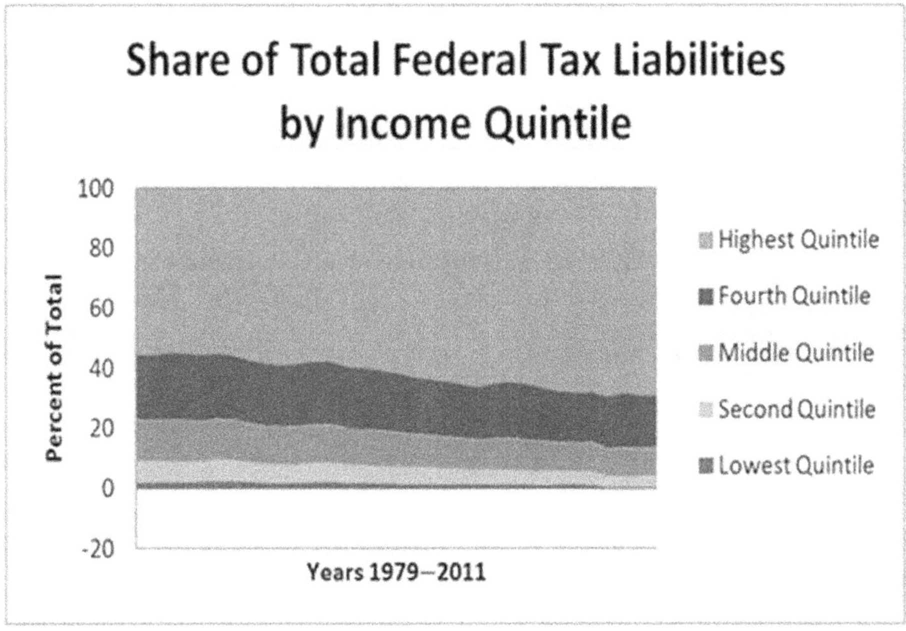

When we add in state and local taxes, the burden is even higher, although whether the extra burden is largely on the rich or is spread across all income levels depends on which state you live in. For example, in the state of New York, an admittedly high-tax state, residents at most income levels pay total state and local taxes at a rate of about 12 percent of income, although both the bottom 40 percent and the top 1 percent by income pay about 10 percent of their income in state and local taxes. This is because of the interaction of New York's fairly progressive income tax and the fairly regressive nature of property taxes, sales taxes, and the like. For example, the bottom 20 percent of New York households by income actually have a negative state income tax rate (-3.5 percent), while the higher tax brackets pay closer to 7 percent. Still, a typical New York resident one-percenter would pay about 44 percent of their income in federal, state, and local taxes, after factoring in the recently increased federal tax rates applicable to capital gains, the higher top marginal tax rate, and other changes in the recent tax-law changes.

Even at the state and local levels, where in general overall effective tax rates are more consistent over income levels, the rich pay much more in taxes (although in proportion to their income, at least in New York State). For example, in New York, the bottom 50 percent of returns by income paid 6.9 percent of all state income tax in 2010 (the state income tax makes up approximately 54 percent of all New York State taxes), while the top 10 percent by income paid 65 percent of all state income tax.

Again, when you think about it, this is maybe as it should be. At the state and local levels, where most of the actual governmental services are performed, taxes are levied at rates more closely proportional to income. (This is not true in all states, particularly those without a progressive income tax. In Washington State, for example, in 2010, the bottom 20 percent by income paid 16.9 percent of their incomes in various state and local taxes, while the top 1 percent paid only 3.3 percent of their incomes in state and local taxes.) At the federal level, however, there is no question that the higher-income taxpayers pay the preponderance of taxes, both as a share of income and in total.

Despite preconceptions to the contrary, the US tax system is as progressive as that of most European countries. According to data cited by the *Wall Street Journal* in 2011, a worker earning a $25,000 salary in the United States keeps a little over 90 percent of his salary after income tax and social security payments, the highest of any G8 nation (other than Japan, which is about the same), compared to, say, the United Kingdom at 83.2 percent and Germany at 72.6 percent. For someone with a $200,000 annual salary, the percentages are 70 percent for the United States, 61 percent for the United Kingdom, and 56 percent for Germany. I guess you could argue about how to interpret the data since the tax burden in the United States is lower at all income levels, but certainly lower-income earners in the United States are not overly taxed relative to the rest of the developed world. Throw in the much higher taxes on goods and services in Europe, which by their nature generally extract more of a toll on lower earners as a percent of income, and the relative tax burden in the United States on lower-and middle-income earners compared to Europe is even lighter.

Americans Are a Generous Bunch

The rich also give their wealth away. Americans gave away $217 billion in 2009, according to the Center on Wealth and Philanthropy. This organization further estimated that roughly half of the amount given was donated by households with a net worth of $1 million or more. As a percent of GDP, Americans are more than twice as generous as most other rich nations. According to one study, the United States gave 1.67 percent of GDP to charity, compared to second place, the United Kingdom at 0.73 percent of GDP, and lowly France at 0.14 percent of GDP. Americans seem to have more of a tradition of giving charitably to causes we support rather than relying on government to address every need.

According to Giving USA Foundation, total charitable contributions for 2011 were almost $300 billion, if giving by foundations, bequests, and corporations is included. Giving USA estimated that individuals accounted for 73 percent of total charitable giving in the United States, or over $200 billion. Recipients of charitable giving include religious organizations at 32 percent of the total giving; education at 13 percent; human services at 12 percent; health at 8 percent; arts, culture, and humanities at 4 percent of the total; and international affairs at 8 percent. Foundations and public-society-benefit organizations received a total of 16 percent of giving. Since these organizations make subsequent charitable grants, there is probably a little double-counting in the totals, but there is no denying that Americans are a generous bunch.

Another study, conducted by the *Chronicle of Philanthropy* in August 2012, looked at giving patterns (by income and residence) for taxpayers who took itemized deductions and earned $50,000 or more in 2008. The study found that these taxpayers donated an average of $2,564 to charity, representing 4.7 percent of their discretionary incomes and accounting for nearly two-thirds of the $214 billion donated by individuals to charity in 2008. The study also found that middle-class Americans gave a bigger share of their *discretionary* income to charities than the rich:

> Households that earn $50,000 to $75,000 give an average of 7.6 percent of their discretionary income to charity compared with an average of 4.2 percent for people who make $100,000 or more. Taxpayers with an income of $200,000 or higher gave an average of $14,088 to charity, representing 4.2 percent of their average discretionary income. This group accounted for 11 percent of the tax returns, but accounted for 41 percent of the money given to charity.

Since the study compared giving rates after taxpayers paid taxes and expenses for housing, food, and other necessities, this would seem to imply that the results may be different if one looked at giving as a percent of total income rather than discretionary income. For those at the lower end of the income scale, their discretionary income would be a much smaller share of their total income, while for the very wealthy, presumably, their discretionary income could be expected to represent a fairly large share of their total income, even with their higher level of taxes and their "necessities." One thing is clear, though—as a general rule, Americans across most income levels give actively to charities.

A number of charitable foundations have been established over the years by the nation's leading entrepreneurs, including the Bill & Melinda Gates Foundation, the Howard Hughes Medical Institute, the Ford Foundation, and the W. K. Kellogg Foundation, among many others. Andrew Carnegie—founder of the Carnegie Steel Company, which was later sold to US Steel—was a dedicated philanthropist, giving most of his money away to support various educational endeavors, including many public libraries and universities as well as numerous philanthropic organizations. The Carnegie Corporation of New York—which, when established by Andrew Carnegie in 1911 with an original endowment of $135 million, was the largest philanthropic trust in the world—had approximately $2.5 billion in assets at the end of 2010 and made annual grants of approximately $100 million during the year.

The country's largest charitable foundation is the Bill & Melinda Gates Foundation, funded largely by Bill Gates and Warren Buffet, with assets of $40 billion as of March 2014.

> Guided by the belief that every life has equal value, the Bill & Melinda Gates Foundation works to help all people lead healthy, productive lives. In developing countries, it focuses on improving people's health and giving them the chance to lift themselves out of hunger and extreme poverty. In the United States, it seeks to ensure that all people—especially those with the fewest resources—have access to the opportunities they need to succeed in school and life.

From 1994 through September 30, 2013, the foundation had made grants exceeding $28 billion.

Another joint philanthropic effort of Bill Gates and Warren Buffet is the "Giving Pledge" whereby they are encouraging the wealthiest individuals and families in America to give a majority of their wealth to charitable causes of their choosing, either during their lives or at death. As of April 15, 2015, the total number of pledge signatories was at 129 and counting (specific focus on billionaires, so that kind of limits the size of the pool).

Of course, you might not like the specific charities to which people donate their money. Many have a political bent with which you may not agree. Maybe you don't think it worthwhile that Mitt Romney gives millions of dollars to the Mormon Church. Maybe you are not a fan of the opera or the symphony. Maybe, in your opinion, Harvard University, with an endowment of $30 billion, doesn't need another $10 million donation. Or maybe you don't share the view of Peter B. Lewis, who, according to his Giving Pledge letter, has given away nearly $500 million, a portion of which went to fund "much of the movement to enact laws that give patients access to marijuana as relief for pain and nausea." Or, based on recent trends in public opinion, maybe you do.

According to the online magazine *Slate*, the largest American charitable contribution in 2010 was the $332 million given by George Soros to the Open Society Foundations and other similar grant makers. The mission of the Open Society Foundations is as follows:

> The Open Society Foundations work to build vibrant and tolerant societies whose governments are accountable and open to the participation of all people.
>
> We seek to strengthen the rule of law; respect for human rights, minorities, and a diversity of opinions; democratically elected governments; and a civil society that helps keep government power in check.
>
> We help to shape public policies that assure greater fairness in political, legal, and economic systems and safeguard fundamental rights.
>
> We implement initiatives to advance justice, education, public health, and independent media.
>
> We build alliances across borders and continents on issues such as corruption and freedom of information.
>
> Working in every part of the world, the Open Society Foundations place a high priority on protecting and improving the lives of people in marginalized communities.

Number two on the *Slate* giving list, Michael R. Bloomberg (founder of Bloomberg L.P. and mayor of New York City from 2001 through 2013), donated $279.23 million in 2010 for the arts, human services, public affairs, and other groups. Irwin and Joan Jacobs pledged $119.5 million, which includes a pledge of $75 million to the University of California at San Diego Health System to build a new medical center. Facebook founder Mark Zuckerberg pledged $100 million to Startup: Education to support programs that are working to improve public schools in Newark, New Jersey. (William and Karen Ackman's Pershing Square Foundation also donated $25 million to help improve the Newark public school system.) Terrence M. and Kim Pegula pledged $88 million to Penn State University to build a new athletics arena, to support the university's men's and women's hockey programs, and to provide scholarships to hockey players who attend the university.

Now again, you might not like George Soros's politics, much care about the public schools in Newark, New Jersey, or think that the Penn State hockey program needs $88 million, but there are worse things these philanthropists could do with their money—and it is their money. And in this country, we have a long history of individuals supporting causes in which they believe, often with their own money. We also have an amendment guaranteeing citizens the right of free speech, and that includes the right to put your money where your heart is.

Summary

And so that is why I appreciate most successful and ambitious individuals and don't begrudge their resulting financial reward. I benefit as a consumer of the broad range of products and services available to the average American. I benefit as a citizen from the large share of taxes paid by high-income taxpayers. And I benefit as well from the income I earn as a participant in the economy. And it is not just the rich but the collective efforts of all the capitalists, the entrepreneurs, the managers, the small-business people, and the workers that contribute to the economy. As Adam Smith said, "Where little wealth circulates, there is little to be got, but where a great deal is in motion, some shares of it may fall to [me]."

CHAPTER 10

Poverty and the Social Safety Net

Surely you are not saying we have the resources to save the poor from their lot? There will be poor always, pathetically struggling. Look at the good things you've got!

JESUS, IN *JESUS CHRIST SUPERSTAR*

THERE IS NO QUESTION THAT poverty remains a problem in the United States, with the poverty rate at 14.5 percent in 2013, representing 45.3 million people, according to data from the US Census Bureau. That is a lot of poverty in an otherwise rich nation. But what is one to do? As the overall poverty rate has been largely static for the past forty years, the question arises, can we do better, or have we reached the "natural" level of poverty? Will there be poor always, pathetically struggling? Probably there will be, and we should certainly do better than 14.5 percent of Americans living in poverty. Still, as we shall see, the poor are not without substantial governmental assistance.

Since the mean household income of the bottom 20 percent of households has increased in real terms by only about 10 percent since 1968, and in fact has declined by 11 percent since it reached its peak in 2006, it is not surprising that poverty remains a pervasive problem in the Unites States. The government's official level of poverty in 2013 was based on an income level of $12,119 for one person under the age of sixty-five and $23,834 for a family of four. For simplicity's sake, I use the reported weighted average for a family of four since a household of four can consist of two adults and two children, or one adult and three children, et cetera. Depending on the makeup of the household, the poverty threshold differs slightly. Based on the official measure, the number of people below the poverty threshold in 2013 was 45.3 million, up from 36.5 million in 2006, reflecting the impact of the recession on unemployment and on household incomes, particularly on lower-income households. For 2013, this represented 14.5 percent of the population living in poverty compared to an estimated poverty rate of 12.3 percent in 2006 and 22.4 percent in 1959, the first year for which poverty estimates are available in this data series. Since 1970, the poverty rate has ranged between a low of 11.1 percent in 1973 and a high of 15.2 percent in 1983. Basically, the rate of income poverty in the United States has not improved much at all over the past forty years.

The poverty rate varies greatly by race. For example, the poverty rate for blacks was 27.2 percent in 2013, while for non-Hispanic whites, it was 9.6 percent. While the poverty rate for blacks at 27.2 percent is unacceptably high, it is less than half that in 1959, when 55.1 percent of blacks were estimated to live below the poverty level. What is clear from looking at the data is that one of the most important determinants of whether a person is living in poverty is family status. For example, only 5.8 percent of all married-couple families (of all races) were below the poverty threshold in 2013, while the poverty rate for families with a male head of household with no wife present was 15.9 percent and the poverty rate for families with a female head of household with no husband present was 30.6 percent. The poverty rate for blacks in families with a female head of household and no husband present was a very high 42.5 percent!

Let me make two important points about the official poverty measure, which was originally developed in the early 1960s and has undergone only minor changes since it was adopted in 1969. First, as indicated earlier, the poverty rate is based on a money income threshold, which for one person is about $12,000 and for a family of four is about $24,000 (in 2013). Thus a family of four with income of $25,000 per year is living above the poverty line but is clearly not living a life of luxury, really just getting by. In 2013,

19.2 percent of the population had a money income of less than 125 percent of the poverty threshold. Also, the poverty estimates reported by the Census Bureau are based on money income before taxes and do not include the value of noncash benefits, such as food stamps, Medicare, Medicaid, public housing, and employer-provided fringe benefits. As we shall see later, the value of these benefits can be substantial. For example, including the value of Supplemental Nutrition Assistance Program benefits (food stamps) in income would move four million people above the poverty line, and taking into account the value of the federal Earned Income Tax Credit would reduce the number of children in poverty by about 2.9 million.

In addition, the official poverty thresholds were developed over forty years ago and do not take into account rising standards of living or such things as childcare expenses, other work-related expenses, variations in medical costs across population groups, or geographic differences in the cost of living. While one could argue about the precise definition of poverty, the official measure does give a good indication of the number of families and individuals living at a low income level over time. Also, see the discussion of the Supplemental Poverty Measure in the appendix.

Finally, not surprisingly, the main cure for poverty is jobs, jobs, and more jobs. Even at the federal minimum wage of $7.25 per hour, a worker who works 1,920 hours (forty-eight weeks at forty hours per week) would earn almost $14,000 per year. Again, not a life of luxury, but presumably enough to at least support oneself above the poverty line (but forget the family). Adding a working spouse at the same minimum-wage rate would increase household income up to $28,000, well above the official poverty level for a family of four. Significantly, the official poverty rate for full-time year-round workers is only 2.7 percent. Obviously, the difficulty in holding a steady job for a single mother with children at home is one of the reasons the poverty rate for families with a female head of household with no husband present is as high as it is at more than 30 percent. It is hard to earn much cash income without a full-time job.

Despite the continuing problem of poverty, people are surviving. A difficult life to be sure, but I am not aware of many systematic cases of people not getting enough to eat, for example. (See the discussion on food insecurity in the appendix.) Consider the following support available to people of little and modest means: cash support in the form of refundable tax credits and direct payments, government-paid medical care, nutritional support, housing support, energy assistance, education grants, occupational training, childcare support, et cetera, not to mention all of the other government services available to all Americans regardless of income. We now consider the details of the current arsenal in the war on poverty.

Government Services

There is much to consider when looking at the social safety net and government aid to the poor. I will start at a very high level by looking at *all* government services. After all, each of us benefit from some government services and programs to some extent, even the rich. For purposes of this discussion, I will divide the various government services into five basic categories: (1) pure public goods; (2) population-based services; (3) public education; (4) direct benefits; and (5) means-tested benefits. In addition to spending on current programs, federal, state, and local governments pay interest on debt incurred to support prior spending that was not covered by government revenues. I listed the types of government services above in order from least directly applicable to lower-income persons to directly applicable to lower-income persons.

Pure public goods are goods from which we all benefit and for which consumption by one does not reduce the ability for all others to benefit. National defense is probably the best example and definitely the largest category of spending on pure public goods. Population-based services are items such as police and fire protection, roads and public transportation, sanitation, and other services that generally require more spending as more people are served. Public education includes public primary and secondary schooling, as well as governmental support of postsecondary schooling and vocation training. Direct benefits include non-needs-based income programs such as social security and unemployment insurance, as well as Medicare. Finally, means-tested benefits include programs with income requirements such as food stamps, Medicaid, and housing assistance. When you add it all up, it encompasses quite an extensive list of actual services provided by the government as well as an extensive social safety net.

Please note that I have adopted many of the conventions and specific numbers utilized by Robert Rector and Jason Richwine in their May 6, 2013, report, *The Fiscal Cost of Unlawful Immigrants and Amnesty to the US Taxpayer*, as well as Robert Rector's April 17, 2012, "Testimony before Committee on the Budget, United States House of Representatives." Robert Rector and Jason Richwine are affiliated with the Heritage Foundation, which, according to their website, is "a research and educational institution—a think tank—whose mission is to formulate and promote conservative public policies based on the principles of free enterprise, limited government, individual freedom, traditional American values, and a strong national defense." As such, you might think that they bring a conservative mindset to the issue of government aid to the poor, and you would be correct. However, the data they use, which I have independently verified, is primarily from the budget of the US government and from the US Census Bureau, and the means-tested spending methodology is based on that used by the Congressional Research Service in their report, *Cash and Noncash Benefits for Persons with Limited Income: Eligibility Rules, Recipients and Expenditure Data, FY2002–FY2004.*

According to Rector and Richwine, total federal, state, and local spending in all categories (including interest) was $5.4 trillion in 2010. This comes to almost $45,000 per US household. That is quite an impressively large number for total government spending per household given that median household income is about $50,000. The total $5.4 trillion in all government spending is in line with the figures we reviewed on total government spending in Chapter 5. Average government revenues per household (according to Rector and Richwine) were only $30,584, with the difference made up by government borrowing. If we exclude interest and spending on pure public goods, the total remaining government spending is $3.8 trillion, or an average of $31,584 per household. The rationale for excluding interest is perhaps obvious since it reflects a current cost related to prior spending, but that does not provide any current benefit to US households (other than compensating the bondholders for making the loan to the government). While we all benefit from pure public goods, it is kind of hard to quantify on a per-person basis. I guess it could be argued that pure public goods such as national defense benefit higher-income people more than lower-income people because higher-income people have more to lose. In addition, many military personnel come from lower- to middle-income households, and thus many of these households are big contributors to our national defense beyond any taxes they may pay. But for the sake of simplicity, let's say that mostly all Americans benefit equally from our national defense and other spending on public goods and leave that out of the equation.

Okay, so big picture, based on the Rector and Richwine analysis, the average American household received the benefit of $31,584 in government spending in 2010 (plus national defense thrown in, which is certainly worth something). Of course, being an average, this may be completely unrepresentative of your personal situation. For example, this number includes spending for social security and Medicare, which benefit the elderly. It also includes spending for education and other child-support services, which benefit households with school-age children. Of course, over a lifetime, the age-related items tend to average out for each of us. It also includes spending for means-tested benefits, which benefit lower-income households. On the tax side of the ledger, the average household paid $30,426 in total federal, state, and local taxes in fiscal 2010, so on *average*, a US household had a net benefit of $1,158 from government (again, excluding the benefits of pure public goods and not accounting for net government interest and deficit borrowing, which is substantial). But beware the averages!

Rector and Richwine did some further work to estimate the benefits received and taxes paid by type of household defined by level of education attained by the head of the household. They found that households headed by persons without a high school degree (typically lower income) received an average of $46,582 per year in government benefits and services (again, excluding public goods such as national defense), while paying an average of $11,469 in taxes, for a net benefit of $35,113 per household. That's not such a bad deal for lower-income households. Conversely, households headed by persons with a college degree or more (typically higher income) received $24,830 in government benefits and services in 2010, while paying an average of $54,089 in federal, state, and local taxes, for a net contribution of $29,250. Again, while acknowledging the dangers of averages, this does give a representative view of the relative net benefit received by a lower-income household from the rest of society compared to the net contribution made to the rest of society from an average higher-income household. One might imagine that the numbers would be even more dramatic for a truly lower-income household (say annual income of under $20,000, which would have a very low overall tax burden) and a truly higher-income household (say an annual income of over $400,000, which would typically have a much higher overall tax burden of maybe $150,000 in taxes).

So that is the overall picture, and it's really no big surprise. Lower-income households typically receive more government benefits and pay less in taxes, while higher-income households receive less in government benefits and pay more in taxes. The poor are net users of governmental resources, and the more affluent are net contributors to governmental resources. Similar conclusions were reached by the Congressional Budget Office based on a review of 2006 data for federal spending and taxes only. The CBO estimated that in 2006, the lowest income quintile of nonelderly households received an average of $15,200 in federal transfers and $9,800 in other federal spending for goods and services (allocated mostly equally across all households), and they paid $2,600 in taxes, for a net household benefit of $22,500. In contrast, nonelderly households in the highest income quintile received an average of $2,000 in transfers and $9,700 in other federal spending for goods and services, and they paid $68,100 in taxes, for a net contribution of $56,400. Excluding elderly households from the analysis dramatically reduces the transfers because the largest federal transfer programs are social security and Medicare, which largely benefit the elderly.

Direct Benefits

Now let's look at some of the specifics of direct benefits and means-tested benefits, which are mostly direct benefits to individuals, rather than, say, the general benefits available to all of us, such as public schools, public roads, and police and fire protection.

Rector and Richwine calculate a total of over $1.3 trillion being spent by federal, state, and local governments on non-means-tested direct benefits in 2010, with $1,185 billion being spent by the federal government and $148 billion being spent by state and local governments. By far the largest direct-benefits programs are the social security and Medicare programs run by the federal government. Total spending by the federal government on social security, including old-age and survivors insurance and disability insurance, was $773.3 billion in fiscal 2012, according to the Office of Management and Budget. The total spending on the Medicare program was $471.8 billion in 2012, so just those two federal programs totaled $1.25 trillion in 2012 (up from a total of $1.16 trillion in the 2010 figures used by Rector and Richwine). I discuss social security and Medicare in other chapters, but a few important points are relevant here. First of all, these programs are generally open to all Americans, subject to having worked and meeting other eligibility requirements. Secondly, as of now, the receipt of benefits is not means tested. Since all benefits participants have contributed taxes into the program (or their spouses have), it has the appeal of being a fairly inclusive program with much popular support. However, because of the way that benefits are calculated and taxes are assessed, these programs are much more beneficial to lower-income households than to higher-income households. See the discussion in Chapter 5.

The other sizable direct-benefits program provided by the government is unemployment-compensation insurance. The unemployment-compensation program is a joint federal-state program created by the Social Security Act of 1935. The program is based on federal law, but each state designs and administers its own program within the federal requirements. All states finance unemployment compensation primarily through contributions from employers on the wages of their covered workers. In addition, three states (Alaska, New Jersey, and Pennsylvania) collect contributions from employees. Compensation is payable to individuals who are out of work, generally through no fault of their own, and who are able and available for work. Most states pay a maximum of twenty-six weeks, and in periods of very high and rising unemployment in individual states, benefits are payable for up to thirteen additional weeks (twenty in some cases). Extended compensation funding is payable under the provisions of the Federal-State Extended Unemployment Compensation Act of 1970. Extended compensation is generally shared by the states and the federal government, but during the most recent recession, the federal government paid 100 percent of most extended benefit costs through December 31, 2013. In addition, the Emergency Unemployment Compensation (EUC08) program provides for additional weeks of benefits (ranging from fourteen to up to fifty-three weeks) paid 100 percent by the federal government. The EUC08 program was effective from July 2008 through January 1, 2014.

Not surprisingly, benefits payable from the unemployment-compensation program increase during recessions and decline during times of economic growth. This is due to the dual effects of higher unemployment, and thus more unemployment-compensation claims, plus the longer benefit periods resulting from extended unemployment compensation and any emergency unemployment legislation that may be in effect. Thus, in fiscal 2010, total benefit outlays totaled $156.4 billion, including $63 billion of regular benefits, compared to total benefits of $43.1 billion in 2008, including $38.1 billion of regular benefits. By fiscal 2013, total benefit outlays had declined to $66.5 billion, including $39.6 billion of regular benefits.

Once again, unemployment compensation is a universal program in that it covers nearly all private-sector workers. It is designed to be social insurance to provide temporary support to those who have lost their jobs due to a general reduction in the workforce. Theoretically, unemployment could happen to anyone, and thus each of us could potentially benefit from the program. Still, it is a social benefit, paid for by those who are working (indirectly, through taxes paid by the employers), just as an unemployed person effectively paid into the program while he or she was working. But for our purposes, as is the case with social security and Medicare, we will exclude unemployment compensation as a benefit targeted to lower-income individuals.

Means-Tested Benefits

Now let's focus on government programs that pay benefits based on the recipient's "need." There are roughly eighty benefit programs that provide cash and noncash aid that is directed to persons with limited income, which, according to Rector and Richwine, accounted for $927 billion in spending in 2011. The 2006 report from the Congressional Research Service, *Cash and Noncash Benefits for Persons with Limited Income: Eligibility Rules, Recipient and Expenditure Data, FY2002–FY2004*, lists eighty-four need-based programs, with total spending of $583 billion in fiscal 2004. The report points out that the number of programs is somewhat arbitrary based on how one wants to define a program. For example, the Temporary Assistance for Needy Families (TANF) program is listed as four programs under cash, services, childcare, and work activities, but it could also be considered one program. Robert Rector's April 2012 testimony before the Committee on the Budget, United States House of Representatives, examined seventy-nine programs accounting for $927 billion in spending. Another study by Michael Tanner, *The American Welfare State, How We Spend Nearly $1 Trillion a Year fighting Poverty—and Fail*, lists 126 separate federally funded programs but comes up with similar figures for total spending. For our purposes, let's just call it eighty programs targeted at lower-income persons. Nearly $1 trillion in spending to support the poor, representing approximately 6 percent of the economy, would seem to be a hefty amount. For myself, I was surprised at how large the number is, given all the buzz about how the United States does not serve its most vulnerable citizens, but let's look at the details.

Using Rector's and Richwine's figures, the breakdown of spending in 2011 by major category is as follows:

2011 Needs-Based spending by Federal and State Governments
(In Billions)

Medical	$ 458.7
Cash Support	182.2
Food	109.4
Housing	56.1
Energy and Utilities	6.4
Education	60.2
Training	8.4
Services	15.3
Childcare and Development	22.7
Community Development	7.9
Total	$ 927.3

Source: Robert Rector and Jason Richwine, *The Fiscal Cost of Unlawful Immigrants and Amnesty to the US Taxpayer*.

MEDICAL CARE

As can be clearly seen, the largest category is spending on health, accounting for nearly half of total needs-based spending, with the vast majority of that coming from the Medicaid program at $432.6 billion. We have already discussed Medicaid in the chapter on health care, but to review, Medicaid is the federal-state medical program for people of limited means. According to the

Centers for Medicare and Medicaid Services (CMS), benefit outlays under Medicaid were $412 billion in fiscal 2011 (excluding administrative costs), of which $262 billion was funded by the federal government. By fiscal 2013, this had reached $437 billion, of which $265 billion was funded by the federal government. A 2013 report by the Congressional Budget Office shows federal spending on Medicaid at $251 billion and spending on the Medicare Part D low-income subsidy at $21 billion in 2012, for a total of $272 billion. The CBO projected this to grow by a factor of 130 percent to a total of $625 billion *in real terms* by 2023, reflecting expected growth in health-care costs and new assistance to be provided under the Affordable Care Act. So federal spending in this category is expected to grow dramatically. Presumably, state spending would grow as well since Medicaid is a joint federal-state program.

In addition, benefits payable under the Children's Health Insurance Program (CHIP) in fiscal 2011 was $12 billion, increasing to $14 billion by fiscal 2013. The average monthly enrollment in Medicaid in fiscal 2013 was 57.4 million people, so average benefits per beneficiary were about $7,600. (The unduplicated annual enrollment in fiscal 2013 was 72.8 million, which is higher than the monthly average because people move in and out of the program during the year.) Presumably, the average benefit paid per household would be higher than the average benefit per beneficiary because of multiple beneficiaries per household.

While Medicaid is the primary medical benefit program for people of need, other needs-based medical programs include medical general assistance, Indian Health Services, Consolidated Health Centers/Community Health Centers, Maternal and Child Health, Medical Assistance to Refugees, and Healthy Start. According to Rector and Richwine, of the total $458.7 billion spent on health-care benefits targeted to people of low income in 2011, the federal government provided approximately 63 percent of the funding while state and local spending came in at 37 percent of the total.

Cash Assistance

The next-largest category of means-tested aid is cash assistance, totaling $182.1 billion in 2011. About half of this consists of the refundable portion of various tax credits, namely the Earned Income Tax Credit (EITC), the Child Tax Credit, and the Making Work Pay Tax Credit. The "refundable portion" is included in these numbers (and is counted as spending in the official budget of the United States) because the credit is refunded even though the individual had no federal tax liability. The portion that is simply used to reduce taxes otherwise owed is treated in the government's numbers the same as any other tax credit or benefit inherent in the tax code. The Making Work Pay Tax Credit was effective beginning in 2009, but it was allowed to expire after 2010 when it was essentially replaced by the reduction in payroll taxes as part of the Tax Relief, Unemployment Insurance Reauthorization, and Job Creation Act of 2010. The new provision applied to all workers subject to payroll taxes and thus was not a means-tested program. The reduced rate on payroll taxes was itself allowed to expire on December 31, 2012.

Still, for consistency we'll stick with the fiscal 2011 numbers as presented by Rector and Richwine. On that basis, the total refundable tax credits were $92.2 billion, consisting of $55.7 billion from the Earned Income Tax Credit (EITC), $22.7 billion from the Child Tax Credit, and $13.9 billion from the Making Work Pay Tax Credit. The numbers are similar for fiscal 2012 based on the 2014 budget of the United States, except for the previously mentioned Making Work Pay Tax Credit, which has expired. The EITC is a federal refundable tax credit, meaning the EITC can reduce the taxpayer's federal tax obligation to zero and refund any excess. For 2012, the EITC was available to taxpayers with adjusted gross income of up to $50,270 (married, filing jointly) if they had at least three qualifying children. The adjusted gross income limit for taxpayers without children was $19,190 (married, filing jointly). The amount of the credit is based on adjusted gross income, filing status, and number of qualifying children, and it can be as high as $5,891 for taxpayers with at least three children. The EITC is designed to provide support to lower- and middle-income individuals and to encourage work since individuals must file a tax return and have earned income to qualify for the credit.

Based on data from the IRS, for the 2011 tax year, over twenty-seven million taxpayers received nearly $63 billion in EITC. Presumably the total amount includes the total amount of the credit, including the tax-offset portion as well as the refundable portion. The average amount of EITC received nationwide was $2,250. According to the Center on Budget and Policy Priorities, the EITC lifted about 6.2 million people out of poverty in 2013, including about 3.2 million children. When combined with the Child Tax Credit, the total lifted above the poverty line was 9.4 million, including about 5 million children.

The Child Tax Credit is fully available to taxpayers who have a qualifying child and an adjusted gross income of less than $110,000 (married, filing jointly). The child tax credit is reduced for taxpayers with adjusted gross income above $110,000 (married filing jointly) or $75,000 (single and head of household or qualifying widow[er]). The maximum credit is $1,000 per qualifying child. The "Additional" Child Tax Credit is for certain individuals who receive less than the full amount of the child tax credit. As such, the additional child tax credit may provide a refund even if the taxpayer owes no tax. According to the Internal Revenue Service, in 2012, 22.9 million returns claimed $27.7 billion in the child tax credit and 19.8 million returns claimed $26.5 billion in the refundable portion of the child tax credit. Again, individuals must have income and must file a tax return to receive either the child tax credit or the additional child tax credit.

After the various refundable-tax-credit programs, the largest cash-assistance program is the Supplemental Security Income program (SSI), managed by the Social Security Administration but paid for by US Treasury funds. The SSI program makes payments to people with low income who are sixty-five or older or are blind or have a disability. In addition, many states add money to the basic federal benefit. This program is distinct from the Old-Age and Survivors Insurance Trust Fund and the Disability Insurance Trust Fund, which are a part of social security. According to the Rector and Richwine figures, total spending on the SSI program in fiscal 2011 was $61.2 billion, comprising $56.5 billion in federal spending and $4.7 billion in state spending.

SSI is meant to be "assistance of last resort." As such, eligibility depends on a person's income and resources. Generally, the Social Security Administration determines the monthly benefit by computing an individual's "countable" income (after certain small exclusions) and subtracts this from the applicable federal benefit rate. The federal monthly benefit rate for 2013 is $710 for an eligible individual and $1,066 for an eligible couple. In January 2012, 8.2 million individuals received federally administered monthly SSI benefits averaging $517 (includes both federal payments and state payments), so that's about $6,200 on an annual basis. During calendar year 2011, federal SSI benefit payments totaled $49 billion, of which 63 percent went to disabled individuals aged eighteen to sixty-four, 19 percent went to disabled individuals under the age of eighteen, 9.8 percent went to the aged, and 8.2 percent went to disabled individuals aged sixty-five years or older. Total state expenditures for federally administered supplements totaled $3.5 billion in 2011.

Next on the cash-assistance list is Temporary Assistance for Needy Families (TANF), which began on July 1, 1997, and succeeded the Aid to Families with Dependent Children program. According to the Office of Family Assistance, "TANF is a block grant program to help move recipients into work and turn welfare into a program of temporary assistance." The four purposes of TANF are as follows:

- "Provide assistance to needy families so that children can be cared for in their own homes
- "Reduce the dependency of needy parents by promoting job preparation, work, and marriage
- "Prevent and reduce unplanned pregnancies among single young adults
- "Encourage the formation and maintenance of two-parent families"

Rector and Richwine show total cash assistance under the TANF program as $13.8 billion in fiscal 2011, of which $6.9 billion was provided by the federal government and $6.9 billion was provided by the states. TANF expenditures can be for "assistance" or for "nonassistance." Assistance spending includes basic cash assistance, childcare, transportation, and supportive services and assistance allowed under prior law. Nonassistance includes work-related expenses, childcare, transportation, individual development accounts, refundable EITC (very small portion), nonrecurrent short-term benefits, prevention of out-of-wedlock pregnancies, two-parent family formation and maintenance, administration and systems, nonassistance allowed under prior law, and other. In fiscal 2011, based on data from the US Department of Health and Human Services, total spending under the TANF program was $33.3 billion, of which $17.9 billion came from the federal government and $15.4 billion came from the states. The total spending provided $11.1 billion in "assistance," $19.5 billion in "nonassistance," and $2.7 billion in transfers to other programs. A total of 1,795,631 families (4,208,808 recipients) received TANF or separate state program assistance in December 2012. The average monthly amount of assistance for TANF recipient families was $392 in FY 2010 (about $4,700 on an annual basis), with monthly cash payments to TANF families averaging $327 for one child, $412 for two children, $497 for three children, and $594 for four or more children. Some TANF families who were not employed received other forms of assistance such as childcare, transportation, and other supportive services.

Other forms of needs-based cash assistance referenced by Rector and Richwine, totaling $15 billion in federal and state spending, include the Title IV-E Foster Care program, Title IV-E Adoption Assistance, general cash assistance, refugee assistance, general assistance to Indians, and Assets for Independence. While recognizing that some of the spending numbers I referenced differ slightly from the Rector and Richwine figures, their total of needs-based cash assistance of $182 billion is a good working number.

Food Aid

Next on the list is food assistance, coming in at a total of $109.4 billion. By far the largest food-assistance program is the Supplemental Nutritional Assistance Program (SNAP), commonly referred to as food stamps. Rector and Richwine show $84.6 billion combined federal and state spending on food stamps in fiscal 2011, of which $77.6 billion was from the federal government and $7.0 billion was from the states. The United States Department of Agriculture reports $75.7 billion as the total federal cost of the program in fiscal 2011 and $74.1 billion in fiscal 2014. The 2014 budget of the United States lists $80.3 billion in federal spending on food stamps in fiscal 2012 (including Puerto Rico), so we are easily in the ballpark at an all-in figure of about $85 billion (including state spending). The costs of the food stamp program have increased greatly over the last seven years. As recently as fiscal 2008, total federal costs for SNAP were less than $38 billion.

The Supplemental Nutrition Assistance Program is basically designed to assure that nearly all Americans receive enough to eat. A couple of relevant highlights of SNAP follow, primarily from *Building a Healthy America: A Profile of the Supplemental Nutritional Assistance Program* (USDA, Food and Nutrition Service, Office of Research and Analysis, April 2012).

- In fiscal 2011, SNAP served nearly forty-five million people, about one in seven Americans. This increased to almost forty-seven million people in fiscal 2012.
- SNAP is available to nearly everyone who qualifies with little income and few resources. Unlike many other needs-based programs, it is not limited to the elderly, the disabled, or families with children.
- On average, in fiscal 2011, SNAP provided $134 per month per recipient ($284 per month per participant household).
- Generally, households must have monthly gross income less than 130 percent of the federal poverty level and monthly net income (after certain allowed deductions for other living necessities) of less than 100 percent of the poverty level.
- Maximum benefits are reduced by 30 percent of a household's net income.
- SNAP benefits are based on the Thrifty Food Plan (TFP). Families with no net income receive the full cost of the TFP. The maximum benefit for a family of four in fiscal 2012 was $668 per month, or about $8,000 on an annualized basis. Forty percent of SNAP households receive the maximum benefit for their household size.
- The diets of SNAP participants, as measured by the Healthy Eating Index, are similar to higher-income Americans.

Other significant food-assistance programs include the Special Supplemental Nutrition Program for Women, Infants, and Children (WIC), and the school lunch and breakfast programs. The WIC program provides federal grants to states for supplemental foods, health-care referrals, and nutrition education for low-income pregnant, breastfeeding, and nonbreastfeeding postpartum women, and to infants and children up to age five who are found to be at nutritional risk. The total cost of this program was $6.8 billion in fiscal year 2011, according to Rector and Richwine. In fiscal 2012, the monthly average number of participants in the program was 8.9 million, and the average monthly food cost per person was $44.98.

The National School Lunch Program is a federally assisted meal program that provided low-cost or free lunches to more than thirty-one million children each school day in 2011. Children from families with incomes at or below 130 percent of the poverty level are eligible for free meals, while those with incomes between 130 percent and 185 percent of the poverty level are eligible for reduced-price meals. According to the USDA, the National School Lunch Program cost $11.1 billion in fiscal 2011 (compared to Rector and Richwine's figure of $10.3 billion). The School Breakfast Program is a similar program, and it served over 12.1 million children each day in fiscal 2011, costing $3 billion.

Other food-assistance programs include the Child Care Food Program, the Nutrition Program for the Elderly, the Summer Food Service Program, the Commodity Supplemental Food Program, the Emergency Food Assistance Program, the Farmers' Market Nutrition Program, and the Special Milk Program. Again, the all-in total for the various food assistance programs was almost $110 billion in 2011.

Housing

Once again, housing assistance comes in the form of many different programs. Rector and Richwine show a total of $56.1 billion in needs-based housing assistance. The largest of these programs is Section 8 rental assistance provided under Section 8 of the US Housing Act of 1937, either in the form of tenant-based rental assistance or project-based rental assistance. The *tenant*-based program (Housing Choice Vouchers) is the federal government's major program for assisting very low-income families, the elderly, and the disabled to afford "decent, safe and sanitary housing in the private market." The *project*-based voucher program provides rental assistance for eligible families who live in specific housing developments or units. The total cost of Section 8 housing assistance was approximately $28 billion in fiscal 2011. (Rector and Richwine show a total cost of $28.4 billion, while the 2014 US budget shows $28 billion in fiscal 2012.) Section 8 housing assistance is funded by the US Department of Housing and Urban Development and administered locally by public housing agencies (PHAs). To be eligible for housing-choice vouchers, in general, the family must have an income not exceeding 50 percent of the median income for the county or metropolitan area in which the family chooses to live. The maximum housing assistance is generally the lesser of the amount generally needed to rent a moderately priced dwelling in the local housing market minus 30 percent of the family's monthly adjusted income.

The other major housing program managed by HUD is public housing. HUD administers federal aid to local housing agencies that manage the housing for low-income residents at rents they can afford. There are approximately 1.1 million households living in public housing units. Other federal assistance programs for housing include the Low Income Housing Tax Credit for developers, the Home Investment Partnership Program, Homeless Assistance Grants, Rural Housing Insurance Fund, Rural Housing Service, Housing for the Elderly, Native American Housing Block Grants, Housing for Persons with Disabilities, and Housing Opportunities for Persons with AIDS, in addition to various state and local housing initiatives. When one adds it up, it comes to over $56 billion, according to Rector and Richwine.

Best as I can tell from data from the US Department of Housing and Urban Development, as of fiscal 2011, a total of 5,341,515 families were in occupied rental units receiving HUD assistance. Of these, 3,362,574 were in multifamily project-based rental assistance or tenant-based rental assistance. According to the 2014 budget of the United States, total discretionary housing assistance for fiscal 2012 is $43.8 billion, or over $8,000 per family. The averages are similar for the Section 8 housing programs. At a total cost of approximately $28 billion, that comes out to over $8,000 per family receiving section 8 assistance. So an average of $8,000 per family receiving government housing assistance seems like a good working number.

Education

The next major category of needs-based assistance is education, which Rector and Richwine calculate to be $60.2 billion, with the Pell Grants being the largest program by far at $41.5 billion. Pell Grants are the primary federal program providing grant aid to low-income and middle-income undergraduate students. In general, the amount of needs-based financial aid a student can receive is based on the difference between the relevant school's cost of attendance (COA) and the student's expected family contribution (EFC). The EFC is a formula-based calculation that takes into account the family's income, assets, and benefits, as well as its size and number of dependents who will be attending college. For the 2012–2013 award year, a student automatically qualifies for a zero EFC (meaning the family is not expected to contribute anything towards the cost of higher education) if the income of the student's parents is $23,000 or less.

In fiscal 2012, the United States Department of Education disbursed $33.3 billion in Pell Grants averaging approximately $3,653 to more than nine million students. The maximum Pell Grant for both the 2011–12 and 2012–13 award years was $5,550.

Other needs-based federal aid programs for higher education include Federal Supplemental Educational Opportunity Grants (FSEOG), Direct Subsidized Loans, Federal Perkins Loans, and Federal Work Study. Non-needs-based federal student aid programs include Direct Unsubsidized Loans, Federal PLUS Loans, and Teacher Education Access for College and Higher Education (TEACH) Grants. In total, Federal Student Aid, a principal office of the United States Department of Education, disbursed $141.9 billion in aid to fifteen million students (a large portion of this in the form of loans and thus excluded from the other figures cited for spending on needs-based education). With such a large component of federal assistance, it is not surprising that costs for higher education have been increasing so rapidly, just as they are in the health-care sector.

The other major federal effort for needs-based education assistance is Title I grants to local education agencies (LEAs), more formally known as Improving Basic Programs Operated by Local Education Agencies (Title I, Part A). This program provides financial assistance to LEAs and schools with high numbers or percentages of children from low-income families. Funds are allocated based on census poverty estimates and the cost of education in each state. Appropriations for fiscal year 2012 were $14.5 billion.

Now I think that most people would agree that it is our nation's collective responsibility to provide a quality education for all of our children and youth, regardless of income. Title I grants are included in the list of needs-based assistance because they comprise a program targeted to lower-income school districts, which perhaps require more funding and have more special needs in order to help low-achieving students meet education standards. As a specific example, let's compare two districts in Westchester County, New York: the Mamaroneck Union Free School District and the Yonkers City School District. The Mamaroneck school district is a relatively well-off suburban district near New York City with approximately 5,265 students, while the Yonkers school district is a less well-off city district, also near New York City, with approximately 25,311 students. The Mamaroneck school district is 75 percent white, while the Yonkers school district is 17 percent white. To give an idea of the relative wealth of the districts, approximately 10 percent of the students in the Mamaroneck school district received free or reduced-price lunch, while the comparable percentage in Yonkers is 67 percent. Total spending per enrollee is approximately $23,608 in Mamaroneck and $20,286 in Yonkers, so about 16 percent higher in Mamaroneck (although spending in both districts is higher than the overall national average). However, about 95 percent of the budget in Mamaroneck is funded from local taxes, with state aid comprising about 5.4 percent of the budget. No wonder the property taxes are so high in the town of Mamaroneck. In Yonkers, however, over 40 percent of the budget is funded through state and federal aid. State aid per enrollee in Mamaroneck is $1,271, while in Yonkers it is $8,391.

So we have a system whereby well-off districts essentially pay for their own local schools (at least in New York), while less well-off districts receive substantial state and federal aid. So if you are a higher-income taxpayer living in a well-off district, you are paying substantial taxes to support your local schools, which do not receive much in the way of state or federal aid, while you would also be paying substantial state and federal taxes, which help support less well-off districts. Now I am not saying that is fair or unfair. I am just reporting the rather unsurprising reality that lower-income families and communities are benefitting substantially from the support of higher-income taxpayers. Yet despite this education-funding dynamic, a 2013 study claims that there is an $8,601 per student spending gap between the wealthiest and the poorest districts in New York State.

——

It's Not Just the Government Supporting Education

Now let's turn to an example in higher education where higher-income households pay their own way while also helping to subsidize costs for lower- and middle-income households. This example does not involve the government, and so is perhaps a little out of place in this chapter, but it is still a widespread practice that benefits lower-income and moderate-income households. At Colgate University as an example, the 2012–2013 combined student charges were $55,715, consisting of $44,330 in tuition and $11,985 in room, meals, and activities fee. Estimated personal expenses were $2,030, so the total cost of attending Colgate University was $57,745 per year.

That is a boatload of money, and it's more than the median household income in the United States. About 60 percent of families with children at Colgate are fortunate to be able to pay the full amount or at least somehow manage to scrape the required funds together. However, 40 percent of the class of 2016 at Colgate receives financial aid, averaging a little over $40,000 per student, of which almost $36,000 per student is in the form of a Colgate Grant from the school. That is a hefty amount of needs-based student aid provided by the university, paid for by endowment fundraising and indirectly from families able to afford the full amount of tuition and fees. Colgate's policy is to meet 100 percent of admitted students' financial need.

The financial-aid story is similar at many other prestigious colleges and universities. That is a large part of the reason why, in a 2013 report on trends in college pricing, the CollegeBoard found that the real average "net" price of tuition, fees, room, and board at private nonprofit four-year institutions had remained largely flat since 2003–04, while the published price had increased 22 percent in real terms after inflation. The definition of *net price* is the average price paid by all full-time students, after all grant aid from all sources in addition to federal tax credits and deductions. Since the average includes students who do not receive financial aid as well as those who do, the net price paid by those who do receive aid has actually declined in real terms over that period.

In Colgate's case, financial aid is available for many income levels depending on the particular situation. Almost half of the students admitted for the class of 2016 receiving financial aid reported family income of over $100,000 per year. So the assistance goes well up the income ladder, as I guess it should at an annual cost of over $57,000. More affluent families can theoretically afford to pay the full "list price" and therefore subsidize moderate-income families, but that sure is a big check to write.

Childcare and Child Development

Spending on needs-based childcare and child development comes in at over $22 billion. Head Start is probably the best-known child-development program, with a total cost of $9.5 billion, including both the federal and the state portion, according to Rector and Richwine. The federal appropriation for Head Start for the 2012 fiscal year was approximately $8 billion. According to the Health and Human Services website, Head Start is a federal program that promotes the readiness of children ages birth to five from low-income families by enhancing their cognitive, social, and emotional development. The program aims to support language and literacy, cognition and general knowledge, physical development and health, social and emotional development, and approaches to learning. Over a million children are served by Head

Start programs every year, which, if I did my math right, comes to about $9,500 per child in the program. The Office of Head Start (OHS), within the Administration of Children and Families of the Department of Health and Human Services, awards grants to public and private agencies on a competitive basis to provide these comprehensive services to specific communities.

Rector and Richwine show $13.2 billion in other spending on childcare and child-development programs. The Child Care and Development Fund (CCDF), for one, made available $5.2 billion to states, territories, and tribes in fiscal 2012. Subsidized childcare services are available to eligible families through certificates or grants and contracts with providers. Parents may select a childcare provider that satisfies any applicable state and local requirements. Approximately 1.6 million children receive a childcare subsidy from the Child Care and Development Fund every month, so about $3,250 per child on an annual basis. Other childcare programs include TANF Child Care and childcare entitlements to the states.

Other Needs-Based Spending

The remaining $60.7 billion of needs-based spending falls under the categories of energy and utilities, training, services, and community development. The primary energy and utility programs include the Low Income Home Energy Assistance Program (LIHEAP) and the Universal Service Fund providing subsidized phone service for low-income persons (including subsidized cell phone service). Training programs include Temporary Assistance for Needy Families Work Activities, Job Corps, and Youth Opportunity Grants, among others. Services programs include Temporary Assistance for Needy Families Block Grant Services, Title XX Social Services Block Grants, and Safe and Stable Families, among many others. TANF Block Grant Services, in particular, comes in at a cost of a little over $10 billion. TANF services include transportation subsidies, parental-skill-building services, home-energy aid, housing aid, rehabilitation services (mental health/substance abuse counseling and treatment), and domestic-violence counseling. Community-development programs total $7.9 billion in spending, the largest of which are Community Development Block Grants and related development funds. The Community Development Block Grant (CDBG) program provides annual grants on a formula basis to entitled cities, urban counties, and states to develop viable urban communities by providing decent housing and a suitable living environment, and by expanding economic opportunities, principally for low- and moderate-income persons.

Needs-Based Summary

So there we have it, $927 billion of needs-based spending in 2011 on roughly eighty different programs. Hopefully I didn't overwhelm you with the details of the various individual programs. I only mean to provide you with an appreciation of the very wide variety of programs targeted to low- and moderate-income Americans.

How are we to give some perspective to the more than $900 billion in spending? Here are some easy calculations. If we compare the total spending to the 46.2 million Americans living in official poverty in 2011, that comes to about $20,000 per person. Of course, many individuals are part of larger households, so this figure would *understate* the amount of spending per poor *household*. If we compare the $927 billion in spending to the sum of the 9.5 million families living in poverty and the 12.4 million unrelated individuals living in poverty (an estimated 21.9 million households living in poverty), then we get a figure of over $42,000 per household in poverty as defined, regardless of the size of the household. That sure seems like a large number, given that the figure is roughly double the poverty threshold for a family of four and not that far off from the median household income in the United States of about $50,000.

However, the number of people living in poverty may not be the most relevant criteria for our analysis, since many programs extend to people with income above the poverty threshold, and sometimes materially above the poverty level (such as Pell Grants). A very broad calculation would be to compare the total needs-based spending to the bottom 50 percent of all households—basically, the US households that pay little or no income tax. That would be approximately 60.5 million households with an income of less than the approximately $50,000 national median income. Even on this very broad basis, means-based spending comes to over $15,000 per household, covering half of all Americans. Now, again, some needs-based programs provide support to households with more than $50,000 in income (but not many). In addition, you may consider some needs-based programs to be investments in educating our children, training, or other investment-type spending. So let's look at it another way. Let's look at total spending excluding education, training, services, childcare and development, and community development. That leaves the categories of cash support, medical care, food, housing, and energy and utilities. That totals $813 billion in needs-based spending to cover life's basic expenses. Then pick your denominator. This still results in a figure of over $37,000 per household living in poverty, over $20,000 per household for the bottom one-third of US households based on income (my personal choice for the most relevant denominator), and over $13,500 per household among the bottom one-half of US households based on income. No matter how you look at it, those are fairly material numbers.

I'll mention two other studies that provide estimates of the amount of assistance provided to low-income households. The first is a study conducted by Michael Tanner and Charles Hughes of the Cato Institute. According to the institute's website, "The Cato Institute is a public policy research organization—a think tank—dedicated to the principles of individual liberty, limited government, free markets and peace. Its scholars and analysts conduct independent, nonpartisan research on a wide range of policy issues." So again, they are not in favor of big government, but they are a respected organization, and, at least according to them, their research is nonpartisan. The authors looked at a number of direct needs-based assistance programs, including TANF, food stamps, housing assistance, Medicaid, and others to arrive at an estimated total value of "welfare" benefits to a representative recipient (jobless single mother with two children in their analysis) depending on the state in which the recipient lives. They found that the annual total value of welfare benefits ranges from a high of $49,175 in Hawaii to a low of $16,984 in Mississippi. New York State comes in at number seven on the list at $38,004. As a specific example, the New York State amount consists of $8,292 from Temporary Aid for Needy Families, $5,251 from food stamps, $12,044 from housing assistance, $10,464 from Medicaid, and $1,953 from other programs. The pretax wage equivalent of $43,700 (basically $38,004 in benefits grossed up to account for taxes) is 110 percent of the median salary in the state of New York, implying that our representative "welfare" recipient is 10 percent better off than a full-time worker earning the median wage in the state of New York.

The authors rightly point out that not all welfare recipients receive all forms of governmental aid. For example, only 20.6 percent of TANF recipients receive housing assistance in New York. Still, the analysis perhaps gives an upper range for what a low- (or no-) income household could receive. In addition, the numbers they cite for each category of assistance are not far off from the averages received by recipient from the overall numbers discussed earlier in this chapter.

In another analysis, the Congressional Budget Office looked at the disposable income for a hypothetical single-parent household with one child living in Pennsylvania based on a range of earnings of the parent. Disposable income in the study is defined as the sum of earnings and transfers (TANF, SNAP, and the Housing Choice Voucher Program) and the market value of Medicaid and the Children's Health Insurance Program (CHIP), less tax liability. At a zero level of earnings, the household disposable income is approximately $20,000 (excluding the value of Medicaid, and CHIP lowers the disposable income to approximately $13,000). If the hypothetical adult were to have a job and earn $20,000, then total household disposable income would increase only to about $23,000 or so. So an extra $20,000 of household earnings at this level of income only results in the household improving its situation by about $3,000. How is that as an incentive to get a full-time job? This is reflective of the marginal "tax rate" for a low-income household if one includes lost transfers, which can be as high as 95 percent and sometimes exceed 100 percent if a certain rise in income results in the complete loss of benefits that are not subject to a phaseout.

So, maybe we have a possible range of assistance per household of between $20,000 and, say, $40,000 per household, depending on how you want to look at it. As another point of reference, the Cato Institute study comes up with a total value of benefits of $29,817 for a single parent with two children in Pennsylvania (the CBO assumed one child), so the two analyses are actually somewhat consistent. In addition to the absolute dollar cost involved, both analyses also illustrate how needs-based assistance can be an impediment to employment, even with the impact of the Earned Income Tax Credit, which is only available to low-income workers. Why would one work forty hour weeks for an incremental $3,000 per year (about $58 per week) in additional disposable income? A purely rational person certainly wouldn't.

Now I am not making a case against the many federally sponsored needs-based support programs we have. I am not even making an argument against *any* of the various programs. Based on the descriptions, they mostly look pretty good to me. For example, SNAP "is the nation's first line of defense against hunger and offers a powerful tool to improve nutrition among low-income people." That certainly sounds worthwhile.

"TANF provides assistance and work opportunities to needy families by granting States the Federal funds and wide flexibility to develop and implement their own welfare programs."

"Public housing was established to provide decent and safe rental housing for eligible low-income families, the elderly, and people with disabilities."

"The Tenant Based Rental Assistance program is the federal government's largest program generally recognized as a cost-effective means for assisting families, the elderly, and the disabled to afford decent, safe, and sanitary housing in the private rental market."

And who can argue against education support? It all sounds fine to me (although I am not so sure about the free or subsidized cell-phone program). My point is that we as a nation do provide material assistance to those in need. And at nearly $1 trillion, it certainly doesn't come cheap.

So once again, when we are looking at ways to balance the federal budget, it is not like we are drastically underfunding the needs-based social safety net. You can even argue that we could afford to cut some programs without dramatic consequences.

CHAPTER 11

A Quick Note on Corporate Welfare

Socialism for the rich and private enterprise for the poor.

Charles Abrams

In the prior chapter, we focused on traditional needs-tested social welfare programs—but let's not forget about the various corporate welfare programs that the government funds. Estimates of the amount spent on corporate welfare can range dramatically, depending on what one wants to include. Is spending on the national highway system a form of corporate welfare because it benefits the trucking industry? I don't think many people would look at it that way, but really, any infrastructure or business development spending could be deemed to be corporate welfare.

A 2012 analysis by the Cato Institute identified a number of corporate welfare programs costing approximately $100 billion based on data from the 2013 US budget. That is maybe only 10 percent of government spending on the needs-based assistance for individuals, but $100 billion is still a material number. And that is federal spending only, which does not include the various tax and other incentives provided to business by state and local governments. The biggest federal corporate welfare program is for agricultural support, totaling approximately $25 billion in fiscal 2012, and it includes direct payments, price-support programs, credit support, and crop insurance. As has been widely reported, many of these programs support large corporate and wealthy farmers. Other significant programs include the Broadband Technology Opportunities Program, applied research-and-development spending by the Department of Defense, $17 billion of spending by the Department of Energy for various programs (including the Advanced Technology Vehicle Manufacturing Loan Program), Federal Housing Administration mortgage subsidies, foreign military financing, National Institutes of Health applied research-and-development spending, and the Small Business Administration. As you might expect, there are many separate targeted programs, and in many cases, the benefit of the program to the beneficiaries is large, while the cost of each individual program in relation to the total federal budget is not that material. Thus the momentum to continue the program is hard to reverse.

The $100 billion of federal spending does not include the various "tax expenditures" that are targeted to businesses. Based on data from the Office of Management and Budget, these totaled approximately $160 billion in 2012. Many of these tax benefits are provisions of the tax code applicable to a wide range of businesses, such as the deferral of income from controlled foreign corporations and the accelerated depreciation of machinery and equipment meant to encourage investment, to mention two of the largest provisions. However, a number are tied to specific industries or activities, such as the energy-production credit and the energy-investment credit, the exemption of interest on life-insurance savings, the credit for low-income housing investments, and the tax credit for orphan drug research.

And lest you think that businesses are benefitting from these tax preferences at the expense of individuals, consider that the tax expenditures targeted toward individuals total about $1 trillion, the largest being the exclusion of employer contributions for medical insurance premiums and medical care, the deductibility of mortgage interest on owner-occupied homes, and the tax deferral on defined contribution employer plans. Just these three categories total almost $400 billion in tax benefits. Since the US tax code is riddled with numerous tax preferences targeted toward both businesses and individuals, I will not include these in the discussion on corporate welfare, but in terms of amending the tax code as a way of balancing the budget, these are up for discussion in their own right.

Also excluded from the estimated cost of corporate welfare is the cost of the various emergency credit programs of the past few years. The largest of these is the Troubled Asset Relief Program (TARP), established under the Emergency Economic Stabilization Act of 2008. According to March 2015 estimates by the Congressional Budget Office, $440 billion of the initially authorized $700 billion will eventually be disbursed through the TARP. The CBO estimated that the net cost to the federal government will be $28 billion, based on an estimated profit to the government of $24 billion for the aid to banks, a cost of $15 billion for aid to AIG, a cost of $12 billion for aid to the automotive industry, a profit of $3 billion for support for various investment partnerships, and a cost of $28 billion for mortgage programs, primarily the Home Affordable Modification Program.

Now $28 billion is $28 billion, but in my opinion, TARP, in conjunction with the emergency credit programs of the Federal Reserve, was a hugely successful program. Did the government provide assistance to the financial industry, which in many ways created their own problems? Why yes, the government certainly did. And with no guarantee of success—the government could have lost much more. In fact, the earlier March 2009 CBO estimate of the total cost of the TARP was $109 billion. However, other than various speculators, not many people would have benefitted from a complete collapse in the financial system. The resultant impact on the real economy would have been rapid and severe, leading to even greater loss of jobs and national income. We could have had another Great Depression, not just the Great Recession. At a total cost of $28 billion, it was actually quite a bargain. And as it turns out, most of the cost of the TARP came from the automotive bailout and the cost of the mortgage-assistance programs targeted toward individuals, not the support for the financial system.

Also in 2008, the government placed the government-sponsored mortgage enterprises (GSEs) Fannie Mae and Freddie Mac into receivership due to the collapse of the mortgage and housing markets that occurred at that time. The government did this in order to support the overall credit markets, which were large holders of Fannie Mae and Freddie Mac debt, and to provide support to the mortgage and housing markets. Total agency (including Ginnie Mae) share of mortgage-backed issuances went from 44 percent of the market in 2006 (precrisis) to 95 percent or more in each year from 2008 through 2012. The total Treasury draws of the GSEs totaled $187.5 billion as of the end of 2012. After suffering massive losses from 2008 through 2011, the GSEs each reported profits in 2012, 2013, and 2014, totaling over $180 billion, so maybe the Treasury can recoup some or even most of its investment in this case as well.

So we really have two main categories of corporate welfare provided by the federal government. The first is what might be called emergency relief, such as TARP, the various lender of last-resort activities of the Federal Reserve, and Treasury support of the GSE mortgage-finance companies and other entities. Most economists and the general population are generally not in favor of bailouts. After all, Bank of America, Citicorp, AIG, and Morgan Stanley are large and sophisticated institutions that should have known the risks of the investments they were making. And they were hugely profitable when the going was good, which was reflected in the compensation of their senior managers. In addition, if people or firms know that they will be bailed out if things go poorly, this could encourage them to take outsized risks. Guess correctly, and make a pile of money; guess wrong, and the government will bail you out. This is the classic moral-hazard issue. Granted, this approach didn't work for Lehman Brothers or Bear, Stearns, which either went out of business or were sold at fire-sale prices. I am sure that many members of congress held their noses while voting to support the $700 billion TARP program while ordinary Americans were losing their jobs. Still, it is hard to say what would have happened if not for the various emergency credit and bailout programs. My guess is that at the end of the day, the total cost is nothing compared to what could have happed if the whole system had come crashing down.

The second type of aid comprises the various direct business-support programs totaling $100 billion on an annual basis, and secondarily through the various tax expenditures endemic to the tax code. Again, many of these look good in theory. Support American farmers? Sure. Support high-speed rail or electric cars or medical research or rural broadband or clean-coal technology or the financing of small business? Why not? But it does add up and diverts resources on other than a free-market basis. In addition to the absolute cost involved, the various corporate welfare programs create a number of other problems. These include supporting favored industries at the expense of the rest of the economy and creating a corrupting relationship between business and government by fostering an environment whereby businesses lobby for favored treatment.

One of the more notorious examples of this was the $535 million government loan guarantee to Solyndra Corporation, a manufacturer of solar panels. In March 2009, Solyndra announced that it was the first company to receive an offer for a US Department of Energy loan guarantee under Title XVII of the Energy Policy Act of 2005 to expand its solar-panel manufacturing capacity in California.

"The leadership and actions of President Barack Obama, Energy Secretary Steven Chu and the US Congress were instrumental in concluding this offer for a loan guarantee," said Solyndra CEO and founder Dr. Chris Gronet.

"DOE, in consultation with independent consultants, performed a thorough investigation and analysis of our project's financial, technical and legal strengths," said Solyndra's vice president of marketing, sales, and business development.

However, on August 31, 2011, Solyndra announced that it was suspending its operations, laying off 1,100 full-time and temporary employees, and intending to file a petition for relief under the bankruptcy code. The government is expected to receive little or nothing for its investment in the company.

A December 2011 article by the *Washington Post* described how politics infused many aspects of the management of the government loan guarantee for Solyndra, including the fact that "Solyndra's strongest political connection was to George Kaiser, a Democratic fundraiser and oil industry billionaire who had once hosted Obama at his home in Oklahoma. Kaiser's family foundation owned more than a third of the solar panel company, and Kaiser took a direct interest in its operations." According to the *Washington Post* article, there is no hard evidence that Kaiser directly lobbied the government to approve the loan guarantee, and let's assume that everything was completely aboveboard. Still, the political connection cannot be missed by all who were involved in the decision-making process. And the point isn't that there was any illegal or unethical behavior in this particular case. The point is that we don't want these potential conflicts of interest to exist, period. We have enough unethical behavior in government without adding additional opportunities.

So there are a number of reasons to keep politicians from picking their favorites in the business world. It is expensive, it misallocates resources, and it leads to ethical issues. If the budget is tight, isn't this an area to consider cutting? Seriously, how bad would it be if we cut almost all corporate welfare spending?

CHAPTER 12

The Problem of Income Inequality

Clever, well educated people are increasingly marrying each other and raising clever, well educated children. The children of ordinary households find it hard to compete with them.

The Economist, January 22, 2011

So far in this book, I have been a solid champion of the benefits of the classical liberalism philosophy of politics and economics. We have seen how this system appeals to our sense of fairness, in that people are free to make their own choices in life and keep the fruits of their own labors. It is, as well, a very dynamic system in terms of economic development—a very effective meritocracy. The democratic free-market system has proven itself throughout world history to be far superior to any other political or economic system in improving the lives of all citizens. However, of course, not all citizens participate in the benefits of the free-market system equally. There are necessarily relative winners and losers, although many initially unsuccessful individuals and companies eventually find success and vice versa. *Creative destruction*, as Joseph Schumpeter called it. Also, based on a person's ability, background, ambition, and luck, there can be a wide disparity in the distribution of income among citizens. This is true of most other political or economic systems as well, but in countries without political inclusiveness or economic freedom, much more of the population typically lives in abject poverty.

I also reviewed the fairly substantial government services provided to all US citizens, which include public education, public infrastructure, police and fire protection, unemployment insurance, social security and Medicare, as well as support provided to citizens based on need, including cash support, food, housing, medical care, education assistance, and other direct means of support. A very high percentage of government services and social support are paid for by the taxes levied on citizens of above-average income, so it is not like we have an inherently unfair or uncaring society. Those who are talented and ambitious can earn a substantial reward for their efforts, while those who are not so successful can and do receive substantial government support. While many on the left would argue that the wealthy receive too much of society's output, and many on the right would argue that the poor don't deserve the support they receive, in a way, with the United States landing somewhere in the middle, it all kind of works.

However, premised on this arrangement are two fundamental concepts that theoretically underlie our political and economic systems. The first of these is that the relative income of those at the top is not *too* far removed from the rest of society and that it maintains its relationship to the economic or social value created by these individuals. The second premise is that America remain the land of opportunity where anyone has the chance to succeed based on talent and hard work. In an ideal world, an unfettered system would work just fine, as the market would basically take care of itself. We would all act ethically, market-distorting monopolies or oligopolies would not exist, and we would all be economically motivated to finish high school, go to college perhaps, develop marketable skills, stay healthy, and work hard to earn a living. Unfortunately, the world doesn't quite work that way. Not all markets are free, not all individuals can be relied upon to act responsibly, and most importantly, not all of us have an equal opportunity to be successful. And so, now we turn to the issue of equity—the question of the fundamental fairness of income inequality and whether we are all truly masters of our own economic fates.

Income Equality in the United States

As discussed earlier, the median household income in the United States was \$51,939 in 2013, which, in real terms, was 9 percent *lower* than it was in 1999, so that statistic doesn't seem to be moving in the right direction. At the same time, income levels for much higher-paid individuals in 2013 had nearly recovered to their prior peak. To provide some perspective on the variation of household income, consider that the household income level at the twentieth percentile (the point at which 20 percent of US households have a lower household income and 80 percent have a higher household income) was approximately \$20,900 in 2013, and the household income required to make it into the top 5 percent of households was approximately \$196,000, so the household income at the 95 percent level was about 9.4 times that of a household at the 20 percent level, and 3.8 times the median family household income level. As a share of national income, the top 20 percent of households received 51 percent of total income, and the top 5 percent of households received 22.2 percent of total income. The disparity grows even more if we look at the top 1 percent of households, members of which earn a household income of about \$400,000; as a group, the top 1 percent takes maybe 15 percent of total income in the United States, depending on how income is measured. By comparison, the bottom 20 percent of households account for only 3.2 percent of total household income. The trend has been toward more concentration of income at the top over the past forty-five years, as shown in the graph below.

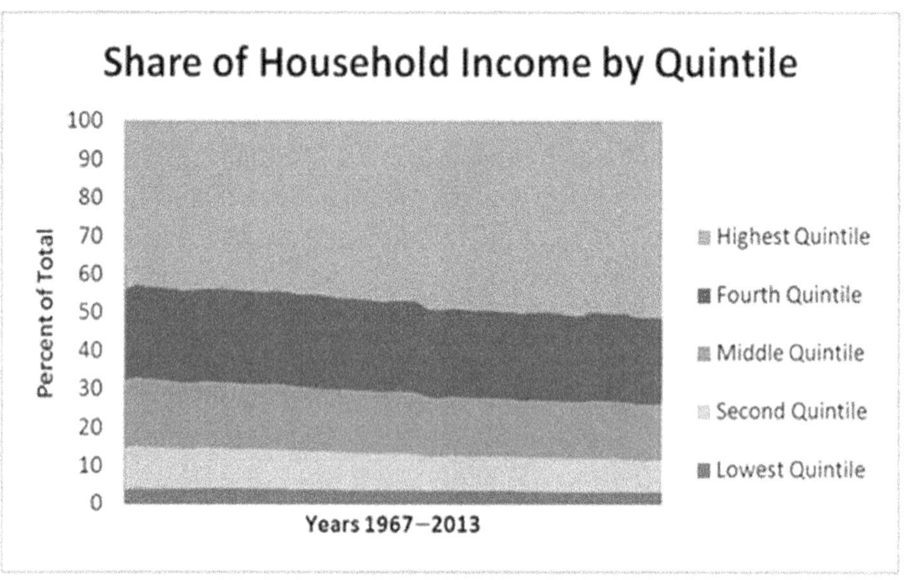

Okay, so maybe the graph above isn't that compelling. After all, the share of income earned by the bottom 20 percent of households moving from 4.2 percent of total income in 1973 to 3.2 percent of total income in 2013 is fairly significant, but it's not so impressive graphically on a scale of zero to one hundred. The following graph, showing the mean household income of the five quintiles and the top 5 percent of households, perhaps more dramatically illustrates the relative economic advancement of higher-income households compared to lower-income households. The average household income of the bottom 20 percent of households increased in real terms by 10 percent since 1968 to 2012, a rather meager advancement over a forty-five-year period of fairly healthy economic growth, while the average household income for the middle 20 percent of households increased by 16 percent in real terms. In contrast, the top 40 percent of households did much better, with the fourth-highest quintile showing 33 percent real income growth and the highest quintile showing 70 percent real growth. The top 5 percent of households almost doubled their real average household income over the same period, and I am guessing that the top 1 percent did even better. So during a period when the average American family, as represented by the middle household income quintile, saw its real income increase by 16 percent over forty-five years, the income of the top 1 percent of households most likely saw income more than double. And it is not like those in the top 1 percent were unduly suffering back in the late 1960s.

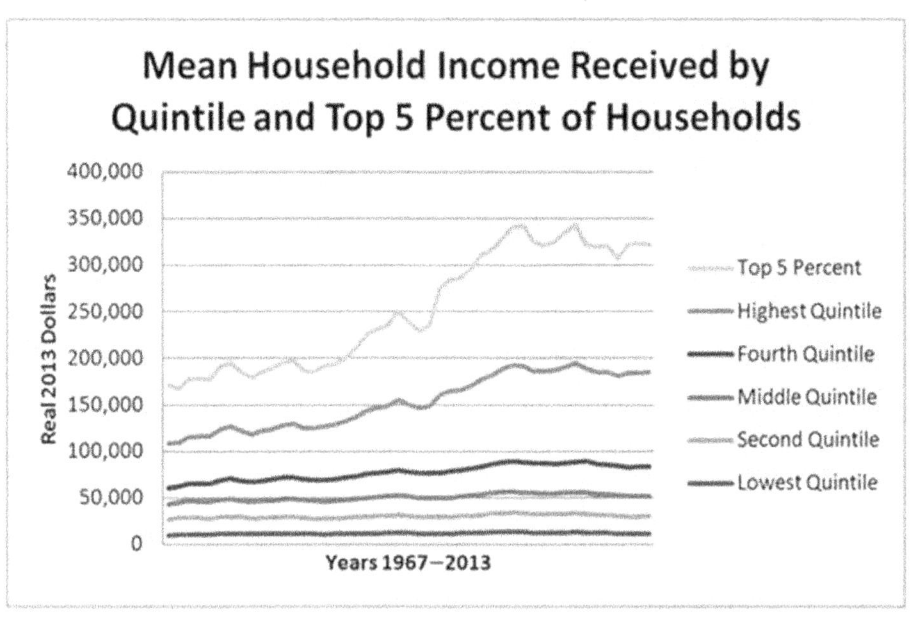

In addition to tracking the share of aggregate household income received by various strata of households, the Census Bureau and others use the Gini Index as a measure of income inequality. The Gini Index can vary from 0, where all households would have the same income, to 100, where all income is received by one household (or from 0 to 1, which is basically the same thing). More technically:

> The index is calculated from the Lorenz curve, in which cumulative family income is plotted against the number of families arranged from the poorest to the richest. The Index is the ratio of (a) the area between a country's Lorenz curve and the 45 degree helping line to (b) the entire triangular area under the 45 degree line. The

> more nearly equal a country's income distribution, the closer its Lorenz curve to the 45 degree line and the lower its Gini Index, e.g., a Scandinavian country with an index of 25. The more unequal a country's income distribution, the farther its Lorenz curve from the 45 degree line and the higher its Gini Index, e.g., a Sub-Saharan country with an index of 50. If income were distributed with perfect equality, the Lorenz curve would coincide with the 45 degree line and the index would be zero. If income were distributed with perfect inequality, the Lorenz curve would coincide with the horizontal axis and the right vertical axis and the index would be 100.

The Gini Index for the US in 2013 as reported by the Census Bureau was 47.6, so I guess we are closer to a sub-Saharan country than a Scandinavian country when it comes to income equality.

Examples of Lorenz Curves and the Gini Index

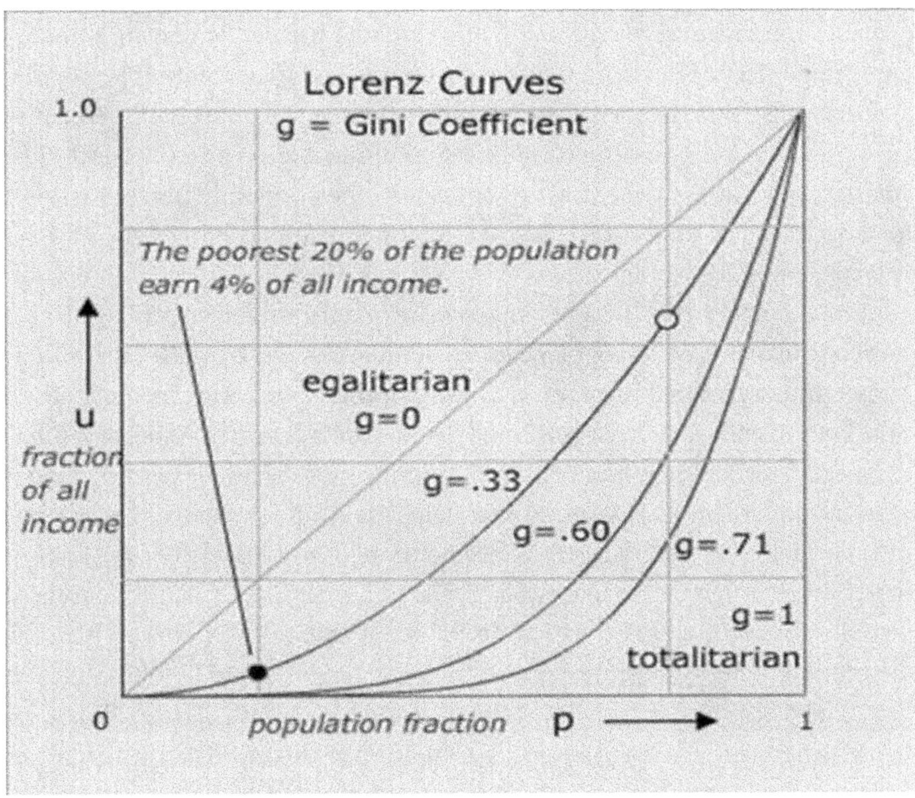

Source: http://kmuletmapcatalog.blogspot.com/2009/04/
accumulative-line-graph-or-lorenz-curve.html

The United States has the highest level of income inequality among the major advanced economies based on most international rankings. The *World Factbook* published by the CIA lists the United States at number forty-one (ranked from most unequal to most equal) on the list with a Gini Index of 45, after many African and South American nations—such as South Africa, Namibia, Chili, and Brazil—but before Canada and most European countries—such as the United Kingdom, Germany, and Sweden, which is the most equal with a Gini Index of 23. Interestingly, China (officially, the People's Republic of China) has more income inequality than the avowedly capitalistic United States. The same is probably true of most other "people's republics."

Of course, the Gini Index may not be the most intuitive measure of income equality. What does a Gini Index of 45 mean to you? The CIA also provides information for the share of household income or consumption by percentage share. For the United States, the richest 10 percent of the population receives 30 percent of the total income while the poorest 10 percent of the population receives 2 percent of the total income, so a ratio of 15:1. The comparable ratios of the richest 10 percent to the poorest 10 percent are 43:1 for South Africa, 28.5:1 for Chile, 13.5:1 for the United Kingdom, 9.5:1 for Canada, and 6.2:1 for Sweden.

On the other hand, higher income inequality might not be too bad if everyone was at least doing okay. In the United States, with one of the highest per-capita national incomes in the world, there is certainly some truth to this. For example, gross national income per capita is nearly 20 percent higher in the United States than Sweden, and it's more than 30 percent higher than in the United Kingdom, so that helps make up for some of the relative income inequality. In fact, the aforementioned household income level at the twentieth percentile level of $20,900 is higher than *median* household income of many countries, including Poland, Portugal, and Turkey. And the distinction is even more pronounced if one compares the United States to countries with higher income inequality, such as South Africa, Brazil, or Chile, where the United States has a higher per-capita GDP by a factor of four or more.

The recent income-distribution trend in the United States has been toward less overall equality. For example, in 1973, when the median household income was $49,262 (in 2013 dollars), only 5 percent lower than in 2013, the bottom quintile received 4.2 percent of total household income compared to 3.2 percent in 2013, and the top quintile received 43.9 percent of household income compared to 51 percent in 2013. The Gini Index was 40 in 1973 compared to 47.6 in 2013, and the income ratio of the ninety-fifth percentile to the twentieth percentile was 6.6:1 in 1973 compared to 9.4:1 in 2012.

A recent study by the Pew Research Center found that "Since 2000, the middle class has shrunk in size, fallen backward in income and wealth, and shed some—but by no means all—of its characteristic faith in the future." Based on their definition of *middle class*, they found that the size of the middle class went from 61 percent of adults in 1971 to 51 percent of adults in 2011, while the total share of income earned by the middle class went from 62 percent in 1971 to 45 percent in 2011. (For the purposes of their analysis, they define *middle income* as households with an annual income that is two-thirds to double the national median.) At the same time, the share of adults who are upper income went from 14 percent in 1971 to 20 percent in 2011, while the share of income earned by upper-income adults went from 29 percent in 1971 to 46 percent in 2011. On the other side of the ledger, the share of adults who are lower income went from 25 percent in 1971 to 29 percent in 2011, with a total share of income declining from 10 percent to 9 percent (more people but less aggregate income). So basically, the United States has seen a shift of people from the economic middle to the lower-and the higher-income categories, and a shift in the total share of income to higher-income individuals. The trend is similar if one looks at median net worth, with a concentration of household net worth moving toward higher-income households. For example, the median net worth of middle-income households was $93,150 in 2010, up a little over 2 percent in real terms from 1983, while the median net worth for upper-income households was up 87 percent in real terms, to $574,788 in 2010. Over the same seventeen-year period, real median net worth for lower-income families actually fell by 7 percent.

So we see that income inequality is higher in the United States than for almost all of our international peers and has been increasing for most of the past forty years. This is a fact. Many conservatives argue that inequality of incomes is not a problem in and of itself so long as there is mobility between income groups. For example, if people in the lowest income group can improve their lots and move to higher income groups, maybe that mobility helps with the fairness issue. There is certainly some truth to this. For example, a 2007 report of the Department of the Treasury (during a Republican administration) found that of those taxpayers in the bottom income quintile in 1996, 42.4 percent remained in the bottom quintile in 2005, while the rest were able to move to higher income groups (28.6 percent to the second quintile, 13.9 percent to the middle quintile, 9.9 percent to the fourth quintile, and 5.3 percent to the highest income quintile). Of those in the highest income quintile in 1996, 69.4 percent remained there in 2007, while the rest moved to lower income quintiles. So there is some ability to move between income groups, maybe about what you would expect intuitively. Some of this is simply income or career progression of the sample group over the ten-year period. Some change is inevitable as, perhaps, a person unemployed in 1996 (and thus in the lowest income group) manages to be gainfully employed in 2005, or an person employed in 1996 finds himself or herself unemployed in 2005. Or some movement may just be a reflection of irregular income in certain jobs or professions.

A more recent study by Raj Chetty, Nathaniel Hendren, Patrick Kline, and Emmanuel Saez looked at cross-generational income mobility, which is perhaps more relevant for our purposes. One would think we would see more income mobility in this case since we like to believe that all of us have more of an equal shot at birth than we do later in life when most of our education, training, and career achievement have already been established. To some extent this is true, since the study found that children born to parents in the lowest quintile (in this case, between 1980–1982) had a 33.7 percent chance of themselves being in the lowest income quintile and a 7.5 percent chance of being in the highest income quintile. Children born to parents in the highest income quintile had a 36.5 percent chance of themselves being in the highest income quintile, compared to a 10.9 percent chance of being in the lowest income quintile. (A 20 percent chance in each case would represent equal opportunity.) So while there is indeed a higher incidence of transgenerational income mobility as compared to the statistics in the 2007 Treasury study, it remains the case that children whose parents are from the lowest income group are three times as likely to end up in the lower income group themselves, compared to children whose parents are in the highest income group, and that children whose parents are in the highest income group are almost five times as likely to be in the highest income quintile themselves, compared to children whose parents are in the lowest income group. This is a bit of a simplification of a fairly exhaustive statistical analysis of income tax data in the study, but I believe it adequately reflects the results of the study and gets the point across.

In any case, the questions of income mobility and income equality are really separate issues. Even with perfect equality of income mobility, I believe that extremely high levels of income inequality are detrimental to the country.

Why Income Equality Is Important

Why is income equality important? First of all, in a nation where a large percentage of the population consider themselves middle class, the financial health of the middle class is important for social cohesion. The Pew study found that in 2012, 49 percent of US adults identified themselves as middle class, which was down from 53 percent in 2008. In fact, 35 percent of adults with family incomes of less than $30,000 identified themselves as middle class, while 46 percent of adults with a family income in excess of $100,000 identified themselves as middle class. So a large number of Americans within a range of income groups consider themselves middle class. The Pew study classified those who identified themselves as upper-middle class in the upper-class category and those who classified themselves as lower-middle class in the lower-class category, so the propensity for Americans to associate themselves as somewhere in the broad middle is even greater. In fact, only 2 percent of respondents identified themselves as upper class, while only 7 percent identified themselves as lower class, leaving 89 percent who identified themselves as upper-middle class, middle class, or lower-middle class (plus 2 percent who didn't know or refused to answer).

The simple fact is that, in their pursuit of happiness, people need to know that they have a reasonably fair chance of achieving their simple goals. Despite the recent downward trends in income equality, the Pew study found that 63 percent of all adults and 67 percent of the middle class agree that "most people can get ahead if they are willing to work hard" (this is down from 74 percent of all adults in 1999). In addition, the study found that while 60 percent of middle-class adults say that their standard of living is better than that of their parents, only 43 percent of adults expect that to be true of their children. The one bright spot here is that nearly 70 percent of middle-class blacks and Hispanics say they have a standard of living better than that of their parents, *and* a similar percentage expect their children's standard of living to be better than their own. It would seem that a vibrant democratic society would need to maintain the size and the positive outlook of the middle class in order to survive. Otherwise, we are prone to class conflict or a tyranny of the majority—and not a majority of the middle, which actually might not be so bad.

The other important reason for a strong middle class is its beneficial impact on the overall health of the economy. A number of studies have been undertaken to demonstrate that some measure of income equality is necessary for sustained economic growth. For example, a research note by Andrew G. Berg and Jonathan D. Ostry of the International Monetary Fund, looking at data across countries, found a strong correlation between high income equality and economic growth duration. Many other economists have made similar points, including, for example, Robert B. Reich (*Aftershock: The Next Economy and America's Future*) and Joseph E. Stiglitz (*The Price of Inequality*).

However, I prefer to address the issue from a philosophical point of view rather than an empirical one. Consider the following two opposite extremes. It seems logical that a society where everyone earns the same income cannot allocate resources efficiently. Where is the profit motive to drive people to jobs that are necessary but may be demanding or may require a high degree of training or apprenticeship? What is the incentive to work at all? What is the driver of innovation or capital formation if there is no ability to earn an exceptional return? On the other hand, it seems that a modern industrial society that is made up solely of a small number of very rich capitalists and a large number of low-paid workers is inherently unstable economically. How are the low-paid workers able to afford to purchase the production that the economy is theoretically able to produce? How many large houses, jets, and expensive cars can the very rich demand? A very large number, it seems, but not enough to sustain the economy. In this case, there is a fundamental mismatch between the productive capacity of the economy and the consumptive demand of the citizenry because of limited incomes. The economy is stunted. This is somewhat the case in China today, with an economy largely dependent on exports and capital investment. It may work for a while, but at some point, balance has to be restored to the domestic and world economies. Overinvestment can only last for so long before it all comes crashing down. Consider instead the historical economic dynamism of the US economy, where the average middle-class household is able to afford decent housing, public services, one or two cars, a washer and a dryer, dishwasher, flat-screen television, cable television, cell phones, dinners out, et cetera. This income generation and consumption demand is what ultimately drives innovation, capital investment, and economic growth. You need both sides of the supply-demand equation.

We now turn to the theories of John Maynard Keynes, who, while he may not have the same status in the economic field as he once did, is still a giant in economic thought. His book *The General Theory of Employment, Interest and Money*, published in 1936 during the worldwide depression, provides the basis for much of prevailing macroeconomic theory and the various "stimulus" programs that the United States and other nations have embarked upon recently and over the past seventy-five years. Under the classical theory of economics largely prevalent prior to Keynes, what is produced is consumed, since the act of production creates the income with which to purchase the production. (Remember from Chapter 3 that net domestic product, by definition, equals net domestic income.) Under the classical theory, prices will clear the market. However, under Keynesian economics, all that is produced is not necessarily consumed. In Keynes's words:

> Thus, to justify any given amount of employment there must be an amount of current investment sufficient to absorb the excess of total output over what the community chooses to consume when employment is at the given level. For unless there is this amount of investment, the receipts of the entrepreneurs will be less than is required to induce them to offer the given amount of employment. It follows, therefore, that, given what we shall call the community's propensity to consume, the equilibrium level of employment, i.e. the level at which there is no inducement to employers as a whole either to expand or to contract employment, will depend on the amount of current investment. The amount of current investment will depend, in turn, on what we shall call the inducement to invest; and the inducement to invest will be found to depend on the relation between the schedule of the marginal efficiency of capital and the complex

> rates of interest on loans of various maturities and risks. Thus, given the propensity to consume and the rate of new investment, there will be only one level of employment consistent with equilibrium; since any other level will lead to inequality between the aggregate supply price of output as a whole and its aggregate demand price. This level cannot be greater than full employment, i.e. the real wage cannot be less than the marginal disutility of labour. But there is no reason in general for expecting it to be equal to full employment. The effective demand associated with full employment is a special case, only realized when the propensity to consume and the inducement to invest stand in a particular relationship to one another. This particular relationship, which corresponds to the assumptions of the classical theory, is in a sense an optimal relationship. But it can only exist when, by accident or design, current investment provides an amount of demand just equal to the excess of the aggregate supply price of the output resulting from full employment over what the community will choose to spend on consumption when it is fully employed. (John Maynard Keynes, *The General Theory of Employment, Interest and Money*)

Maybe that all sounds a bit confusing, but in reality it is really quite simple. Basically, consumer and investment demand don't necessarily equal production, which can lead to a drop in investment, which can lead to a drop in income, which can lead to a further drop in demand. The equilibrium position is not one that necessarily equates to full employment or the position equal to the theoretical potential of the economy. As Keynes writes:

> Moreover, the richer the community, the wider will tend to be the gap between its actual and its potential production; and therefore the more obvious and outrageous the defects of the economic system. For a poor community will be prone to consume by far the greater part of its output, so that a very modest measure of investment will be sufficient to provide full employment; whereas a wealthy community will have to discover much ampler opportunities for investment

> if the saving propensities of its wealthier members are to be compatible with the employment of its poorer members.

It is well established that the marginal propensity to consume is much higher for lower-income individuals than for wealthier individuals. After all, a person who is barely getting by will tend to spend all of a small additional bit of income, while a wealthier person might not change his or her spending at all upon receiving some additional income. That is why many stimulus-centered tax rebates and the like are focused on lower- and middle-income Americans; if you want to stimulate consumer demand, get the money to the people who will spend it.

Finally, to come full circle to my point, we now have an economic theory that supports the thesis that a more equitable distribution of incomes is beneficial to the economy by providing a more stable base of demand, which of course provides the greatest incentive to capital investment. As Keynes said, "Moreover, experience suggests that in existing conditions, saving by institutions and through sinking funds is more than adequate, and that measures for the redistribution of incomes in a way likely to raise the propensity to consume may prove positively favourable to the growth of capital."

This is particularly true today as a large portion of the savings in the United States required to support capital formation is from the undistributed profits of the business sector. And lest you think he is simply in favor of the redistribution of income for its own sake, Keynes goes on to say, "For my own part, I believe that there is social and psychological justification for significant inequalities of incomes and wealth, but not for such large disparities as exist to-day [written in 1935]. There are valuable human activities which require the motive of money-making and the environment of private wealth-ownership for their full fruition."

So that is the view of one brilliant economist who makes sense to me. Now I turn to another well-known economist, John Kenneth Galbraith. His book *The Affluent Society* was originally published in 1958, with the fortieth-anniversary edition coming out in 1998. One of the central themes of the book is that the Western world has reached a level of affluence that has implications for how we are to manage our economy and distribute the output of our production. In the “affluent society,” our basic needs are easily met. For example, in 1900, 41 percent of the US workforce was in agriculture, while in 2000, 1.9 percent of the workforce was working in agriculture. And we still produce plenty of food. That frees up 39 percent of the workforce to focus on other activities, like building cars and designing smartphones. So, according to Galbraith, we are left in a situation where producers need to create their own demand through advertising and the like to convince us of needs we didn’t even know we had. Production becomes less important for the goods produced than for the need to sustain employment opportunities for the people, since the lost production will be barely missed by society as a whole, while the reduced incomes of the unemployed will be greatly missed by those without jobs. In addition, the need to maintain a high level of production and employment is necessary to keep the masses happy. As Galbraith said:

> In the advanced country, in contrast, increased production is an alternative to redistribution. And, as indicated, it has been the great solvent of the tensions associated with inequality. Even though the latter persists, the awkward conflict which its correction implies can be avoided. How much better to concentrate on increasing output, a program on which both the rich and the poor can agree, since it benefits both.

Not to say that approach is a bad thing. It is in many ways a win-win. The rich and the successful entrepreneurs are able to keep the rewards of their efforts and good fortune, the middle class can enjoy a reasonably comfortable lifestyle, and the poor can get by with life’s basic necessities. Of course, this happy situation is dependent on an economy that has enough innovation, want creation (which admittedly seems to have no limit), and aggregate demand to sustain itself. Galbraith makes the point that “consumer demand thus comes to depend more and more on the ability and willingness of consumers to incur debt.” In a way, the creation of consumer debt serves as a substitute for more even distribution of incomes in maintaining demand and balance in the economy.

Galbraith originally wrote *The Affluent Society* in 1958, and the book was last updated in 1998. Since 1958, our overall level of affluence as measured by real per-capita GDP has about doubled, so we are now literally twice the "affluent society." Income inequality and consumer debt have increased significantly as well. In 1958, consumer credit (excluding mortgage debt) was $49.5 billion, which by 1998 had increased twenty-nine-fold to $1.4 *trillion.* Total household debt, including mortgage debt, was $176.5 billion in 1958 and by 1998 had increased by thirty-three-fold to $5.9 trillion. By way of comparison, over the same forty-year period, disposable personal income increased by a factor of about twenty, from $330.4 billion to $3.7 trillion. From 1998 to 2007, consumer credit increased by 86 percent to $2.6 trillion, and total household debt more than doubled to $13.2 trillion. Growth in disposable personal income again lagged the growth in debt, increasing by 60 percent to $10.4 trillion. There is a fair bit of inflation in all these numbers, of course, so let's look at consumer credit as a percentage of disposable personal income, which went from 15 percent in 1958, to 22 percent in 1998, to 25 percent in 2007. Total household debt increased from 53 percent of disposable personal income in 1958, to 91 percent of disposable income in 1998, to a staggering 127 percent of disposable personal income in 2007. Much of this growth was fueled by the mortgage boom, which was, of course, one of the great drivers of consumer demand and economic growth over the nine years from 1998 to 2007. So what Mr. Galbraith saw as a real problem back in 1958 was even more of a problem in 2007 and 2008.

Theoretically maybe, this could continue on forever as sources of consumer finance proliferate and Americans are more comfortable borrowing against future earnings to finance current expenditures. After all, Galbraith's concerns in 1958 weren't realized by 1998, even though household debt had increased dramatically. Does this disprove the theory? I do not think so. As we have seen recently, the collapse of consumer credit can have a dramatic effect on the economy, directly through reduced spending as well as through the shock to the financial system. From 2007 to 2014, total household debt declined by 3.8 percent to $12.7 trillion, driven by the decline in mortgage debt outstanding. Some of this debt reduction is certainly due to households paying down debt and minimizing new borrowings, but a significant portion of the reduction was driven by mortgage defaults, short sales, and foreclosures that didn't fully satisfy the outstanding obligation. If the lender accepts a $200,000 short sale in satisfaction of a $250,000 mortgage obligation, that certainly helps the debt statistics, as the lender takes a $50,000 loss. While consumer credit, excluding mortgages, has increased somewhat since 2007, there is no question that the lack of household debt growth is a major reason why the recession was so deep and the recovery so anemic, accentuated by tight state and local government budgets and credit, which were also constrained. The recession surely would have been much worse if not for the rapid increase in federal spending and government debt, which somewhat offset the decline in other credit. Another mitigating factor over the last few years was the rapid increase in student-loan debt, which more than doubled between 2007 and 2014 to over $1.3 trillion. Hopefully, this is not the next credit bubble to burst, although I am not optimistic on this front.

Now we find ourselves in a period of record-low interest rates, which has the effect of lowering debt-service payments and allowing consumers to handle a higher level of debt. In fact, the debt-service ratio, an estimate of the ratio of debt payments to disposable personal income, was the lowest in 2014 as it had been in the past thirty years, even though the level of debt today is still very high historically. But again, this is largely a function of the record-low interest rates that have been engineered by the Federal Reserve. What is to happen when rates increase to more normal levels? Has the household debt boom ended its run? I think yes, probably so. The only sustainable solution for better balance in the economy is higher incomes (which benefit everyone) and a more equal distribution of incomes (which, while it may not benefit everyone directly, should benefit society as a whole).

Factors Driving Income Inequality

The reason incomes have become less equal is a difficult question to answer. Probably many factors are involved, including increased globalization, which brings bigger markets for successful businesses; a global labor pool, which puts pressure on wages for low-skill jobs; increased technology; the rewarding of highly skilled individuals; weaker labor unions; and the like.

A paper by Jon Bakija, Adam Cole, and Bradley T. Heim lists a number of reasonable explanations that have been the subject of study by others. These include (1) globalization, which may increase the demand for skilled workers in the United States while depressing the demand for lower-skilled workers in the United States; (2) skill-based technological change; (3) the "superstar" theory, which combines the elements of each of the first two trends; (4) executive compensation practices, including the use of stock options, which can lead to very high levels of compensation, and the fact that senior executives' pay is in many cases set by their peers on the board of directors; (5) technological change and compensation practices in financial professions; (6) a change in social norms, which may have reduced the social norm against extremely high pay; and (7) various changes in tax laws that have occurred over the past few decades.

All of the above certainly make sense to me, particularly the impact of globalization and technology. Apple is one of the most valuable companies in the world today because it has been successful in a worldwide market. The same can be said of Boeing, Microsoft, Google, Exxon Mobil, The Coca-Cola Company, Samsung, and many, many other companies. In the financial world, a successful hedge-fund or private-equity manager can raise huge sums of money for investment on very advantageous terms, the favorable economies of scale leading to very large personal compensation. In any case, it seems to me that we are more and more in a world where the winners take all. Once again, this is not an entirely new phenomenon. The famous economist (at least to other economists) Alfred Marshall wrote:

> The relative fall in the incomes to be earned by moderate ability, however carefully trained, is accentuated by the rise in those that are obtained by many men of extraordinary ability. There never was a time at which moderately good oil paintings sold more cheaply than now, and there never was a time at which first rate paintings are sold so dearly. A businessman of average ability and average good fortune gets now a lower rate of profits on his capital than at any previous time; while yet the operations, in which a man exceptionally favoured by genius and good luck can take part, are so extensive

> as to enable him to amass a large fortune with a rapidity hitherto unknown.
>
> The causes of this change are chiefly two; firstly, the general growth of wealth; and secondly, the development of new facilities for communication, by which men, who have once attained a commanding position, are enabled to apply their constructive or speculative genius undertakings vaster, and extending over a wider area, than ever before.
>
> It is the first cause, almost alone, that enables some barristers to command very high fees; for a rich client whose reputation, or fortune, or both are at stake will scarcely count any price too high to secure the services of the best man he can get; and it is this again that enables jockeys and painters and musicians of exceptional quality to get very high prices. In all these occupations the highest incomes earned in our own generation are the highest that the world has yet seen.

Of course, this was written in 1890, with the eighth edition being published in 1920, and the trend toward improved communication, global trade, and other factors leading to concentration of income is even more pronounced today. However, because of the great increase in overall wealth and income since 1890, even a moderately capable businessman or skilled worker can earn a decent living compared to his predecessors in the 1800s.

The reality of the situation is that a number of trends tend to increase the inequality of incomes, based largely, I believe, on knowledge, skills, capability, ambition, and luck. Of course, to some extent, you can make your own luck, but most supremely successful careers have had some good fortune thrown in along the way. Having established that income inequality has been increasing, we will once again turn our attention to whether such success is available to all Americans equally or just a select group.

Equal Opportunity for All?

Is it a fact that anyone can make it in America? There are certainly numerous examples of rags-to-riches stories. John Paul DeJoria was basically homeless when he founded John Paul Mitchell Systems (hair products). Ursula Burns was raised in the "projects" and is now the CEO of Xerox and the first African-American woman to be the head of a Fortune 500 company. Oprah led a very difficult life before she became Oprah, and she is worth approximately $3 billion, according to *Forbes*. And the list can go on and on. So we know it can be done.

But it is not that easy. These are all extremely talented people. Statistically, the upper class comes largely from the upper class. Even those college dropouts who famously made good—Bill Gates (Microsoft) and Mark Zuckerberg (Facebook)—weren't overcoming great hardship. First of all, they each left Harvard University to pursue their business passions, so that's a pretty good place to quit for something better. Bill Gates's father was a prominent lawyer, and his mother was a director of First Interstate BancSystem and the United Way. Bill Gates graduated from Lakeside School, a private school near Seattle, Washington. According to the school's website, they send 100 percent of their students to four-year colleges. Mark Zuckerberg's father is a dentist, and his mother is a psychiatrist. Mark Zuckerberg graduated from Phillips Exeter Academy, a private college preparatory school founded in 1781 and with an endowment of approximately $1 billion. That's a pretty impressive endowment for a high school! Bill Gates and Mark Zuckerberg are also both really, really smart and driven to succeed. (Have you seen the movie *The Social Network*?) Now, they may have been very successful without such advantages, but it isn't like they had to overcome great obstacles early in their lives. Plus, did I mention that they are really, really smart and driven to succeed?

Why do the successful frequently come from the upper class, broadly defined? In many ways, success breeds success. First, take a look at education. The best way to make it comfortably into the middle class and beyond is to get a good full-time job, and the best way to get a good full-time job is to get a good education. For full-time male workers with a bachelor's degree, the median earnings in 2010 were $71,778, 79 percent higher than the $40,055 in median earnings for a high school graduate and more than twice the median earnings for a nongraduate of high school ($29,435 for full-time workers who have at least completed the ninth grade but have not graduated high school). Statistically, the simple accomplishment of graduating from high school increases one's earnings by about 36 percent. Given that, one would think that high school graduation rates should reflect the very high return earned by finishing high school, but sadly they do not. According to *Building a Grad Nation*, the overall national high school graduation rate was 75 percent in 2008 (one out of four students failed to graduate), and close to 40 percent of minority students (African American, Hispanic, and Native American) failed to graduate high school with their class. So that is 25 percent of all Americans and almost 40 percent of minority Americans who are starting out in the workforce already at a very distinct disadvantage.

Fortunately, some limited success has been recently reported on this front. The *Building a Grad Nation* February 2014 annual report found that the 2012 graduation rate reached 81 percent, up from 73 percent in 2006. Even more significantly, the graduation rate for African American students increased from 59 percent in 2006 to 68 percent in 2012, and for Hispanic students, the rate increased from 61 percent in 2006 to 76 percent in 2012. Even so, nearly one-third of African American students failed to graduate, and we still have a long way to go to narrow the gap between white and minority graduation rates and to achieve an overall national graduation rate of 90 percent. Although the trends are in the right direction, that still leaves nearly one out of five American students without a high school degree, with its resultant impact on the ability to earn a decent living.

Children from higher-income households graduate from four-year colleges at a much higher rate than children from lower-income households. According to data collected by the US Department of Education, the overall public high school graduation rate of twelfth graders in 2007 was 81.2 percent, and of those who graduated, 39.5 percent attended a four-year college or university in 2007–2008, so a little less than one-third of US high school students go on to attend a four-year college immediately following high school. (A fairly significant proportion of graduating seniors attended two-year institutions. For example, for those graduating in 2003, 26.7 percent were attending a two-year institution the following year.)

For those high schools in which over 75 percent of students are approved for free or reduced-price lunch, the comparable figures are a graduation rate of only 63.7 percent, and only 26 percent of those who graduated were attending a four-year college or university in the following year, so about 17 percent of that group of high school students went on to attend a four-year college immediately after high school. For comparison, in high schools in which less than 25 percent of students are eligible for free or reduced-price lunch, students graduate at a rate of 91.1 percent, and 52.1 percent of these graduates attend a four-year college or university, so about 46 percent of that group of high school students go on to attend a four-year college immediately after high school. The comparable statistics are even higher for private high schools. So we can see a definite correlation between family income and the academic performance of children (using reduced-price or free school lunches as a proxy for lower income and assuming that it is not the school lunches themselves that are causing the problem).

As a specific example, let's take another look at two high schools in Westchester County, New York: Mamaroneck High School, where approximately 10 percent of the students receive free or reduced-price lunch, and Yonkers City High School, where approximately 67 percent of the students receive free or reduced-price lunch. For Mamaroneck, for those students entering ninth grade in 2008, the on-time graduation rate four years later was 91.9 percent with a 1.9 percent dropout rate, while the comparable figures for Yonkers were a 66 percent on-time graduation rate with a 10.9 percent dropout rate. Here the definition of *graduation* is slightly different from the national figures used above, as it compares students in ninth grade four years ago and tracks whether they graduated four years later (so an "on-time" graduation). Looked at over a six-year outcome, Mamaroneck eventually graduates approximately 95 percent of its students, and Yonkers eventually graduates approximately 75 percent of its students.

And I don't mean to pick on Yonkers—it is just a convenient urban district in Westchester County. The Yonkers results are similar to or better than many other urban or less well-off districts in New York and across the country. In fact, the Yonkers school district was recently named number 147 on *Newsweek*'s list of the top schools for low-income students performing better than expected for their level of poverty. The overall on-time graduation rate in the state of New York for the 2012 graduation class was 74 percent, while the comparable rates were only 60.4 percent in New York City, 46.8 percent in Buffalo, 43.3 percent in Rochester, and 48 percent in Syracuse. So some major New York State school districts have less than half the class graduating on time. And believe it or not, New York State's overall graduation statistics are in line with the national average.

And that is just high school. Students from wealthier districts are typically much more prepared for college. For example, the standardized test scores are on average much higher at wealthier school districts such as Mamaroneck than they are at lower-income districts such as Yonkers. Many studies have indicated that, of students admitted to college, students from wealthier backgrounds tend to graduate at a higher rate than students from less well-off backgrounds, due to academic preparedness, family and other social support, or other factors.

So, on average, children from wealthier backgrounds tend to achieve a higher overall level of education, which is one of the biggest predictors of future income. But the disparity goes much deeper than this simple analysis. The advantages are many times evident at birth. There is a rather famous quote-counterquote exchange (mythical, according to QuoteCounterquote.com) that goes like this: F. Scott Fitzgerald says, "The rich are different from you and me." And Earnest Hemingway responds, "Yes, they have more money." However, as we shall see, the differences are more material than simply financial.

For example, in his book *Coming Apart*, Charles Murray describes the formation of a new broad upper class and a new lower class, based on economics but with a number of social differences as well. First of all, members of the broad upper class tend to congregate with each other, professionally, socially, and geographically. Murray refers to the neighborhoods where members of the broad upper class tend to live as "super zips." These zip codes are generally populated with well-educated and affluent white families. Maybe two-thirds of the adults living in these super zips have at least a college degree, and the median family income is in the $150,000 range, so three times the national median. While a number of residents of these super zips send their children to private schools, the public schools typically provide a high-quality education, and the students are generally engaged in learning. Serious crime is very low. In short, these are expensive but very nice places to live.

To keep with the local example of zip code 10538 (Larchmont postal district) within the town of Mamaroneck, New York, the median household income was $149,347 in 2011, and of the population twenty-five years and older, 42.9 percent have a graduate or professional degree and another 35.9 percent have a bachelor's degree (so nearly 80 percent of adults have at least a college degree). Many residents have degrees from Ivy League schools or other elite institutions of higher learning. I know of Princeton-Princeton couples, Yale-Yale couples, Stanford-Stanford couples, Harvard Business School-Harvard Business School couples, and multiple Harvard Law School graduates, just to name a few. And there are many other examples of smart and successful people, including local business entrepreneurs and those with less glamorous academic credentials. The median sale price of a house in the town of Mamaroneck is approximately $1 million, which maybe buys you a 2,500-square-foot house, about the same size as the average new house built in the United States. Property taxes are among the highest in the nation. Residents are clearly paying a premium in terms of housing costs and local taxes to live in 10538. The story is very similar in other "super zips" across the country.

The broad upper class has many social advantages as well. First of all, they tend to marry, and while divorce is not out of the question, they tend to stay married during the child-raising years at a much higher rate than much of the rest of America. Charles Murray looked at data for white adults aged thirty to forty-nine. Basically he researched the prime adult years, and he focused on white Americans to try to control for the impact of race, if any, in his analysis. He categorized the broad elite as having a bachelor's degree or higher and working in a profession or management position (or being married to such a person), while the contrasting lower earning group has no more than a high school education and a less prestigious and lower-paying job. He found that 83 percent of the higher-income prime-age adults were married compared to only 48 percent of lower-income whites. This was due to both a lower percentage of lower-income adults ever marrying and a higher divorce rate among the lower income group.

Again, Murray focused his research on white adults. Unfortunately, the marriage rate for African Americans is much lower than for white Americans. Average data over the 1999–2002 period showed that of white adults (eighteen years and older), 61 percent were married compared to only 38 percent of African American adults. Not surprisingly, this distinction carries over to births by unmarried women. In 2011, 29 percent of births to non-Hispanic white women were to unwed mothers, while 72 percent of births to non-Hispanic black women were to unwed mothers. While both of these statistics seem unfortunately high to me, the fact that nearly three out of four births to non-Hispanic black women were to unwed mothers seems distressingly high. Talk about starting off at an economic disadvantage; as we know, households headed by a single mother have a very high incidence of poverty.

To give a specific example on a similar metric across all races, in the Larchmont, New York, zip code of 10538, 89 percent of all households with children under the age of eighteen had both a husband and a wife present. By comparison, in the city of Buffalo, New York, with a median household income of $30,230, only 35 percent of family households with children under the age of eighteen were headed by both a husband and a wife. Again, and focusing just on the economic implications without regard to any social judgments, that seems like a distressingly low statistic.

Members of the broad upper class also tend to have their children later in life when perhaps they are more mature and able to devote more resources to raising their children. And they certainly do put effort into raising their children. Within 10538, even though almost all wives are college graduates and have had viable careers before having children, many, if not most, leave the workforce in order to raise their children. Some men with working spouses do the same. If both parents continue to work, they take great pains to arrange quality care for their children. The parents make sure their children attend good schools and receive extra tutoring if needed. The children take music lessons, play organized sports, go to summer camp, and go on enriching family vacations. The kids are expected to do well, they expect themselves to do well, and by and large, they do have high levels of achievement. They don't just strive to attend college, they expect to attend highly selective colleges (as many of their parents have), and they frequently do.

Charles Murray cites data from Roger Geiger that found that ten schools enrolled 20 percent of all of US students who scored in the top five percent on the SAT or ACT college-admission tests, and that 105 schools, which accounted for just 19 percent of all freshmen in 1997, enrolled 74 percent of the top high school students. As Murray says:

> The segregation of the college system now means that the typical classroom in a third-tier public university is filled with students who are not that much brighter than the average young person in the nation as a whole, whereas the typical classroom in an elite school has no one outside the top decile of cognitive talent, and many who are in the top hundredth or thousandth of the distribution. Both sets of students are technically "college educated" when they get their BAs, but that's where the similarity stops. The cognitive pecking order of schools is apparent to everyone—to employers looking at applicants' resumes, to parents thinking about where they want their children to go to college, and to high school students thinking about how to best make their way in life.

Charles Murray also presents evidence that despite affirmative action, the elite colleges are largely populated with students from the upper-middle class. For example, Joseph Soares found that 79 percent of students at Tier 1 colleges as of the 1990s came from families in the top quartile of socioeconomic status, while only 2 percent came from the bottom quartile. Murray finds that the main reason "upper-middle class children dominate the population of elite schools is that the parents of the upper-middle class now produce a disproportionate number of the smartest children."

How can this be? The simple (perhaps uncomfortable) answer is that by and large, their parents are smart, and smart parents, on average, produce smart children. Not *only* smart children, of course, since genetics tends to revert to the mean. Two absolutely brilliant parents typically won't produce equally brilliant children, but they would tend to produce children with above-average intelligence—and most likely well-above-average intelligence. The same is true of parents with below-average intelligence, and I'm sorry to say it, but by definition, half of all adults have below-average (or below-median, anyway) intelligence. They would tend to produce children of below-average intelligence, although again the trend would be toward the mean, and of course, some children of parents with below-average intelligence would be very smart.

So we have bit of a "virtuous" circle here. The most-able children attend the most prestigious colleges and universities. They tend to have access to the best job opportunities and earn the most income. They tend to meet and marry other highly intelligent people. They tend to maintain a traditional nuclear family and to live in the most desirable communities, where they tend to associate with each other. Their children tend to be intelligent as well and attend high-quality public or private schools. They are driven to do well and frequently attend the most prestigious colleges and universities, which then open up the best job opportunities for them. And so on.

Now, of course, all of this is a gross generalization. At each step, large variations occur. Many families remain together in low-income neighborhoods and provide nurturing environments for their children. Many adults of average intelligence have very smart children, and many adults of above-average intelligence have children with below-average intelligence. Graduating from an elite college is no guarantee of a successful career, just as many people from lower-tier educational institutions or even with no college education achieve great success. But in general, when looking at large groups of people, the children of the broad elite have the best chance of earning high incomes, while the children of lower-income families tend to be lower income themselves.

In a way, this isn't necessarily unfair. After all, it is hard to argue against the fundamental right of parents to try to advance the prospects of their children by spending money on schooling in the forms of private-school tuitions or higher local property taxes—or by providing enriching summer experiences, or by providing a home environment where personal achievement is encouraged and even expected. It is also hard to argue against a system of higher education whereby the best students are attracted to the most prestigious colleges and universities or then become the most coveted new hires by businesses. They are in fact the best prospects. If you believe in a meritocracy, then they deserve it. If you believe in the capitalist system, then they are simply reaping the benefits of their abilities and their substantial investments in money and effort.

But the point is that the broad elite do have a material advantage compared to, say, the bottom half or bottom quarter of America. Some of the advantage is environmental, and some of the advantage is natural. It is not fair to say that everyone has the chance to make it in America. It is fair to say that every smart, talented, energetic, hard-working person can make it in America (recognizing that some individuals may have economic, social, racial, or other prejudices or obstacles to overcome). But by definition, half of us have less-than-average intelligence, have less-than-average ambition, come from families with below-average parenting skills, et cetera. Ten percent of us are in the bottom decile of intelligence, and ten percent of us constitute the laziest ten percent of the population. If those individuals don't have other advantages, or if in fact they have other social disadvantages, then their economic livelihood doesn't seem so promising. Is it their fault? What are their options? Do they deserve at least some level of comfort or at least some chance in their pursuit of happiness? Most of us would argue that they do deserve such a chance. Not a life of luxury, of course, but a reasonable shot at a "middle-class" lifestyle as broadly defined.

The difficult question is, what is one to do about this situation, and how should we factor this into our discussion of the federal budget? That will be partially dealt with in the next chapter.

CHAPTER 13

A Spirit of Compromise

And so, my fellow Americans: ask not what your country can do for you—ask what you can do for your country.

JOHN F. KENNEDY, INAUGURAL ADDRESS, JANUARY 20, 1961

LET'S REVIEW WHERE WE ARE so far. We started out by reviewing the overall fiscal situation of the United States. We saw that the federal government is running deficits that are not sustainable over time, and in fact the US government has made additional future financial promises with no plans to fund those promises.

Despite the troubling fiscal situation, we can't just focus on the negative. We reviewed the impressive historical economic performance of the United States and saw that the United States remains the world's economic super power by a fairly wide margin. The country's real output per person has quadrupled since 1929 and has doubled since 1960, resulting in a material increase in America's standard of living.

We then reviewed the founding principles of our country, which are based on a belief in individual freedom and a concept of a limited government that governs with the consent of the governed. We also explored the basic principles of the free-market system, which is a natural complement to a free democratic political system and is based on the interactions of producers, workers, and consumers to most efficiently produce the goods and services that consumers desire. This "classical liberal" philosophy is based on individual political freedoms and individual economic freedoms. Not only does it appeal to our sense of individual rights, it also happens to be the most economically successful political and social system in human experience.

In Chapter 4, we reviewed how the free market rewards individuals for their contributions to the economy in the form of wages, just as the pricing system rewards producers for their contributions to the economy. Together, this market mechanism allocates resources and establishes values for labor, capital, and goods and services. In short, in economic terms, you are what you produce. In Chapter 5, we reviewed the historical basis for money and learned that, in and of itself, money has no value, but it rather serves as a common medium of exchange and a store of value. Money is just a way to keep score, if you will.

After reviewing these fundamental economic concepts, we detailed the spending and taxing policies of government, and then turned our attention to a discussion of the primary contributors to our economic production, government support for low- and moderate-income Americans, and the extent and causes of income inequality in the United States. In Chapter 9, I extolled the virtues of successful people because of their impacts on the economy and the very large taxes that highly compensated people pay to fund government services and transfer payments. In Chapter 10, I reviewed the extensive social safety net available to all citizens and the needs-based welfare programs that benefit low- and moderate-income Americans. And finally, in Chapter 12, we saw that poverty and income inequality remain pervasive problems in the Unites States. We also explored the nature of income inequality and the relative tendency of the children of the broad upper class to remain in the broad upper class, while those from lower-income parents tend to be lower income themselves.

We have seen from the previous chapters that there is a tension between the haves, who generally represent the most productive members of society and pay the most in taxes to support our governmental services, and the less fortunate, whose economic skills are less valued by society and who receive the greater share of government support. We know that, from a fiscal standpoint, something has to give. Either taxes have to go up, spending has to go down, or both. Are we to add to the tax burden of our most productive citizens, or are we to cut the benefits of our most vulnerable citizens?

It would seem to be a tough choice, but here is the good news. Either way, I believe, we have room to maneuver. The rich are actually quite well off, and while the affluent do pay the preponderance of taxes, most could afford to pay a bit more if it were required. And they would still lead very nice lives, at least in terms of their material lifestyle. The middle class has been squeezed for the past twenty years, but they really aren't doing too badly either. They have to keep to a tight budget, but a typical middle-class household can afford a modest house, a nice car, flat-screen TV, smartphones, and an annual family vacation. And the absolute middle-class family of four (at say a $50,000 household income) pays very little federal income tax, so they are not overly burdened from that perspective. The poor are poor, of course. So by definition, they are struggling, perhaps really struggling. But there is quite an extensive menu of needs-based support programs including cash, health care, food, housing, and energy assistance, totaling over $900 billion on an annual basis. So really, it could be worse, such as in Haiti, where the annual gross domestic product is $650 per person. And that is an average, not the bottom strata of society. That is real poverty.

So at the end of the day, it comes down to one's personal perspective of what is right or fair. Is there an absolute moral obligation or one true answer, or is it just a political battle between the haves and the have-nots? I guess each of us has to reach our own personal conclusions on what is right or fair when it comes to taxation and income redistribution. But fairness is sometimes a variable concept, or else it seems we would all agree.

Since I am not a philosopher or a moralist, I offer up the thoughts of Jonathan Haidt in his book *The Righteous Mind: Why Good People Are Divided by Politics and Religion*, which at least resonate with me. Professor Haidt considers the moral matrix across six foundations: (1) care/harm, (2) liberty/oppression, (3) fairness/cheating, (4) loyalty/betrayal, (5) authority/subversion, and (6) sanctity/degradation. In his opinion, these are fairly universal foundations of human morality with a basis in innate human evolution. Let's briefly review each of these in turn.

The Care/Harm Foundation would seem to be one of the most basic human moral instincts. This would include the maternal instinct to care for a child or the urge to come to the aid of someone in distress. How many volunteers do we get if a child falls down a well or is lost in the woods? The public support is extensive. The parable of the good Samaritan may be a classic example of the appeal of the Care/Harm Foundation. We can also add to this the belief of many that society should provide food to those who do not have enough to eat, clothes to those who do not have clothes, and shelter to those who are homeless. The other side of the Care/Harm Foundation is harm—we generally are against murder (the Fifth Commandment) and are for the Golden Rule ("Do unto others as you would have them do unto you"). Maybe the harm side of this foundation is a little more absolute, as in "you *shall* not murder," while the care side is more of a *should* standard. In general, though, this is a foundation of moral behavior that most of us can agree on in concept, if not always in degree or practical application.

Haidt's next universal moral foundation is the Fairness/Cheating Foundation. While the concept of fairness may be nearly universal, it can mean different things to different people. For liberals (and, I suppose, socialists), fairness often means equality—as in, all people should share equally, or at least more equally, in the economy's production. In the simple hunter-gatherer society, perhaps, the tribe would apportion the available food in whatever method they deemed fair. Presumably, the tribe had ways of ensuring that everyone contributed to the group as well. This is not to say that all primitive human tribes were egalitarian or met our modern sense of fairness—some primitive societies practiced infanticide or killed or abandoned the old or the sick as a way of dealing with the rigors of survival, for example.

In our much larger, more dispersed, and individualistic free-choice society, the contribution-reaping dynamic is not as easily controlled, which leads to tension along the fairness foundation. For example, why is it fair that some people own multiple large houses and can afford to have nearly every material want satisfied in abundance, while others are homeless and don't have enough to eat? If we have enough houses and food to feed everyone (which we do), shouldn't we provide housing and food to all? This is the side of fairness more often associated with the liberal point of view. On the political right, fairness more often means proportionality—as in people should be rewarded in proportion to what they contribute. For example, why is it fair that I went to school for twenty years to earn my advanced degree and work sixty hour weeks to provide for my family, while I am taxed at 40 percent or more of my income to support others who don't contribute as much or perhaps anything at all? And by definition, if you are not working, for any reason, then you are not contributing economically. I suggest that each interpretation of fairness has some validity.

Haidt's third moral foundation that we will consider is the Liberty/Oppression foundation. Once again, this can take somewhat different meanings depending on your perspective. To many liberals, this takes the form of an emphasis on oppression of less-advantaged groups, leading to a focus on a fight for civil rights, support for the economically disadvantaged, et cetera. This can, according to Haidt, easily be expanded beyond equality of rights to equality of outcomes. Conservatives tend to be more concerned with the liberty side of the foundation—as in, don't tell me what to do, or as the Gadsden flag says, "Don't tread on me." As a result, they tend to favor low taxes, low regulations (at least as it applies to them), and a general "leave me alone" belief. An example of the Liberty/Oppression foundation conflict might be minimum-wage laws, which some business people may consider an infringement on their right to hire a willing worker at a wage that the worker is willing to accept, while others may consider minimum-wage laws necessary to prevent the economic oppression of unskilled workers who may not have many employment options or bargaining power with potential employers. Again, perhaps each view has validity, and it all depends on one's personal perspective which attribute should be valued more highly.

The next three moral foundations described by Haidt have perhaps more to do with one's personal code of behavior, or how one might like others in society to behave in their personal lives, so while important, we will deemphasize here.

The Loyalty/Betrayal Foundation is loyalty to your group, however defined. Consider the marine corps motto of *semper fidelis* ("always faithful") and the code "Unit, Corp, God, Country" as examples. And notice that *unit*, the most immediate group, is listed first.

The Authority/Subversion Foundation is basically respect for authority, such as for your ranking superiors, parents, or elders.

The Sanctity/Degradation foundation is the "don't be gross" side of morality, including respecting your body, not practicing cannibalism, and not desecrating religious or secular symbols such as the flag, et cetera, even if doing so would have no practical harm to anybody.

Haidt ties it all together by attributing weight to each of the six Moral Foundations for a liberal moral matrix and a conservative moral matrix. In his construct, the Liberal Moral Matrix is highly weighted to the Care/Harm Foundation above all others, with the Liberty/Oppression foundation receiving secondary importance (focus on oppression) and the Fairness/Cheating foundation also a factor (focus on fairness of outcomes). Based on my casual observations, this characterization seems largely accurate to me. My most liberal friends basically ascribe to an "if someone needs something, then of course they should get it" type of approach, almost without any regard for the cost.

The conservative moral matrix is more equally weighted among all six moral foundations, including Care/Harm, Liberty/Oppression (focus on liberty), Fairness/Cheating (focus on proportionality), as well as the Loyalty/Betrayal, Authority/Subversion, and Sanctity/Degradation Foundations, traits which some liberals (but certainly not all) dismiss as quaint relics of an unenlightened time. Again, I doubt if this characterization would surprise anyone.

Libertarians, not surprisingly, are focused mostly on the Liberty/Oppression Foundation as the basis for their moral philosophy. This approach focuses on individual freedom with a "let the chips fall where they may" attitude.

So why is this relevant, and what does it all mean when it comes to the federal budget? As a first step, perhaps we should all acknowledge that each side of the political argument has some moral validity. Let's face it, most of us believe that we shouldn't harm people, and most of us feel at least some measure of the care impulse. We mostly all believe in the importance of fairness, although that can mean different things to different people. The liberal side can argue very strongly that the less fortunate deserve our support because they need it, whether their predicament is due to events beyond their control or even due to their own actions. The conservatives can argue just as strongly that taxing some Americans to provide support to other Americans is inherently unfair. After all, if some people believe it is proper to support lower-income Americans or the less fortunate, they are certainly free to do so individually. As Thomas Jefferson said in his first inaugural address, "Government…shall not take from the mouth of labor the bread it has earned." Once again, it depends on where one comes out on the spectrum.

As a result, I think we should at least tone down the moral rhetoric on both sides of the political aisle. It is not an all-or-nothing proposition. From my perspective somewhere in the middle, the scales seem relatively balanced. In a land of plenty, we should do what we can to provide some minimum level of support for all Americans. And we certainly do. In a free society and a free economy, we should allow our citizens to reach their full employment potential and keep the rewards that they have rightfully earned. For the most part, we have, in the modern context—if you consider keeping 60 percent of your earnings a success. When President Obama infamously said, "You didn't build that," he was right in one respect. And that is that we live in a society that has certain natural advantages in terms of infrastructure, an educated population, and a system that still does reward work and effort. We all live in a society based on the "consent of the governed," and that includes all Americans, not just the successful people among us. So, maybe the bottom 20 percent of the population economically live at the expense of the rest of us, but the top 20 percent of the population economically live at the expense of the rest of us as well. It's a package deal.

Since both sides of the argument have some valid points, we should recognize that a middle-ground approach is reasonable, rather than a spirit of compromise being considered a betrayal of one's philosophical views. Despite the rancor in the political system, this is mostly where we are today, with a tax system that is progressive, but not overly confiscatory, and a reasonable social safety net. I recognize that many will disagree with each of these separate assessments, but as I said before, the poor are surviving, the middle class can enjoy a comfortable lifestyle through hard work, and the rich are still able to get rich. So something must be in balance—or at least not dramatically off.

As a practical start, we need to bring a more positive attitude to the political discussion. On the left, this means not demonizing the portion of the population that funds the social welfare system. Perhaps instead of simply saying that the top 20, 10, or 1 percent (pick your percentage) don't pay their "fair share," let's recognize that the top economic echelon is filled with the difference makers when it comes to the economy and public finance. This is the old 80 percent–20 percent rule in action. How about appealing to their higher emotions rather than scolding the hard working and successful for being "unfair"? That is what most charities do, since they can't simply confiscate funds through taxation but have to compete in the free market for donations.

As an example, consider the giving levels at the Bronx Zoo. A family annual membership costs $139 and gives the family admittance to the zoo, parking and attractions not included. But for $1,500, you can get free parking and attractions, a free water bottle, free admission for two additional guests on every visit, plus exclusive tours and events with curators, scientists, and program specialists. A family membership at the Metropolitan Museum of Art in New York City costs $200 and entitles a family to unlimited admission to the museum and to certain members-only events. But a family who gives $20,000 becomes a member of the President's Circle and gets not only free admission to the museum but the following additional benefits (among others): reciprocal membership privileges at fifteen other museums, attendance at the Spring Garden Party at the Cloisters, patrons' lounge privileges, special evening reception with the museum's director, and invitations to a private event with the museum's president and to behind-the-scenes events with museum curators and conservators. If I were a civic-minded art lover with an extra $20,000 to give, that sure seems like a really nice package of benefits that would make me feel good about the museum and myself, even though it says right on the museum's website that the fair-market value of this package of benefits is about $1,500. So it's not like it is a great deal financially.

What does a taxpayer receive for supporting the government? A letter of thanks? An IRS water bottle? A US Treasury ballpoint pen? A private White House tour? How about none of the above, although one can probably get many special benefits by giving to a political party or campaign, such as the practice of offering overnight stays in the Lincoln bedroom in the White House for major political donors. How much sense does that make?

In my opinion, Scott Adams got it right in his *Wall Street Journal* article "How to Tax the Rich." Scott Adams is the creator of *Dilbert*, so he knows a little bit about pointing out life's simple absurdities. First of all, let me give the caveat that he knowingly proposes some "bad" ideas for how to raise revenue from the rich in order to perhaps inspire some good ideas. His five "bad" ideas of benefits that the country could offer the rich in exchange for higher taxes are (1) time, (2) gratitude, (3) incentives, (4) shared pain, and (5) power.

Maybe some are bad ideas, but maybe some aren't. Or at least in concept they aren't. The country could offer the rich some extra time. For example, Adams suggests, maybe the top 2 percent of taxpayers could get priority service at the Department of Motor Vehicles. That would be a perk really worth something—kind of like concierge service, and better even than free parking at the Bronx Zoo. And, as Scott Adams points out, the extra 2 percent wait time for everyone else would be barely noticeable. Probably worth it for having 2 percent of the population pay so much of the total tax burden. Or maybe we could offer some other perks, like unlimited access to the carpool lanes (Adams's suggestion) or maybe an exclusive White House Christmas ornament or an FBI cap or fleece or something (some of my suggestions). Wouldn't that be cool? Maybe that doesn't appeal to your sense of fairness, but as a benefit for someone who pays $100,000 a year or more in taxes (just to pick a number), that seems like a pretty cheap price to pay.

The government could arrange for a little gratitude. Scott Adams's "bad" idea is that the government could make it a requirement that anyone applying for social services has to write a personal thank-you note to a nearby rich person. Maybe a truly heartfelt thank-you note for paying for free health care would bring more support for Medicaid among those who have to pay for it. Maybe that truly is a bad idea. But, how do you feel about some generic gratitude? Like a form letter from the president thanking you for your substantial contribution to the government. Or maybe an accounting of how your money was spent and whom it has helped? Others do this. For example, if you give $1 a day to CARE, you are helping to:

> **Help children beat malnutrition** and stay healthy through programs that improve the livelihoods of poor families.
>
> **Help communities establish clinics** and immunization campaigns to stop needless deaths from common, preventable diseases.
>
> **Help families build new wells** and sanitation systems for safe drinking water.
>
> **Help make it possible for poor children to go to school,** so they can fulfill their dreams and escape poverty forever.
>
> If you give enough to qualify As a Partner for Change, you'll also enjoy the following benefits:
>
> You'll receive **monthly stories and photos** of women and families that your gift has helped.
>
> You'll be invited to attend **exclusive conference calls** with CARE's president and special guests to hear about CARE's work and priorities.

Maybe the top thousand taxpayers should get a framed certificate hand-signed by the president or a special tour of the White House conducted by the first lady. Then people might *want* to be among the top taxpayers in the country. Members of the top 1 percent are so competitive (in my experience) that they would work their damnedest to get on the invite list.

How about a little shared pain? As Scott Adams points out, shared pain makes all of us feel like we are in this together. That is why large donors to charities sometimes choose to make a matching challenge gift. As in "if you can increase donations from your existing base of donors, I'll match whatever the increase is." As it applies to the federal budget, it can include a shared burden of any increase in taxes, such as an increase in top rates, which impacts higher-income Americans, in conjunction with an increase in the gas tax, for example, which impacts most Americans. Or maybe make it a condition that obese people lose weight or smokers quit smoking in order to qualify for Medicaid. That's never going to happen, but you have to admit there's a certain fairness aspect to it—you can have free health care if you adopt some healthy habits, helping to keep the overall cost down.

Or it can mean combining an increase in taxes with spending cuts. No matter where you start, this makes everyone feel like it is a group effort—not an effort of the 1 percent or the 10 percent or just a cut-spending approach, which alienates a larger portion of the population. How many times have you applied this concept within your own family or other group? Probably many times, such as whenever one of your kids wants to purchase a major item (smartphone, for example). In many households, this might take the form of "if you can come up with half of the purchase price, I'll pay for the other half." Of course, the parents are expected to cover the monthly cellular plan, which is the real cost.

Scott Adams also suggests ways to provide financial incentives and more power for the rich (like an extra vote), but I tried to focus on what I thought were the good "bad" ideas. Try to come up with some of your own. And remember, there are no bad ideas, so get creative.

Of course, the political right has to tone down the rhetoric as well. The incomes earned by the very rich are truly phenomenal and have increased much more quickly than incomes for the vast majority of Americans. During the same timeframe, the top marginal tax rate has generally been declining until just recently. The concentration of wealth (as opposed to incomes) is even more centered at the top. So while the rich do indeed pay the preponderance of taxes, and there is much governmental support available for Americans of lesser means, I would say that the rich are doing quite well, thank you. As Mae West said, "I've been rich and I've been poor. Believe me, rich is better." Or Woody Allen: "It's better to be rich than poor, if only for financial reasons." So stop complaining as if every little tax increase is an attack on the American way of life. As we saw in the last chapter, we don't all have an equal shot in life, and certainly we need to maintain a system with at least some level of equity of outcomes, just to keep everyone in the game. The key to the success of the American system is making everyone a participant in society, in the economy, and in the political process.

The Handicap System in Golf

Leveling the playing field in some way is not a unique concept. Consider the handicap system in golf. As in life, theoretically, we all have an equal opportunity to be good golfers. After all, all one has to do is hit a stationary ball with a golf club. There is no defensive lineman running toward you, physical speed is not required, and while strength and size are helpful, they are certainly not required. All it takes is some skill and coordination. And yet, the variation in ability is huge. To allow for competition among golfers of varying abilities, the United States Golf Association has developed a handicap system "to make the game of golf more enjoyable by enabling players of differing abilities to compete on an equitable basis. The System provides a fair Course Handicap for each player, regardless of ability, and adjusts a player's Handicap Index up or down as the player's game changes." A scratch golfer can play to a course handicap of 0, while a bogey golfer has a handicap of approximately 20 on a course of standard difficulty. PGA tour pros (and other highly skilled golfers) are better than scratch and would have a "plus" handicap.

With a handicap index of 13 (a handicap of 16 on my home course), I consider myself a decent golfer, usually shooting in the high eighties to mid-nineties, but at least among those golfers who keep a handicap (by recording all scores), I am decidedly average. My index of 13 puts me right at about the median of all golfers who maintain a handicap. Only 1.6 percent of male golfers are better than scratch.

Most club level tournaments use the handicap system in some form. As a result, any member, or team if a team competition, theoretically has a chance to win if they play well relative to their ability. This keeps it fun for all (particularly for the high handicap players) and maximizes participation. Don't get me wrong, everyone knows who the best golfers are, and the most prestigious tournaments, including the honor of "club champion," are determined without the benefit of handicaps. But there are probably only about twenty golfers out of a membership of three hundred at a typical golf club who have a realistic chance to win on that basis. But at least for the rest of us, we can enjoy our shot in the "net of handicap" competition. It keeps everyone interested. It keeps the club vibrant and provides the very best golfers a venue in which to shine.

Now, I realize that golf is a game and not real life. Giving extra shots to the lesser-skilled golfers doesn't really have any economic impact relative to the more highly skilled golfers (except when money wagers are involved). So maybe this example is not relevant to the economic game of life, where the winners can reap huge financial awards while the lesser-skilled economic players barely scrape by. But I ask you to consider that maybe it is even more important to give all workers at least a shot at some success in the game. It keeps it interesting for everyone, and that is good for all.

CHAPTER 14

Let's Make a Deal

Everyone wants to live at the expense of the state. They forget that the state lives at the expense of everyone.

Frederic Bastiat

Now that we've set the stage, it's time to get down to balancing the budget. Hopefully, by now you agree that something has to be done to address the excessive federal debt level and the budget deficit that the United States government currently runs. I have argued that a combination of tax increases and spending cuts is required if we are to take a balanced approach to deficit reduction. I hate to be anticlimactic, but to me, the details aren't even that critical once the overall approach is established. However, I will lay out some specific proposals nonetheless.

There are a number of very good deficit-reduction plans and options on both the left and the right that have been the subjects of debate for many years. The bipartisan National Commission on Fiscal Responsibility and Reform—created by President Obama and cochaired by Alan Simpson, former Republican senator from Wyoming, and Erskine Bowles, former chief of staff to President Clinton—released its report in December 2010. The commission's plan called for reducing the deficit to 2.3 percent of GDP by 2015 and 1.2 percent of GDP by 2020, by capping revenue at 21 percent of GDP and reducing spending below 22 percent of GDP and eventually to 21 percent of GDP by 2035, leading to a fully balanced budget. In 2015, the projected revenue and spending under their plan are 19.3 percent and 21.6 percent of GDP, respectively. Their plan has six major components (from *The Moment of Truth: Report of the National Commission on Fiscal Responsibility and Reform*, December 2010):

- Discretionary spending cuts: provide $200 billion in illustrative 2015 savings.
- Comprehensive tax reform: reduces rates, broadens the tax base, reduces many "tax expenditures," and reforms the corporate tax code. Eliminates the Alternative Minimum Tax (AMT).
- Health-care cost containment: reforms physician payments, cost sharing, malpractice law, prescription drug costs, and government-subsidized medical education. Institutes additional long-term measures to bring down spending growth.
- Mandatory savings: cut agriculture subsidies, modernize military and civil service retirement systems, reform student-loan programs, and put the Pension Benefit Guarantee Corporation on a sustainable path.
- Social Security reform: ensure sustainability for the next seventy-five years while reducing poverty among seniors.
- Process changes: reform the budget process to ensure that debt remains on a stable path.

In many ways the commission's plan has some fairly dramatic changes—for example, moving back to a Reagan-era level of income tax rate brackets of 12 percent, 22 percent, and 28 percent, while limiting itemized deductions dramatically and moving capital gains taxes to the same rate as ordinary income. Some of the changes to Social Security are fairly material as well, such as making the benefit formula more progressive (it is already fairly progressive). In addition, their plan would ultimately result in total federal revenues reaching 21 percent of GDP, which is about the highest it has ever been. On the other hand, their plan aims to bring the budget completely in balance by 2035, which is pretty impressive given the current situation and the long-term spending trends. In any case, the commission's plan certainly is well thought out and offers at least a starting point of discussion on how to contain the deficit, but as far as I am aware, after an initial flurry of interest, it has been largely ignored in Washington.

The *Fiscal Year 2016 Budget Resolution* of the Republican-controlled House Committee on the Budget proposes a plan to essentially balance the federal budget by 2025 without raising new taxes. As a result, the projected outlays and government revenue each come to a little over 18 percent of GDP in 2025, compared to the 21 percent of GDP referenced in the National Commission on Fiscal Responsibility and Reform plan above. The Republican plan does this by reducing spending substantially from current trends, particularly by repealing the Affordable Care Act, reducing Medicaid spending by converting the program to provide "State Flexibility Funds" to the states and allowing the states to tailor their own plans, reducing projected spending on other mandatory spending categories, and making more dramatic reductions in discretionary spending than are included in the Budget Control Act of 2011 spending caps. At the same time, spending on national defense is projected at greater than the caps included in the Budget Control Act. While revenues are projected to be largely unchanged from current policy, the Republican plan calls for tax reform that would include lower rates for individuals and families as well as large corporations and small business and recommends repealing the Alternative Minimum Tax, along with broadening the tax base by closing "special interest loopholes." As seems to be the case with most Republican tax plans, the details are lacking on how tax rates are to be reduced materially while leaving total tax revenues unchanged as a share of GDP. Taken together, this is a distinctly Republican plan, with all of the required savings coming in the form of nondefense spending cuts, and with no increased taxes.

President Obama offers his vision for the budget in the *2016 Budget of the US Government.* That document projects a budget deficit of 2.5 percent of GDP in 2025, with receipts coming in at 19.7 percent of GDP and outlays at 22.2 percent of GDP. The administration achieves this by cutting defense- and nondefense-appropriated programs from 6.5 percent of GDP in 2014 to 4.5 percent of GDP in 2025, while social security, Medicare, Medicaid, and other mandatory programs increase from 12.5 percent of GDP in 2014 to 14.8 percent of GDP in 2025. Total receipts, led by personal income taxes and corporate taxes, increase from 17.5 percent of GDP in 2014 to 19.7 percent of GDP in 2025.

The Congressional Budget Office's analysis of the president's budget, in which I would put more analytical stock, has slightly different projections for federal revenues, spending, and resulting deficit inherent in the president's budget. For example, the CBO projects 2025 revenues equal to 19.2 percent of GDP, outlays of 22.1 percent of GDP, and a deficit of 2.9 percent of GDP. According to the CBO, the president's budget proposals would result in revenues being higher in 2025 by 0.9 percent compared to the CBO's baseline (before the president's budget proposals), and outlays would be about in line with the CBO 2025 baseline. In any case, President Obama's budget is a decidedly Democratic plan, with higher revenues, higher spending (other than defense), and a higher deficit than the congressional Republican plan.

Without getting too bogged down in the details, the president's revenue-enhancing proposals include (1) limiting certain deductions and tax exclusions (including employer-paid health care, among others) to 28 percent of their value, (2) enacting immigration reform (which results in more workers paying taxes immediately, while their receipt of government benefit payments is generally delayed for a number of years), (3) increasing estate and gift taxes, (4) increasing the dividend and capital gains tax rate to 28 percent, (5) implementing a "fair share tax" such that very-high-income taxpayers would pay at least 30 percent of their adjusted gross income (after a credit for charitable donations), (6) imposing a one-time tax on the accumulated earnings of foreign corporations controlled by US shareholders, (7) imposing a financial-crisis responsibility fee, and (8) enacting business tax reform that is revenue neutral in the long run. The president also proposes a number of spending proposals, some of which would reduce spending and some of which would increase spending, but I will skip the particulars here.

So there are the bones of three plans: a somewhat bipartisan plan, a House Republican plan, and a Democratic administration plan. The very broad summary for year 2016 and year 2025 compared to the most recent Congressional Budget Office budget projections is as follows:

Projected Revenues, Outlays, and Deficit as a Percent of GDP

	2016			2025		
	Revenues	Outlays	Deficit	Revenues	Outlays	Deficit
CBO June 2015 Baseline	18.4%	20.9%	-2.5%	18.3%	22.2%	-3.8%
CBO June 2015 Extended Alternative Fiscal Scenario	17.9%	21.3%	-3.4%	18.1%	22.9%	-4.9%
House Republican 2016 Budget Resolution	18.5%	20.3%	-1.8%	18.2%	18.3%	-0.1%
President Obama 2016 Budget (CBO Analysis)	19.0%	21.0%	-2.0%	19.2%	22.1%	-2.9%
Commission on Fiscal Responsibility and Reform	19.7%	21.9%	-2.2%	21.0%	21.8%	-0.8%

Notes:
House plan excludes macroeconomic effects.
National Commission on Fiscal Responsibility and Reform document was released in December 2010 and thus did not have the benefit of current data.

These three approaches to the federal budget give us a broad range of outcomes, with the resulting deficits ranging from 1.8 to 2.2 percent of GDP in 2016 and from 0.1 to 2.9 percent of GDP in 2025, and a range of federal spending from a little over 18 percent of GDP to up to 22.1 percent of GDP. The House Republican plan aims to balance the budget by cutting spending and keeping total tax revenue about where it is now, while the commission's plan calls for a balanced budget by restraining some of the growth in spending and increasing total tax revenue to bridge the gap. The president's plan is somewhat of a hybrid, allowing spending to increase as in the commission's plan but not increasing tax revenue in an amount sufficient to balance the budget. So in total, we've got a nice philosophical base from which to work.

For myself, I am going to take a big-picture approach to balancing the budget since it is very easy to get lost in the details. First of all, in my opinion, we should set a goal of achieving a deficit of no more than 1.5 percent of GDP during reasonable economic times. Why did I pick 1.5 percent of GDP? Obviously, a deficit of 1.5 percent of GDP is not the same as a balanced budget, which some might believe to be the appropriate goal, but as I argued earlier, there is no compelling reason we need a fully balanced budget, since if managed properly, the federal debt will never actually have to be repaid. In fact, at a deficit level equal to 1.5 percent of GDP, the total federal debt would tend to decline modestly in real terms and as a percent of GPD in the future, even though it would be increasing in nominal terms.

I also didn't pick a target of an annual deficit of 3 percent of GDP, which is the deficit level generally accepted as sustainable over an extended period of time, and about the level projected by the CBO based on President Obama's 2016 budget proposal. The reason for not targeting a deficit of 3 percent of GDP is straightforward: every plan or budget should have some contingency built in. Do we want to go right to the prudent limit as a basic plan? No responsible CEO, CFO, or individual managing a household budget plans like that, so why should the federal government? And as I said before, this is the goal to meet during normal, nonrecessionary economic times. We want to retain the ability to run larger deficits during recessions, when federal spending naturally increases and federal revenues naturally decline, even before implementing any additional stimulus measures. As recent experience shows, even limited wars are very expensive, and a severe recession can put a real strain on public budgets. I am all in favor of deficit spending when the economy is in recession. If consumers and businesses aren't spending, that is a perfect time for the government to take up some of the slack. This is basic Keynesian economics. However, the ability to undertake stimulus spending is based on the premise that the government isn't already running a large deficit. Just think how it would be if the government had a solid starting fiscal position, which it more or less did in 2007 when the federal debt held by the public stood at 36 percent of GDP. Then we could tackle the recession with both guns blazing (or with a bazooka, as Henry Paulson would say), which in fact the government did with the TARP and the various stimulus programs and five straight years when the deficit exceeded 5 percent of

GDP. However, we are now faced with the inconvenient truth that the federal debt is already above the generally accepted maximum sustainable total debt level. Whatever financial flexibility that the United States had prior to the Great Recession has been eliminated. We certainly don't want to be in this fiscal situation if and when the next crisis hits.

So a target deficit of 1.5 percent of GDP will tend to average out at a higher deficit level than that over time. That's just the way things work. In addition, with current federal debt held by the public at 74 percent of GDP at the end of fiscal year 2014, we already have a federal debt level that, while perhaps not alarmingly high, is higher than it has ever been since the immediate post–World War II period. Could I have picked a target of 1 percent or 2 percent without being too far off the mark? Of course I could have; 1 percent would probably be better from a fiscal standpoint, and a deficit of 2 percent of GDP would at least get us on the right track. But let's see if we can make our target of 1.5 percent work.

This deficit target doesn't seem impossible given historical averages and the most recent trends. The deficit for fiscal 2014 was 2.8 percent of GDP, compared to a peak deficit of 9.9 percent of GDP in 2009, so we've made great progress already. What will it take to get us to our 1.5 percent deficit target? Well, first, it will take an end to the recession (officially ended in June 2009), which has taken a large bite out of federal revenues because of the heavy reliance on income taxes (individual, social security, and corporate) as the primary federal revenue source, in addition to increased spending on recession-sensitive programs such as unemployment insurance and food stamps. In fact, in October 2011, the CBO estimated that the effect of the recession on the deficit for fiscal year 2012 accounted for $343 billion of the total $973 billion deficit that was projected for that year. This estimated $343 billion shortfall due to cyclical factors, made up largely of reduced revenues but including some increased outlays as well, represents a little over 2 percent of GDP.

We will use 2016 as our reference year, when, hopefully, the economy will continue to improve and the United States will be close to a full output and employment condition. In June 2015, the CBO projected that 2016 revenues will equal 18.4 percent of GDP, spending will reach 20.9 percent of GDP, and the deficit will equal 2.5 percent of GDP *based on current law.* While not as much of an issue now due to the passage of the American Taxpayer Relief Act of 2012, which made a number of temporary tax provisions permanent, the federal government, in its infinite wisdom, has a number of policies in effect that are scheduled to expire over the next decade or so. The American Taxpayer Relief Act extended indefinitely a number of tax provisions that were scheduled to expire in 2013 and later years and indexed the Alternative Minimum Tax for inflation beginning in 2013. As a result, the act brought the long-term law closer to current actual practice. However, the CBO still forecasts revenues, spending, and the deficit for an "Extended Alternative Fiscal Scenario," which includes a continuation of certain tax policies that are otherwise scheduled to expire, as well as modifying certain provisions of current law that might be difficult to sustain for a long period. As a result, another reasonable starting point is to look at the CBO projections in June 2015 based on the "extended alternative fiscal scenario," which leads to a projected deficit of approximately 3.4 percent of GDP in 2016. Revenues under that scenario are forecast at approximately 17.9 percent of GDP and spending is forecast at 21.3 percent of GPD.

So depending on what assumptions one wants to make regarding the sustainability of certain governmental policies, the CBO projects a deficit in fiscal 2016 of between 2.5 percent of GDP and 3.4 percent of GDP. For my purposes, I will assume a hybrid projection somewhat between the baseline projection and the extended alternative fiscal scenario. This working assumption results in federal revenues coming in at 18.2 percent of GDP and spending coming in at 21.1 percent of GDP, for a total deficit of 2.9 percent of GDP in 2016.

As a result, to reach our target deficit of 1.5 percent of GDP, we need to find a way to reduce the deficit by 1.4 percent of GDP by 2016, or approximately $260 billion on an annual basis. That is obviously a big number, but as we have seen, we have big numbers with which to work. Periodically, the CBO publishes options for reducing the deficit, the most recent being *Options for Reducing the Deficit: 2015 to 2024*, published in November

2014. That study lists seventy-nine deficit-reducing options as well as over one hundred other options that were the subject of prior CBO analyses. Some of these options are fairly substantial in terms of their potential effect in reducing the deficit, so it's not as if we don't have specific actions to consider.

Increase Revenues

Let's start at a high level and begin with the revenue side of the equation. Assume that, given the current deficit level and the natural pressure on the budget due to demographic factors, we need to set our revenue goal slightly above the 18.3 percent average of GDP for the 1980 to 2008 period, and much higher than the approximately 15 percent of GDP in fiscal year 2010 and the 17.5 percent of GDP in fiscal 2014. For me, the appropriate revenue target is 19 percent of GDP, compared to our working projection of 18.2 percent of GDP for the baseline scenario, so representing a slight increase from current levels.

What would it take to increase projected revenues by 0.8 percent of GDP? We need to raise about $150 billion in tax revenues to meet our goal of federal revenues reaching 19 percent of GDP in 2016. And $150 billion would require almost a 10 percent increase in individual income taxes for all taxpayers, not a small sum. Honestly, if all we did was reinstate the income tax policies in effect prior to the Bush tax cuts of 2001 and 2003, the increase in tax revenues from the higher rates would probably do the trick. Of course, this would mean that all taxpayers would be affected, including low- and middle-income earners. The 10 percent tax bracket for the lowest earners would disappear, tax rates for all levels of income would increase, and qualified dividends would lose their preferential tax treatment. In addition, a number of tax credits targeted primarily to the working poor would expire as well. This, in conjunction with the increased taxes on higher-income Americans restored as a part of the American Taxpayer Relief Act of 2012, would be as broad a tax increase as were the original tax cuts enacted in 2001 and 2003. However, having said this, taxes would return to the levels that were generally prevalent from 1998 to 2001, and the economy mostly hummed along just fine during that period.

So we could do that, but very few are advocating that, at least publicly. I am not a fan of that either, but we need to do something, and so here is my plan.

Embrace the Tax Increases in the American Taxpayer Relief Act

The American Taxpayer Relief Act of 2012 ("ATRA") was already a step in the right direction in terms of reducing the deficit. The basic provisions put to rest a number of uncertainties regarding the existing tax code, many of which were enacted in 2001 and 2003 as part of the Bush tax cuts and were scheduled to expire on December 31, 2012. The ATRA made permanent the 10 percent individual tax bracket and permanently extended the 25 percent, 28 percent, and 33 percent tax brackets on income at or below $400,000 (filing individually), $425,000 (heads of households), and $450,000 (married, filing jointly), which rates had previously been scheduled to increase for 2013 and thereafter. The ATRA increased taxes primarily on higher-income Americans through an increase in the top tax rate from 35 percent to 39.6 percent for income over $400,000 (individual) and $450,000 (married, filing jointly) and an increase in the capital gains tax rate from 15 to 20 percent (which also affects qualifying dividends). A number of other provisions were either implemented or made permanent, including setting the estate tax at 40 percent after a $5 million exemption per person and enacting a permanent AMT patch by indexing the exemptions for inflation. So, all in all, this was not a bad piece of legislation from an otherwise dysfunctional Congress.

To me, the increase in the capital gains rate was a no-brainer. The previous maximum rate on long-term capital gains and qualifying dividend income was 15 percent, which was in effect from 2003 through 2012. I estimate that increasing the maximum rate to 20 percent will raise an additional approximately $30 billion per year (recognizing that capital gains are highly variable year to year, particularly when the rates change). No surprise here, but the two biggest beneficiaries of the favorable rate applied to capital gains are the wealthy and the very wealthy. For example, over 60 percent of the long-term capital gains reported to the IRS on Form 1040, Schedule D, in 2012 were reported by taxpayers who had adjusted gross income in excess of $2 million. The preferential rate on capital gains is a big reason that Warren

Buffet can make the statement that he pays a lower tax rate than his secretary and why Mitt Romney's reported tax rate was less than 15 percent.

The main argument for low or even no capital gains taxes is that capital gains taxes serve as a disincentive to savings and capital investment. If a 20 percent capital gains tax is beneficial to capital formation (as compared to the higher rate applied to ordinary income), then a 15 percent rate is even better. However, I find it very hard to believe that a 20 percent capital gains tax rate is a great detriment to investment. What else is a wealthy person, or indeed anyone with capital, to do? Invest in treasuries yielding 2 to 3 percent, with the income taxable at ordinary income tax rates? Keep the money in cash or short-term treasuries, currently yielding basically nothing? The United States taxes wages up to almost a 40 percent rate (before any state income taxes), and to me that is a much bigger disincentive to economic growth than to tax capital income at a 20 percent rate, particularly since earning income from work requires real work, while earning capital income requires, well, mostly capital.

As a former private-equity investor, I can personally attest that a modest increase in the capital gains tax rate to 20 percent will not be a big factor influencing capital investment. People will still start businesses, and investors will still want to invest in companies. The primary determinant of capital investment is *the ability to earn an attractive return on the investment.* Yes, this is true, on an after-tax basis, but the return is primarily determined by the expected revenues and profits to be generated from the investment and only secondarily by the capital gains tax rate. That is why capital investment is so variable. If investors expect improving economic conditions, then capital investment will take place. If investors expect declining economic performance and overcapacity, then capital investment will decline. That is why at the height of the financial crisis, investors were willing to accept a *negative* return on Treasury bills. People were willing to give the government $100,100 in the present to receive $100,000 in the future, thus locking in a "safe" loss. That is how risk averse people were in 2009, and it's an indication that a 20 percent tax rate on capital gains (15 percent at the time in 2009) pales next to economic fundamentals.

So why not raise the capital gains tax rate even higher? Well, let's not push it! A lower rate of tax on capital is still an inducement to investment.

It's just that in the overall fiscal and tax environment, a 20 percent capital gains tax rate makes sense. Plus, if the provisions of the Affordable Care Act remain in place, the top capital gains tax rate will be 23.8 percent, the highest it has been since 1990.

As to the increase in the top rate on earned income above $450,000 (filing jointly), I accept this provision but with no great enthusiasm. At least it is less burdensome than President Obama's earlier proposal to raise taxes for taxpayers with taxable income of more than $250,000 (married, filing jointly). In my opinion, we want to maintain the work incentive for the $250,000-to-$450,000 income group as much as possible. These are the people who are successful professionals, business people, small-business owners, and other relatively high-income (but typically not rich) citizens, and they should be incentivized to produce, save, and invest. They are striving to build up some capital, and they are heavily taxed already. Of course, people earning more than $450,000 are productive as well and bear a heavy tax burden, but we need help somewhere, so I'll go with the higher tax rate on income over $450,000, which basically affects households in the top 1 percent by income.

The end result is that the ATRA had the effect of increasing taxes on higher-income Americans (particularly when one considers the additional taxes to be paid under the Affordable Care Act) and reducing the uncertainty of the many tax provisions that had expiration dates attached. At the time of the passage of the ATRA, the CBO estimated that it would *increase* deficits by approximately $4.6 trillion over the next ten years compared to prior law, which included a scheduled broad increase in taxes at all income levels. Since very few politicians were prepared to let taxes increase for all Americans, the more relevant comparison is to compare the effect of the ATRA to the tax provisions in effect as of 2012. At the time, the CBO estimated that the ATRA would decrease the deficit by approximately $700 billion to $800 billion over the next ten years. Since most of the impact of the ATRA was on revenues, we'll estimate that the impact of the higher taxes is approximately $70 billion on an annual basis, to fall almost exclusively on higher income Americans.

So the ATRA is a start toward our revenue target, but it's unfortunately only a start as the impact of the ATRA is already reflected in the current debt level and future deficit projections. If we are serious about closing the deficit, we either need to increase taxes substantially on our most productive citizens, or we need to tax more broadly the majority of Americans. Since higher-income Americans already pay the preponderance of taxes, and because rates on higher-income Americans were recently increased, it seems to me that any additional taxes should be a shared burden on all Americans, including high-income Americans. It we are to provide for widespread government services, we should finance this with broad-based taxes. That way, society shares in the benefit and the burden more equally, which should lead to a more balanced political discussion. Not that everyone has to pay equally, but everyone should at least pay something. Otherwise, all we are left with is a direct argument for simple income redistribution without a common civic responsibility.

Institute Additional Taxes on Carbon and Motor Fuels: $130 Billion

I am going to come right out with my biggest tax proposal, even though as of now it has probably no chance of becoming law (although theoretically, it has aspects that should appeal to both liberals and conservatives—go figure). First, I propose that the United States institute a carbon tax equal to $25 per metric ton of carbon dioxide released, which is essentially a tax on fossil fuels. Based on an estimated 5.4 billion metric tons of carbon dioxide released in the United States in 2012, this results in tax revenue of $135 billion, but let's call it an even $100 billion in revenue since it might be hard to capture all carbon emissions, and a carbon tax is intended to reduce carbon emissions. This is in essence CBO revenue option number thirty-five in their November 2013 list of deficit-reducing options, which they estimate to result in additional revenues of $100 billion in 2016, after accounting for reduced emissions of carbon and somewhat reduced income and payroll taxes due to higher business costs. In addition to the carbon tax, I would increase the federal tax on motor fuels by $0.25, raising an additional $30 billion (a reduced version of CBO option number thirty-seven in their November 2014 study, which analyzes an increase of $0.35), resulting in a total of $130 billion from taxes on fossil fuels.

As I argue in Chapter 8, there are a number of advantages to carbon-based taxes, including reducing dependence on foreign oil; reducing carbon emissions, which most scientists believe are the primary cause of global warming; and, most importantly, having the potential to raise large amounts of revenue. Certainly, $130 billion is a large sum of money to go toward deficit reduction.

While this is without doubt a regressive tax, this is a tax that people can choose to minimize if they so desire (which is also the point). They can purchase a more fuel-efficient car. They can choose to drive less by taking public transportation, consolidating trips, carpooling, or living closer to work. They can choose to better insulate their homes, set the thermostat a little lower, et cetera. In this country, *we tax work heavily, so the easiest way to avoid taxes is to not work.* That makes no logical sense whatsoever. In 2014, individual income taxes and social insurance taxes taken together, which are largely levied on wages and personal income, amounted to approximately $2.4 trillion, and that is just federal. Is an additional $130 billion from carbon and fuel taxes so burdensome to the citizenry? In addition, the regressive nature of carbon taxes can be minimized through other changes to the tax code, which I'll discuss later.

Finally, in my view, a carbon-based tax is a preferable alternative to a value-added tax, which is very popular in Europe and is similar to a carbon tax in that it is essentially a sales tax that has the potential to raise vast amounts of revenue. (For example, the CBO estimated in their 2013 deficit-reduction study that a 5 percent VAT can raise revenues of $150 to $270 billion, depending on how widely it is applied.) I believe the carbon tax provides more of a benefit than just raising revenues and that general sales taxes are best left to the states as they represent primary revenue sources for them.

Eliminate All "Green Energy" Tax Breaks: $10 Billion in Tax Revenue and Spending

Another benefit of a carbon tax is that it would enable the United States to eliminate all "green" energy subsidies and tax breaks. These include tax breaks for producing ethanol, tax breaks for purchasing an alternative fuel car, tax subsidies for creating alternative energy sources such as solar and wind power, and government support for development of alternative car technologies and the various green-energy loan programs—which, all totaled, easily comes to over $10 billion per year. In addition, because coal has a higher carbon content than other sources of electricity generation, including natural gas, the Obama administration can focus less on its current campaign to kill coal-based generation of electricity through federal regulation. If the increased cost of carbon-based energy sources doesn't result in these alternative energy sources becoming cost effective, then so be it. Ultimately, the market will find the most efficient energy sources, factoring in an additional cost for carbon.

Limit Deductions to a 28 percent Rate: $15 Billion in Tax Revenue

I propose that the United States limit the extent to which taxes can be reduced by itemized deductions to 28 percent of the deductions, which would affect taxpayers with taxable income roughly in excess of $200,000. (The CBO includes this as an option in their November 2014 study.) This is also a variation of one of the proposals that has been floated by President Obama in various forms, which has some merit. The president's latest proposal in the 2016 budget applies the 28 percent limit to certain exclusions as well (such as the exclusions for tax-exempt interest, employment-based health insurance, and employees' retirement contributions) and so is more comprehensive than what I am suggesting here (and therefore raises more in tax revenue than what I am suggesting here). The 28 percent limit has some appeal since it would not affect lower-income taxpayers at all, most of whom do not itemize deductions, or taxpayers with income less than about $200,000, as they are already in the 28 percent tax bracket or lower. Second, it has a fairness aspect to it for taxpayers who do itemize deductions in that it treats moderate- and higher-income taxpayers equally. For example, if a married taxpayer in the 28 percent tax bracket (taxable income between $148,850 and $226,850 for 2014 taxes) donates $10,000 to charity (or is entitled to any of the other available tax deductions such as mortgage interest or state and local taxes), he or she would be able to reduce his or her taxes by $2,800, while a taxpayer in the 35 percent tax bracket with the same charitable deduction would be able to reduce taxes by $3,500. Under this proposal, each of our hypothetical taxpayers would be able to reduce taxes by the same amount, $2,800.

This proposal has the added benefit of keeping the many tax preferences in place, while limiting their cost, rather than amending some of the specific deductions themselves. For example, as an alternative, we could limit or eliminate the deduction of mortgage interest, which might make some economic sense, but doing this when housing is still in the recovery phase doesn't seem timely. Or we could limit or eliminate the deduction of state and local taxes, which is essentially a federal subsidy to high-tax states, but this would hurt residents of these high-tax states (such as me). Or we could limit the deduction for charitable donations, which would obviously hurt charitable fundraising. In each case, an argument can be made for limiting or eliminating the deduction, but by simply limiting the tax effect of all deductions, we retain the favorable tax treatment of activities deemed desirable, while minimizing the revenue effect to some extent. In addition, limiting the value of all deductions could pave the way for eliminating certain deductions in the future as part of a lower overall tax rate since the impact wouldn't be as severe at that time.

Reduce the Exclusion from Income for Employment-Based Health Insurance: $50 Billion

The exclusion of employer contributions for medical insurance premiums and medical care is the single largest "tax expenditure" in the tax code, accounting for over $200 billion in foregone revenue in 2016 (federal income tax only, excluding the impact on payroll taxes, which would increase the total impact). This tax expenditure results from the fact that although these employer benefits are a part of many employees' compensation, these employer-paid benefits are not subject to individual income taxes and payroll taxes. On the one hand, this exclusion encourages employers to offer insurance coverage to their employees since it is a benefit that can be offered on a tax-free basis. On the other hand, it encourages a noncash form of compensation in place of higher cash compensation, which may be more beneficial to employees. In addition, in my opinion, it contributes to the very high cost of health care in this country compared to the rest of the world, since the true cost of this service is largely invisible to the employee. Finally, it discriminates against employees who do not have employer-provided health insurance since if they were to purchase their own coverage, they would have to use after-tax dollars in many cases.

The CBO has analyzed a number of alternatives that would reduce the exclusion for employment-based health insurance. These include (1) reducing the tax exclusion for employment-based health insurance and the health insurance deduction for self-employed individuals, (2) replacing the income tax exclusion for employment-based health insurance with a deduction, and (3) replacing the income and payroll tax exclusion with a refundable credit. These various options can limit certain deduction amounts and have phase-outs based on income levels. For me, I would simply include in income the value of all employer-paid health insurance above a certain amount per employee or family. This would affect higher-income people more than lower-paid employees because higher-income employees may have more comprehensive and expensive health insurance coverage, and they might be in a higher tax rate bracket, so the net after-tax impact on them would be greater. Depending on how the parameters were set, this provision could easily be structured to raise an additional $50 billion in taxes in 2016, which is less than 25 percent of the total amount that could be raised from a full repeal. In this way, the incentive for employers to provide insurance coverage remains in place, while the employee is more aware of the cost, hopefully leading to a more judicious use of health-care services.

Increase Customs Duties and Fees: $15 billion

Increasing customs duties and fees is perhaps another controversial proposal, particularly since the economic orthodoxy since the Great Depression has been to reduce import duties. I myself am in favor of free trade since free trade is economically efficient. However, let's recognize that *all* taxes, in some way, are an impediment to economic efficiency. Taxes on wages are a disincentive to work, the employer share of social security taxes are an additional cost of business and a disincentive to hire workers, and taxes on profits are a disincentive to invest. So I don't propose an increase in customs duties as an antitrade measure but as a revenue-raising measure. And the suggested increase of $15 billion, while a very significant amount compared to the roughly $30 billion in current federal revenue from this source, represents only about 0.5 percent of the total imports of the United States. So it's not as if an increase in customs duties of this amount would be a great disincentive to import foreign goods if the increase were widely applied. However, having said all that, the United States has consistently been in a foreign trade deficit for many years, and a slight nonpunitive tariff increase certainly can't hurt the trade balance.

I also offer the following two additional considerations on this point. First, since September 11, 2001, the United States has dramatically increased its spending for homeland security, such that the 2013 spending for the Department of Homeland Security was nearly $60 billion. Presumably this includes monitoring goods entering the country. Is it not appropriate to fund a portion of this cost through fees on goods being imported into the country? It just seems an appropriate cost of doing business for countries and firms that export to the United States.

Second, my proposal to institute a carbon tax would undoubtedly result in an increased cost of business for many US firms, and I look at an increase in customs duties as a partial offset to the increased cost of domestic production resulting from a carbon tax. Once again, there is a certain fairness aspect to it.

Enact a Broad-Based Tax Cut Affecting All Workers: $50 Billion Reduction

Since I am proposing that we raise an additional $130 billion in taxes through a broad-based tax on carbon and a higher federal motor-fuels tax, I am also proposing that we cut $50 billion in income-based taxes as a partial offset. This could take many forms, but whatever the form, it should be a widespread reduction since the carbon-based tax is a widespread tax increase. One approach might be to exclude the first $15,000 of earnings from the employer and employee share of Medicare taxes. Since the total Medicare tax rate is 2.9 percent, this would result in a direct tax cut of $217.50 for every person earning $15,000 per year (or more), as well as reducing the share paid by the employer by a similar amount (a self-employed person would save the full $435). The share saved by the employer would reduce the employer's business costs, which could lead to more hiring or offset some of the increased costs borne by the employer due to the increased cost of carbon.

This proposal would cost the Treasury maybe $50 billion as a rough estimate ($435 times 135 million workers). Or, maybe this provision could be included with an increase in the minimum wage, which would help the lowest-income earners. Alternatively, a new or expanded refundable tax credit could be instituted that would have the effect of providing a tax cut to lower-income working Americans. President Obama, for example, has proposed a number of tax changes in his 2016 budget "supporting middle class and working families," including modifying refundable tax credits, which the CBO estimated will cost approximately $35 billion per year once fully implemented. A progressive tax cut, which will serve to offset a portion of the per-person impact of the carbon tax will reduce the tax on work while increasing the tax on carbon fuels. Net, that is a good thing.

This overall concept is not dissimilar to a proposal by Al Gore, who suggested the following way back when:

> For the last fourteen years, I have advocated the elimination of all payroll taxes—including those for Social Security and unemployment compensation—and the replacement of that revenue in the form of pollution taxes—principally on CO2. The overall level of taxation would remain exactly the same. It would be in other words, a revenue-neutral tax swap. But instead of discouraging businesses from hiring more employees, it would discourage businesses from producing more pollution.

That's actually not a bad logical summary, although to replace all payroll taxes would take one heck of a big carbon tax.

Reduce Corporate Income Tax Rates While Eliminating Certain Loopholes: Revenue Neutral

As was discussed earlier, the United States has one of the highest corporate income tax rates in the world. In today's global economy, this creates an incentive for both US and internationally headquartered companies to base operations and profits overseas rather than here in the United States. In fact, it is their fiduciary duty to shareholders to try to do so. In addition, it results in an incentive, once profits have been earned overseas, to leave them there, either in cash or reinvested in international operations. For example, cash held overseas by US corporations totaled nearly $1 trillion at the end of 2012. This is money that could theoretically be reinvested in domestic operations or, alternatively, repatriated to the United States and paid out as dividends to shareholders. In either case, it is a huge tax-policy-induced inefficiency. This noncompetitive US tax system makes no sense today.

As a result, I propose that the corporate tax rate be reduced to 28 percent from the current 34 to 35 percent that exists today. This could reduce tax receipts by about $60 billion depending on the level of corporate profits (20 percent reduction in rate, applied to roughly $300 billion in corporate tax receipts). I propose that all of the lost revenue be recouped through reduced corporate tax breaks, such as tax preferences for the oil and gas industry and other various tax expenditures targeted toward corporations, which totaled about $120 billion in 2014. It may take some time to fully recover all of the revenue lost through corporate tax reform, because the impact of the reduced rates would be felt immediately, while the impact of the increased incentive to invest and retain profits in the United States would happen more gradually over time. But ultimately, the end result would be a more equitable corporate tax system and a greater incentive to base businesses and income in the United States.

By the way, both President Obama and many key Republicans are on the record for being in favor of revenue-neutral corporate tax reform (including a lowering of the tax rate), so you'd think we could make some easy progress on this front.

Revenue Summary

So where do all of these tax increases leave us? We have increased revenues by $220 billion through various tax increases. Taxes will be higher for all levels of taxpayers, with the carbon-based and motor-fuels taxes falling on all Americans and most of the other proposed tax increases falling primarily on higher-income Americans. We have restructured the corporate income tax to be more competitive with international practice. We have also reduced income-based taxes by $50 billion, targeted heavily to lower-income Americans. As a result of all of this, the net increase in tax revenues totals about $170 billion annually, representing about 0.9 percent of projected 2016 GDP, so I've actually exceeded my goal by $20 billion. That's not so bad.

Now I recognize that this represents a fairly sizable tax increase, which is anathema to many and would result in the highest overall federal tax burden as a share of the economy since 2000. However, total federal revenues targeted at 19 percent of GDP would still be less as a share of GDP than during the years 1998–2000 and much less than that proposed by the bipartisan National Commission on Fiscal Responsibility and Reform, for example. And let's face it, the federal government has been outspending revenues for quite some time, and we have some catching up to do to get the overall federal debt down to more manageable levels. So I don't think targeting federal receipts at 19 percent of GDP is out of line at all given the current fiscal situation.

Spending

So that is the revenue side of the equation; now let's look at spending. Here is the quick math. If our deficit target is 1.5 percent of GDP and our revenue target is 19 percent of GDP, then our spending budget is 20.5 percent of GDP. That's not too complicated. This spending target is solidly between the president's target of spending at 21 percent of GDP in 2016 (22.1 percent in 2025) and the House Budget Committee target of 20.3 percent of GDP in 2016 (18.3 percent in 2025), so that seems about right to me. In fiscal 2014, total spending by the federal government was 20.3 percent of GDP, so we have already exceeded our target! However, perhaps that is an unrealistically easy goal since it includes certain spending cuts already, such as continuation of the sequester, and also excludes inevitable increased spending due to the Affordable Care Act and other health-care spending increases. Based on our federal budget operating assumptions, the projected spending in 2016 comes in at 21.1 percent of GDP, so we need to cut spending by 0.6 percent of GDP by 2016, or approximately $115 billion.

Is this hard to do? Total spending by the federal government in fiscal 2016 is projected to be approximately $4 trillion, so our target reduction is slightly less than 3 percent of total spending. That seems doable without too much trouble. One could seemingly cut every spending category by 3 percent without noticeable adverse impact. However, this includes interest, which is truly mandatory, and social security, which is politically mandatory, at least in the short term. Spending before interest and social security is projected to be about $2.8 trillion in 2016, so our spending-reduction target comes to about 4 percent of that amount. Now, 4 percent is a bigger number but maybe still doable. After all, spending in those remaining categories is estimated at about $2.4 trillion in 2014, so to get to $2.6 trillion in 2016 all we are really asking is that the increase in spending be held to about $200 billion (which gets you to very roughly $2.6 trillion compared to the $2.8 trillion projected, thus saving $200 billion from forecast). That is a 4 percent annual *increase* from 2014 levels, which certainly seems reasonable to me. So we can cut projected spending in 2016 by $115 billion by increasing noninterest, non-social-security spending by 4 percent a year over the next two years. That almost seems magically easy.

However, there are a couple of complications to this approach. First of all, a sizable portion of the increase in spending over the next two years is due to the impact of the Affordable Care Act for insurance subsidies and the expansion of Medicaid. So either that has to be repealed or amended, or money needs to be diverted from other spending categories. And any material amendment to the Affordable Care Act could have implications for revenues, which are higher due to the taxes included as a part of the ACA. Second, other spending constraints may have to be applied to other health-care spending, including Medicare, which is another political "third rail" spending category, and Medicaid. But other than that, it doesn't seem so hard. What category of spending couldn't be constrained, or even frozen, for three years? Literally, every area could handle it. What have been the big complaints of living with the impact of the sequester, which began in March 2013? Air-traffic control? Okay, that is important to maintain, and the government was forced to adequately fund this. But other than that, the biggest problem that received any public attention that I am aware of was the closure of national parks and cancelation of the public tours of the White House, and these were largely political moves, which have since been reversed.

Of course, this approach means that national defense would be affected. Also affected would be welfare, food stamps, farm support, NASA, and every other area of government spending. But really, benefits would not be all that dramatically affected if the cuts were spread around. A two-year freeze of SNAP benefits means that a family receiving $500 in monthly food stamps in 2014 would still be receiving $500 a month in food stamps in 2016 (assuming they still qualify), which, granted, may be worth less due to inflation—but if, say, the real value is 4 percent less in 2016, that is still $480 a month (in 2014 dollars) in nutrition support. I recognize that a $20-a-month reduction is a meaningful amount for a family living near the poverty line, but that is less than $1 a day, and they would still be receiving $480 a month of food support, which is certainly something.

But maybe you think we should have a more targeted approach to spending cuts. This would certainly make sense if the politicians could agree on something. The CBO's November 2014 report on options for reducing the deficit lists forty-five separate non-health-related options for reducing spending, each ranging from $3 billion to $397 billion total over a ten-year period, in addition to a number of health-related options. Some of these can result in substantial savings. Here is just a sample of the annual savings for a number of options. (I use the 2017 estimates here to allow for a full phase-in of the impact.) If you are interested in the details, please check the CBO website for the latest spending-reduction analysis.

Reduce crop subsidies in the crop insurance program	$2 billion
Eliminate the add-on to Pell grants	$7 billion

Eliminate the concurrent receipt of retirement pay and disability compensation for disabled veterans	$11 billion
Tighten eligibility and income limits for SNAP	$6 billion
Eliminate supplemental income benefits for children	$12 billion
Replace the Joint Strike Fighter with F-16s and F/A-18s	$2 billion
Reduce funding for international affairs programs	$9 billion
Eliminate human space-exploration programs	$8 billion
Eliminate health-exchange subsidies for people with income over 300 percent of the poverty guidelines	$9 billion
Increase premiums for Parts B and D of Medicare	$12 billion
Change the cost-sharing rules for Medicare and restrict Medigap insurance	$9 billion

Of course, each of these options has its positive and negative implications. For example, while we certainly want to support our veterans, does it make sense for military retirees to receive both full retirement annuity *and* disability compensation? Prior to 2003, military retirees had to choose between the two. As another example, the Supplemental Security Income program provides cash assistance to people who are disabled, aged, or both, and who have low income and few assets. About 15 percent of recipients are disabled children under eighteen years of age. Obviously, households with a disabled child and low income can use the extra money, but is this a well-targeted federal program, since it is otherwise targeted toward people who are unable to work? Human space exploration is certainly exciting, but space exploration can be conducted much more cheaply with unmanned missions. The overall point is that every program presumably has its merits, and choices will have to be made if we are to bring the budget under control.

Other options can result in even greater savings. For example, reducing the size of the military to satisfy caps under the Budget Control Act can save $31 billion in 2016 and $83 billion in 2023 (from the November 2013 CBO report). Of course, this would result in a cut of 10 percent or more in projected military spending and a real reduction in America's military capability, although the United States would maintain the title of the world's largest spender on defense by far. Maybe we can afford to do this from a security perspective, and maybe we can't.

Or we could convert multiple assistance programs for lower-income people into smaller block grants to the states, which would save $52 billion in 2016. This option would provide for funding equal to federal outlays for the impacted programs in 2007, adjusted for inflation, which is much lower than the current spending on these programs. That doesn't sound completely unfair, does it? As such, this option would both reduce the amount spent on assistance programs as well as transfer much control from the federal government to the state governments. Depending on your point of view, this could be a good thing or a bad thing.

Or we could impose caps on federal spending on Medicaid, which covers health care for low-income families with dependent children, the elderly, people with disabilities, and, at states' option, nonelderly adults with family income up to 138 percent of the federal poverty guidelines (this last part is a provision in the Affordable Care Act). Obviously, there can be much variability in the savings depending on how one wants to set and adjust the caps, but the November 2013 CBO report projects savings in 2016 of $10 billion to $28 billion and savings in 2023 of $20 billion to $124 billion. This could result in real savings and provide the states with more flexibility in how they choose to manage their needs-based health-care programs. As the CBO says, "In response, states would have to commit more of their own revenues to Medicaid or reduce services, restrict eligibility or enrollment, cut payment rates for health-care providers, or (to the extent feasible) develop ways to deliver services more efficiently, each of which would raise various concerns." I personally believe this would be a very good thing, but you may disagree.

My objective here is not to burden you with the details of the cost-savings opportunities in the federal budget but to stress the fact that cuts can be made. Across the board if we must, but there are plenty of areas that can be targeted. How about corporate welfare? We could cut that by 25 percent, or about $25 billion, or maybe even more, or entirely. Defense spending? Freeze for two years. Needs-based assistance programs? Freeze for two years. Government spending on health care? That's where the real big money is.

As I said before, the details of federal spending can be a little confusing. So here is at least my big-picture plan to cut $115 billion of spending from the total $4 trillion projected by the CBO for federal spending in 2016.

Cut federal spending for major health-care programs by 5 percent	$50 billion
Cut corporate welfare by 25 percent	$25 billion
Cut defense spending (less than 5 percent)	$25 billion
Cut nondefense discretionary by 5 percent	$30 billion
Reform the Disability Insurance Program (10 percent reduction)	$15 billion
Cuts from other income support programs (less than 5%)	$10 billion
Interest savings from increased revenues and reduced spending	$15 billion

The total comes to $170 billion, leaving social security unaffected (other than the Disability Insurance program), which is exactly equal to the total revenue increases I proposed. I admit that this is a bit of a broad brush, but this at least seems like a good place to start. While the reductions to health-care spending and other social programs might seem harsh, please recognize that in all cases, total spending for these categories would still be *increasing* relative to 2014, and in most cases they would be increasing on a per-beneficiary basis. So these are really more spending "slowdowns" than actual reductions from current levels.

So once again, I have exceeded my goal—by $55 billion in this case. If all of my revenue increases and spending cuts where implemented, projected revenues would come in at about 19.1 percent of GDP, and projected spending would come in at about 20.2 percent of GDP, resulting in a deficit of 1.1 percent of GDP. That would actually be a pretty good goal, but even if not, it provides the politicians with some wiggle room to modify some of the proposed revenue increases or spending reductions. Or consider it a budget cushion for some investment spending or critical defense needs.

Some Additional Investment Spending

One area where I would not cut any capability is in true public services. By this I mean primarily infrastructure—such as roads, bridges, public transportation, and the like—and primary and secondary education. In these two areas, at least, everyone benefits, and they serve to strengthen the overall vitality and competitiveness of the United States. If we are going to spend money, why not have quality public infrastructure, quality public transportation, and quality public education, literally for everyone? And add to this, clean air and clean water. For example, what would you rather have, extended unemployment benefits or quality sewage-treatment facilities, which lead to clean water *and* create jobs? As we know, every dollar spent in these areas stays in the economy in terms of jobs and spending, and in addition, we receive a public benefit. I personally don't mind spending for quality of life in parks, true services, et cetera. I also don't mind spending for public education because I believe that every child deserves a quality education, independent of his or her economic situation or location of residence. Not to say that money is the answer to all of the problems in education or any other area. Certainly we can do better with the resources we currently spend. However, a purposeful lack of investment should never be the problem, since that can be solved.

President Obama dedicates a full fifty-three pages of the *Fiscal Year 2016 Budget of the United States* to "Investing in America's Future." While the title of that section of the budget looks like artful packaging rather than a comprehensive program to invest in America's future, it does include some worthwhile initiatives. Without opining on the particulars, I'll summarize that the president proposes programs to accelerate manufacturing growth, invest in research and development, invest in climate resilience and preparedness, invest in upgrading America's transportation network, improve access to education, and advance national-security priorities. I am sure that the various Republicans have lists of their own. The point is that if we bring balance to the federal budget, then the country could undertake some thoughtful investment spending that would benefit the country in the long run.

Long-Term Fiscal Balance

So we can see that in the near term, we can solve the budget problem without making any drastic changes. Just a little extra revenue and some spending cuts, which really bring us back to historical averages of spending and revenues as a share of GDP. However, in the long term, the United States has a different budget problem that results from a combination of demographics and the increasing cost of health care. For example, in the Extended Alternative Fiscal Scenario (before economic feedback, which, if included in the analysis, would make the deficit worse), the CBO projects a total deficit of 5 percent of GDP in 2023, but a total deficit of 13 percent of GDP in 2038, and total debt held by the public at 156 percent of GDP in 2038. So obviously something has to change, and that something is government spending on health care (Medicare and Medicaid) and, to a lesser extent, social security. In the extended alternative fiscal scenario, spending for social security increases from 4.9 percent of GDP in 2014 to 6.4 percent of GDP in 2038, while spending on Medicare, Medicaid, and other government health-care programs increases from 4.7 percent of GDP in 2014 to 7.9 percent in 2038 (and continues to grow as a percent of GDP forever after). That is a total increase in federal spending for those two areas of 4.7 percent of GDP, while the rest of government spending (other than interest, which increases as the debt increases) actually declines slightly as a percent of GDP.

Social Security can be fixed with a couple of tweaks to slow the growth of benefits without reducing current payments. For example, one option the CBO analyzed was to lengthen the number of years of earnings included in the benefit calculation to thirty-eight from the current thirty-five years for people who turn sixty-two in 2016, 2017, and beyond (from the November 2014 CBO study). The CBO projected savings of $13.1 billion in 2024, which would increase in future years as more and more retirees are affected by the revised calculation formula. This would most affect people who worked less than thirty-eight years because years without earnings are included with a zero-level earnings, thus bringing down the average earnings upon which benefits are based. This would include people who were not able to work for thirty-eight years because of extended periods of unemployment, time off to raise a family, or poor health, and on average, it would affect women more than men because women tend to spend more years out of the workforce. On the other hand, it would treat workers who work more than thirty-five years more fairly since they pay more in social security taxes over their working lives than comparably paid workers who work thirty-five years, but the people who worked for more than thirty-five years do not currently accrue more benefits due to the extra years of work.

Another approach would be to use the chained CPI to index benefits to inflation rather than the traditional CPI. The chained CPI accounts for changes in spending patterns, which the traditional CPI does not, and it historically has grown at an average of 0.25 percentage points more slowly per year than the traditional CPI. As a result, growth in benefits once retired would increase more slowly. The CBO projects that this would save $22 billion in 2024, again growing over time as the impact becomes more pronounced (CBO November 2014 study). If this approach were applied to certain other federal programs, the total savings would come to about $35 billion by 2024. While this would tend to lead to reduced benefits for recipients compared to current law, particularly as recipients age, it would still provide a stable real income stream consistent with a broad measure of inflation for the rest of their lives.

So it would only take a couple of tweaks to bring social security within a sustainable long-term trend. Dealing with escalating health-care expenditures is a bit more problematic because while the growth in social security is mostly a demographic issue, spending on health care has the added burdens of the increasing use and increasing cost of health care. As such, the future spending growth is much larger, and the changes required to address it are more material. However, while difficult, the problem is not unsolvable if we accept the premise that *unlimited* access to *free* health care is not a universal right. The amounts have to be capped at some level tied to GDP, which would allow for some real growth in spending but would be much lower than would occur if present trends continue. That is the only way to do it. That is basically the final health-care recommendation of the National Commission on Fiscal Responsibility and Reform, which recommended that the government "establish a global budget for total federal health-care costs and limit the growth to GDP plus 1 percent." That very simple approach works for me.

Conclusion

Hopefully you agree with me that a balanced budget, or at least a modest and sustainable deficit, is a national goal worth attaining. As we have seen, the steps required to do this are neither impossible nor unduly burdensome to the citizenry. We simply need to raise taxes modestly on all Americans, with the usual skew toward higher-income earners, and contain the growth in government spending, including defense, needs-based assistance, and entitlements. Taxes would be moderately higher on those who can afford to pay more taxes, without damaging the incentive to work and invest, and the social safety net would still be robust. What is not fair or appropriate in this approach? To some people, all of the required deficit reduction should come from spending cuts, but this would require much more drastic cuts, and it ignores the fact that demographics are against us over time as the population ages. To others, all of the required deficit reduction should come from increased taxes on the wealthy because they don't pay their "fair share." However, this approach lacks the appeal of a shared sacrifice and ignores the fact that higher-income Americans already pay the preponderance of federal taxes.

So my plan calls for shared increases in taxes and cuts in spending of less than 1 percent of GDP in each case. This would lead to a sustainable budget that is consistent with historical norms, yet result in a slightly higher overall tax burden than is the case today, recognizing that the aging population of the country will necessarily require higher taxes if we are to sustain our most popular social programs. For a number of ancillary reasons, I propose that the United States institute a tax on carbon (fossil fuels) and limit the tax benefits associated with employer-provided health insurance. To me, this is economically efficient, fair, and just plain sensible.

However, maybe you don't agree with such a drastic change from current tax policy. As a point of comparison, if you wanted to raise additional tax revenue simply by raising the tax rates, the United States could increase all personal income tax rates by about 2.5 percentage points, which, based on analysis by the CBO, would raise approximately $150 billion in additional annual tax revenue. That is another viable tax option (which isn't too far from where the US tax rates were before the Bush tax cuts). If you wanted to limit the impact only to higher-income Americans by increasing the tax rates only for the top two tax brackets (largely affecting taxpayers with $400,000 or more in income), the CBO projects that a one percentage increase in rates would raise approximately $12 billion in revenue. As a result, it would take a much larger increase to raise the required revenues, say an increase of fifteen percentage points, which would bring the top tax rate to about 55 percent. So despite the popular appeal of soaking the rich, it is not that easy to dramatically increase revenues from 1 percent of the population.

If you are a fan of eliminating deductions as a way to raise taxes without increasing tax rates (more of a flat-tax structure), the CBO estimates that eliminating the deductibility of state and local taxes would raise approximately $100 billion in revenue and that curtailing (but not eliminating) the deduction for charitable contributions could raise another $20 billion in revenue, assuming rates stay the same. That won't be too popular in the (generally higher-tax) blue states or with the various charities. However, if this approach were combined with my proposal to limit the favorable tax treatment of employer-provided health insurance, that would be more than enough to get us to the revenue target. So, as it is with spending, we have many options, or a combination of viable options, in order to raise additional revenues.

And we don't necessarily have to get all of this done by 2016; that is just a reasonable year to pick since by then the economy should be close to full output. The United States could phase in the tax increases and spending cuts over a multiple-year period in order to minimize the disruption to businesses and households and to not abruptly impact aggregate demand in the economy. However, as is always the case with excessive debt levels, the sooner we get started, the better.

The minute I finish writing this, the facts on the ground have changed. The prospects for the economy have worsened or improved. Some governmental policy or law has changed—or not changed, as was perhaps expected. Tax receipts and governmental spending have increased or decreased. I am sure that I have missed some relevant information that I should have considered. And, of course, future projections of taxes, spending, and the deficit have changed or certainly will change based on all of the previously mentioned factors.

What have not changed, however, are the overall trends in demographics and government finance. Based on current policies and economic conditions, the United States is on a path to run annual deficits in the range of 3 percent of GDP and maintain debt to the public in excess of 70 percent of GDP for the next few years. Unfortunately, this somewhat stable fiscal situation may have reduced the impetus to reduce the budget deficit. It is easier to talk about deficit reduction when the deficit is in excess of $1 trillion and about 10 percent of GDP than when the deficit is lower by about two-thirds. However, irrespective of the current situation, the long-term trends are obvious, and that is for a natural upward pressure on government spending, with the resultant obvious impact on the deficit. Some would argue that it is silly (or, more likely, bad politics) to address a problem in advance, but a little long-term planning never hurt anyone. The sooner we fix the problem, the easier the fix will be.

So let's get the deal done.

Source Notes

Preface

1. Information on relative defense spending from *The Economist: Pocket World in Figures*, 2012 ed.
2. The quote from President Obama's 2013 State of the Union address comes from the White House website, http://www.whitehouse.gov/the-press-office/2013/02/12/remarks-president-state-union-address. (I left out the "Applause" parts.)
3. Data for total government spending comes from Table 3.1, National Income and Product Accounts, Bureau of Economic Analysis, US Department of Commerce.
4. 2012 presidential election results are based on the "Official 2012 Presidential Election Results" and exit polls conducted by Edison Research of Somerville, New Jersey, for the National Election Pool. Income tax data comes from *The Distribution of Household Income and Federal Taxes, 2010*, Congressional Budget Office, December 2013.
5. Historical deficit information comes from Table 1.1, Office of Management and Budget.

Chapter 1

1. Historical deficit and federal debt information comes from Tables 1.1, 1.2, and 7.1, Office of Management and Budget.
2. Sequester information comes from Wikipedia.

3. Dick Cheney quote on the deficit comes from Ron Suskind's *The Price of Loyalty: George W. Bush, the White House and the Education of Paul O'Neill*, as reported by Wikipedia.
4. Deficit and public-debt information for Japan, Italy, Greece, and Spain comes from *The Economist*, November 19, 2011; the CIA *World Factbook*; Tradingeconomics.com; and the *OECD Factbook 2013: Economic, Environmental and Social Statistics*, OECD Publishing, 2012.
5. US government balance-sheet and off-balance-sheet information comes from the *Financial Report of the US Government for Fiscal Year 2014*, US Department of the Treasury.
6. Projections for future deficits come from *The 2015 Long-Term Budget Outlook*, Congressional Budget Office, June 2015, http://www.cbo.gov/publication/50250#title0. See also *Updated Budget Projections: 2015 to 2025*, March 2015, and *The 2014 Long-Term Budget Outlook*, July 2014, Congressional Budget Office. The "extended alternative fiscal scenario" developed by the CBO and presented in the July 2014 report assumes the following:

> The automatic reductions in spending in 2015 and later required by the Budget Control Act of 2011 as subsequently amended would not occur—although the original caps on discretionary appropriations in that law would remain in place; lawmakers would act to maintain Medicare's payment rates for physicians at current levels; and federal noninterest spending apart from that for Social Security, the major health care programs (net of offsetting receipts), and certain refundable tax credits would rise after 2024 to its average as a percentage of GDP during the past two decades—rather than fall significantly below that level, as it does in the extended baseline."

It also incorporates the following assumptions regarding revenues:

> About 70 expiring tax provisions, including one that allows businesses to deduct 50 percent of new investments in equipment immediately, will be extended through 2024; and after 2024, revenues will equal 18.0 percent of GDP, matching the value they would have had in 2024 given the previous assumptions about expiring tax provisions and standing slightly higher than the average of 17.4 percent over the past forty years—rather than rising over time as a percentage of GDP, as they do in the extended baseline. (CBO, *The 2014 Long-Term Budget Outlook*, July 2014)

I believe the modifications in the June 2015 report were not quite so extensive.

7. Descriptive information on the CBO comes from *An Introduction to the Congressional Budget Office*, Congressional Budget Office, November 2012.
8. Information on foreign holdings of US federal debt comes from the US Department of the Treasury, http://www.treasury.gov/resource-center/data-chart-center/tic/Documents/mfh.txt.

Chapter 2

1. The data for the economic comparison of the United States to the rest of the world is based on information from the *CIA World Factbook*, https://www.cia.gov/library/publications/the-world-factbook/, at official exchange rates.
2. Quote on inclusive economic and political systems from Daron Acemoglu and James A. Robinson's *Why Nations Fail*, 2012, p. 429.

3. Future population projection comes from *World Population Prospects: The 2010 Revision, Highlights and Advanced Tables*, Population Division, Department of Economic and Social Affairs, the United Nations, 2011.
4. United States economic statistics come from Tables 1.1.5, 1.1.6, 7.1, 1.1.1, and 1.1.10, National Income and Product Accounts, US Bureau of Economic Analysis. The data provided by the US Bureau of Economic Analysis is updated on a regular basis and revised from time to time, so minor differences may exist depending on when the data is accessed.
5. US savings and investment statistics come from Table 5.10, National Income and Product Accounts, US Bureau of Economic Analysis.
6. US government borrowing from Table 5.1, line 40, National Income and Product Accounts, US Bureau of Economic Analysis.
7. US international trade and balance of payments statistics come from Table 1: "International Transactions," US Bureau of Economic Analysis.
8. Reference to America's "exorbitant privilege" comes from Barry Eichengreen's *Exorbitant Privilege: The Rise and Fall of the Dollar and the Future of the International Monetary System*, 2011.
9. GDP per-person statistics for various countries come from *The Economist: Pocket World in Figures*, 2012 ed.
10. US household income data come from Carmen DeNavas-Walt and Bernadette D. Proctor, *Income and Poverty in the United States: 2013*, Current Population Reports, US Census Bureau, US Government Printing Office: Washington, DC, 2014, pp. 60–249.

Chapter 3

1. Thomas Edison quote comes from Brainyquote.com.
2. New York City taxi medallion prices come from the New York City Taxi and Limousine Commission, http://www.nyc.gov/html/tlc/downloads/pdf/avg_med_price_2014_may.pdf.

3. Median salary information by occupation comes from the US Department of Labor, http://www.bls.gov/oes/current/oes_nat.htm.
4. "Domestic Product Equals Domestic Income" table derived from *Measuring the Economy: A Primer on GDP and the National Income and Product Accounts*, September 2007; and *Concepts and Methods of the US National Income and Product Accounts*, Bureau of Economic Analysis, US Department of Commerce, October 2009.
5. Automotive employment information comes from the Bureau of Labor Statistics, http://www.bls.gov/iag/tgs/iagauto.htm.
6. Share of employment represented by labor unions comes from the Bureau of Labor Statistics.

Chapter 4

1. Will Rogers quote from Liaquat Ahamed's *Lords of Finance.*
2. John Stuart Mill quote comes from *Principles of Political Economy*, 1848, as referenced in Milton Friedman and Anna Jacobson Schwartz's *A Monetary History of the United States, 1867–1960.*
3. Various Ludwig von Mises quotes come from the new edition of his *The Theory of Money and Credit*, 1952.
4. Statement on setting the silver content of a US silver dollar comes from Wikipedia.
5. Amount of US currency held abroad comes from *The Use and Counterfeiting of United States Currency Abroad, Part 3*, United States Treasury Department, September 2006.
6. Milton Friedman quote comes from Milton Friedman and Anna Jacobson Schwartz's *A Monetary History of the United States, 1867–1960.*
7. Adam Smith quote regarding the gold standard comes from his *The Wealth of Nations.* Winston Churchill quote comes from Liaquat Ahamed's *Lords of Finance.* Original source of the Warren Buffet quote is unknown.
8. US money supply, reserve balances, and similar statistics come from Table H.6: "Money Stock Measures," Table H.3: "Aggregate

Reserves of Depository Institutions and the Monetary Base," and statistical release H.4.1, Board of Governors of the Federal System, January 2, 2015.

9. Information for the behavior of the money supply during the Great Depression comes from Milton Friedman and Anna Jacobson Schwartz's *A Monetary History of the United States, 1867–1960.*
10. Some of the information on the Federal Reserve (and various quotes) come from *The Federal Reserve System Purposes and Functions*, Board of Governors of the Federal Reserve System.
11. Data for inflation during the Civil War and World Wars I and II come from Milton Friedman and Anna Jacobson Schwartz's *A Monetary History of the United States, 1867–1960.*
12. I read Milton Friedman's quote, "Substantial inflation is always and everywhere a monetary phenomenon," in his *Money Mischief*, but I am not sure of the original source.
13. Discussion on the money supply over an extended period of time uses 1929 data from Table A-1, column 9, of Milton Friedman and Anna Jacobson Schwartz's *A Monetary History of the United States, 1867–1960.* Data from 1959 to 2013 comes from Table H.6, Federal Reserve.

Chapter 5

1. Justice Oliver Wendell Holmes quote is found in Thomas Sowell's *Basic Economics.*
2. Information on government spending for consumption and investment comes from Tables 1.1.5, 1.1.10, 3.2, and 3.15.5, National Income and Product Accounts, Bureau of Economic Analysis.
3. Table detailing the government consumption and investment spending by category comes from Table 3.15.5, National Income and Product Accounts, Bureau of Economic Analysis.
4. Government spending for social benefits comes from Table 3.12, National Income and Product Accounts, Bureau of Economic Analysis.

5. Federal nondefense discretionary spending in dollars and as a share of the economy comes from Tables 1.1.5 and 1.1.10, National Income and Product Accounts, Bureau of Economic Analysis. As another point of reference, 2015 Budget Table S-4 shows $522 billion for discretionary nondefense spending, *Fiscal Year 2015 Budget of the US Government.*
6. Much of the detail of US government spending for 2013 comes from Tables 28.1 and 29.1, *Fiscal Year 2015 Budget of the US Government*, Office of Management and Budget.
7. Congressional Research Service estimate of war-related spending comes from Amy Belasco, *The Cost of Iraq, Afghanistan, and Other Global War on Terror Operations Since 9/11*, Congressional Research Service, March 29, 2011.
8. Data on military spending by country come from *The Economist: Pocket World in Figures*, 2012 ed., and *The Military Balance 2010*, Center for Arms Control and Non-Proliferation.
9. Graph on federal social spending as a percent of GDP based on data from Table 3.12, National Income and Product Accounts, Bureau of Economic Analysis.
10. Much of the information on Social Security and Medicare comes from *Status of the Social Security and Medicare Programs: A Summary of the 2014 Annual Reports*, Social Security and Medicare Boards of Trustees; and Table 5.A1, *Annual Statistical Supplement, 2014*, Social Security Administration.
11. Description of the calculation of social security benefits primarily based on information from the *Social Security Policy Options*, Congressional Budget Office, July 2010; and *Your Retirement Benefit: How It Is Figured*, Social Security Administration, January 2014, http://www.socialsecurity.gov/pubs/EN-05-10070.pdf.
12. Poverty data comes from Table B.2 of Carmen DeNavas-Walt, Bernadette D. Proctor, and Jessica C. Smith, *Income, Poverty, and Health Insurance Coverage in the United States: 2012*, Current

Population Reports, US Census Bureau, US Government Printing Office: Washington, DC, 2013, pp. 60–245.

13. Certain statistics on the increasing cost of the Social Security Disability program come from *The 2014 Annual Report of the Board of Trustees of the Federal Old-Age and Survivors Insurance and Federal Disability Insurance Trust Funds*; and Joyce Manchester and Jae G. Song, *What Can We Learn from Analyzing Historical Data on Social Security Entitlements*, Social Security Bulletin, vol. 71, no. 4, 2011.
14. Medicare statistics come from *Status of the Social Security and Medicare Programs: A Summary of the 2014 Annual Reports*, Social Security and Medicare Boards of Trustees.
15. Data on grants to state and local governments come from Table 3.24U: "Federal Grants-in-Aid to State and Local Governments," National Income and Product Accounts, Bureau of Economic Analysis.

Chapter 6

1. Data on total government spending in aggregate and per household derived from Table H1: "Households by Type and Tenure of Householder for Selected Characteristics: 2013," US Census Bureau; and Table 3.1, National Income and Product Accounts, Bureau of Economic Analysis.
2. Sources of total current government receipts come from Table 3.1: "Government Current Receipts and Expenditures," National Income and Product Accounts, Bureau of Economic Analysis.
3. OECD international statistics come from *OECD Factbook 2014: Economic, Environmental and Social Statistics*, OECD Publishing.
4. Data for graphs depicting federal, state, and local government receipts come from Tables 3.2, 3.20, and 3.21, National Income and Product Accounts, Bureau of Economic Analysis.
5. Details on the history of the federal income tax come from the Tax Foundation and from Table 23: "US Individual Income Tax: Personal Exemptions and Lowest and Highest Bracket Tax Rates, and Tax Base for Regular Tax, Tax Years 1913–2012," Internal Revenue Service.

6. Historic return information comes from Table 1: "All Individual Income Tax Returns: Sources of Income and Tax Items, Tax Years 1913–2005," Internal Revenue Service.
7. Information on personal income taxes as a percent of GDP comes from Table 2.3, Office of Management and Budget.
8. AMT statistics derived from *Present Law and Background Relating to the Individual Alternative Minimum Tax*, Joint Committee on Taxation, March 5, 2007.
9. Source of international tax rates comes from Table II.1: "Corporate income tax rate," Organisation for Economic Co-operation and Development, 2013.
10. Information on cash held overseas comes from Moody's Investors Service, https://www.moodys.com/research/Moodys-US-companies-cash-pile-grows-10-in-2012-to--PR_268757.
11. Graph of federal receipts by source derived from OMB Table 2.1: "Receipts by source."
12. W. Kurt Hauser quote comes from "The Tax and Revenue Equation," *The Wall Street Journal*, March 25, 1993.
13. "Federal Income Tax Receipts Versus Top Tax Rate" graph derived from Table 2.3: "Receipts by Source as a Percentage of GDP," Office of Management and Budget; and Table 23: "US Individual Income Tax: Personal Exemptions and Lowest and Highest Bracket Tax Rates, and Tax Base for Regular Tax, Tax Years 1913–2012," Internal Revenue Service.
14. Ibn Khaldun quote comes from Arthur B. Laffer and Stephen Moore's *Return to Prosperity.*
15. Adam Smith quote comes from his *The Wealth of Nations.*
16. Categories of "tax expenditures" comes from *Fiscal Year 2014 Analytical Perspectives, Budget of the Unites States,* Office of Management and Budget.
17. Arthur B. Laffer tax proposal comes from Arthur B. Laffer and Stephen Moore's *Return to Prosperity.*
18. Rand Paul tax proposal from www.randpaul.com/issue/taxes.

Chapter 7

1. US national health-care spending statistics come primarily from Centers for Medicare and Medicaid Services. Spending in 2013 comes from http://www.cms.gov/Research-Statistics-Data-and-Systems/Statistics-Trends-and-Reports/NationalHealthExpendData/Downloads/highlights.pdf. Historical data and projection come from http://www.cms.gov/Research-Statistics-Data-and-Systems/Statistics-Trends-and-Reports/NationalHealthExpendData/Downloads/Proj2013.pdf and http://www.cms.gov/Research-Statistics-Data-and-Systems/Statistics-Trends-and-Reports/NationalHealthExpendData/NationalHealthAccountsHistorical.html.
2. International health-care data come from *OECD Factbook 2014: Economic, Environmental and Social Statistics*, 2014, OECD Publishing.
3. CBO hypothetical projections and graphs on US health-care spending come from *The Long-Term Outlook for Health Care Spending*, Congressional Budget Office, November 2007.
4. Statement that per-capital spending on health care is roughly double for a person over the age of sixty-five is derived from various sources.
5. OMB estimate that as much as $700 billion of health-care spending does little or nothing to improve patients' health comes from the *Budget of the US Government, Fiscal 2011.*
6. FOLFIRINOX study comes from "FOLFIRINOX versus Gemcitabine for Metastatic Pancreatic Cancer," *The New England Journal of Medicine*, May 12, 2011. Estimate of relative cost of FOLFIRINOX from the American Society of Clinical Oncology, http://meetinglibrary.asco.org/print/570169.
7. Study comparing Avastin to Lucentis comes from "Ranibizumab and Bevacizumab for Neovasccular Age-Related Macular Degeneration," *The New England Journal of Medicine*, May 19, 2011.
8. *New York Times* reference to the relative cost of Avastin and Lucentis comes from an editorial in the *New York Times*, May 17, 2011.
9. Estimate on Medicare savings for using Avastin compared to Lucentis comes from *Review of Medicare Part B: Avastin and Lucentis Treatments for Age-Related Macular Degeneration*, Office of Inspector

General, Department of Health and Human Services, September 2011.

10. Cost of Avastin for treating breast cancer comes from an op-ed by Frederick C. Tucker, *New York Times*, May 25, 2011.
11. Cost of various cancer drugs comes from Stephen S. Hall's "The Cost of Living," *New York* magazine, October 28, 2013.
12. Recommendation against PSA screening comes from *Talking with Your Patients about Screening for Prostate Cancer*, US Preventative Services Task Force, May 2012.
13. Cost of American births comes from Elizabeth Rosenthal's "American Way of Birth: Costliest in the World," *New York Times*, July 1, 2013.
14. Example of cost of hip replacement surgery comes from Elisabeth Rosenthal's "For Medical Tourists, Simple Math," *New York Times*, August 4, 2013.
15. International obesity statistics come from *OECD Factbook 2013: Economic, Environmental and Social Statistics*, 2013, OECD Publishing. doi: 10.1787/factbook-2013-en.
16. US obesity statistics come from *Health, United States, 2012: With Special Feature on Emergency Care*, National Center for Health Statistics, Hyattsville, MD, 2013.
17. Statistics on diabetes come from "National Diabetes Fact Sheet," the Centers for Disease Control and Prevention, 2011, http://www.cdc.gov/diabetes/pubs/pdf/ndfs_2011.pdf.
18. OMB estimate of the cost of treating obesity and related diseases comes from the *Budget of the US Government, Fiscal 2011.*
19. Incidence of nonalcoholic fatty liver disease comes from Anahad O'Connor's "Threat Grows From Liver Illness Tied to Obesity," *New York Times*, June 14, 2014.
20. Statistics on the prevalence of smoking in the United States come from the Centers for Disease Control and Prevention website, http://www.cdc.gov/; and *Health, United States, 2012: With Special Feature on Emergency Care*, National Center for Health Statistics, Hyattsville, MD, 2013.

21. International smoking statistics are 2010 data from "Global Trends and Projections for Tobacco Smoking, 2000-2025," World Health Organization.
22. Department of Health and Human Services quote and information come from "The Health Consequences of Smoking—50 Years of Progress: A Report of the Surgeon General." Office on Smoking and Health, National Center for Chronic Disease Prevention and Health Promotion, Centers for Disease Control and Prevention, US Department of Health and Human Services: Atlanta, GA, 2014.
23. *New York Times* article on companies' policies toward smoking comes from Reed Abelson's "The Smokers' Surcharge," *New York Times*, November 17, 2011.
24. Spending on Medicare comes from Center for Medicare and Medicaid Services.
25. Information on New York State spending on Medicaid comes from the 2012 New York State budget.
26. Information on Westchester County spending on Medicaid comes from *Westchester County Proposed 2014 Budget*, November 15, 2013.
27. ACA enrollment information (including for New York State) comes from *Health Insurance Marketplaces 2015 Open Enrollment Period: March Enrollment Report*, Department of Health and Human Services, March 10, 2015, http://aspe.hhs.gov/health/reports/2015/MarketPlaceEnrollment/Mar2015/ib_2015mar_enrollment.pdf. See also http://healthcare.mckinsey.com/individual-market-enrollment-updated-view.
28. Information on the growth in Medicaid enrollment and insurance coverage comes from http://aspe.hhs.gov/health/reports/2015/MedicaidEnrollment/ib_MedicaidEnrollment.pdf and http://aspe.hhs.gov/health/reports/2015/uninsured_change/ib_uninsured_change.pdf, March 16, 2015.
29. Cost and revenue estimates for the ACA primarily come from *CBO's Estimate of the Net Budgetary Impact of the Affordable Care Act's Health Insurance Coverage Provisions Has Not Changed Much over Time*, posted

May 14, 2013; and "Letter to the Honorable John Boehner Providing an Estimate for H.R. 6079, the Repeal of Obamacare Act," July 24, 2012.

30. Data on New York residents purchasing individual health insurance prior to the impact of the ACA come from Roni Caryn Rabin and Reed Abelson's "Health Plan Cost for New Yorkers Set to Fall 50 percent," *New York Times*, July 16, 2013
31. Cost of New York insurance plans under the ACA comes from https://nystateofhealth.ny.gov/individual/searchAnonymousPlan/search, accessed April 10, 2015.

Chapter 8

1. Ronald Reagan quote comes from Notablequotes.com.
2. Much of the scientific data related to global warming comes from Working Group I contribution to the IPCC Fifth Assessment Report: *Climate Change 2013: The Physical Science Basis* (Summary for Policymakers), Intergovernmental Panel on Climate Change, September 27, 2013.
3. Survey of scientific views on global warming comes from John Cook, Dana Nuccitelli, Sarah A Green, Mark Richardson, Bärbel Winkler, Rob Painting, Robert Way, Peter Jacobs, and Andrew Skuce's "Quantifying the Consensus on Anthropogenic Global Warming in the Scientific Literature," *Environmental Research Letters*, IOP Publishing, 2013.
4. Pew Research Center poll on global warming comes from http://www.people-press.org/files/legacy-pdf/10-15-12 percent20Global percent-20Warming percent20Release.pdf.

Chapter 9

1. Ace Greenberg quote I've heard and seen many places, with the *D* referring to *desperate*, *deep desire*, or *determined*, any one of which adequately makes the point.

2. Reference to Emmanuel Saez and the level of income required to be in the top 1 percent of earners comes from his *Striking it Richer: The Evolution of Top Incomes in the United States* (updated with 2012 preliminary estimates), September 3, 2013.
3. Share of top income earners by occupation comes from Jon Bakija, Adam Cole, and Bradley T. Heim's *Jobs and Income Growth of Top Earners and the Causes of Changing Income Inequality: Evidence from US Tax Return Data*, April 2012.
4. According to Willie Sutton in his autobiography, he never said "That's where the money is." Rather that quote was the work of an enterprising reporter, and it took off from there. This is per *Where the Money Was*, first published by Viking Press: New York, 1976.
5. Compensation of Richard Fuld and Angelo Mozilo comes from http://www.forbes.com/lists/2008/12/lead_bestbosses08_CEO-Compensation_CompTotDisp.html.
6. Bernard Mandeville quotes come from his *The Fable of the Bees, or, Private Vices, Public Benefits*, vol. 1, 1705, 1723.
7. Leon Black party description and quote come from *New York Times Deal Book*, August 18, 2011.
8. Share of taxes paid by income group comes from *The Distribution of Household Income and Federal Taxes, 2011*, Congressional Budget Office, www.cbo.gov/publication/49440, November 12, 2014. Supplemental information also used. Related graphs derived from the same.
9. Tax Policy Center study is Rachel Johnson, James Nunns, Jeffrey Rohaly, Eric Toder, and Roberton Williams, *Why Some Tax Units Pay No Income Tax*, Urban-Brookings Tax Policy Center, July 2011.
10. State tax information comes from *Who Pays? A Distributional Analysis of the Tax Systems in All 50 States*, Institute on Taxation and Economic Policy, January 2013.
11. Share of total New York State income taxes paid by income decile comes from *Analysis of 2010 Personal Income Tax Returns, Profile of Income, Deductions, Credits and Tax*, Office of Tax Policy Analysis,

New York State Department of Taxation and Finance, September 2013.

12. *Wall Street Journal* data on how much workers keep after taxes come from Alistair MacDonald's "Europeans Found Taxed Heaviest: Russia's Rich Have Lightest Load," *Wall Street Journal*, June 13, 2011.
13. American charitable giving in 2009 comes from the Center on Wealth and Philanthropy as reported in January/February 2010 edition of *Advancing Philanthropy* magazine.
14. US giving levels compared to other nations comes from *International Comparisons of Charitable Giving*, Charities Aid Foundation, November 2006.
15. Detail on US charitable giving by type comes from *Giving USA 2012: The Annual Report on Philanthropy for the Year 2011.*
16. US giving by income level and quote come from *The Chronicle of Philanthropy*, August 19, 2012.
17. Information on the Carnegie Corporation comes from its website, http://www.carnegie.org/.
18. Information on the Bill & Melinda Gates Foundation comes from its website, www.gatesfoundation.org, accessed on April 24, 2014.
19. Information on the Open Society Foundations comes from its website, http://www.soros.org/about/mission-values.

Chapter 10

1. Most US poverty statistics come from Carmen DeNavas-Walt and Bernadette D. Proctor, *Income and Poverty in the United States: 2013*, Current Population Reports, US Census Bureau, US Government Printing Office: Washington, DC, 2014, pp. 60–249.
2. Information on the Heritage Foundation comes from its website, http://www.heritage.org/about, accessed May 10, 2013.
3. CBO 2006 estimate of federal transfers comes from *The Distribution of Federal Spending and Taxes in 2006*, Congressional Budget Office, November 2013.

4. Much of the information related to federal spending in fiscal 2012 comes from Table 31-1, *Fiscal Year 2014 Budget of the US Government*, Office of Management and Budget.
5. Unemployment insurance information comes from *Unemployment Compensation: Federal-State Partnership*, Office of Unemployment Insurance Division of Legislation, US Department of Labor, April 2013.
6. Data on unemployment benefits paid comes from *UI Outlook, FY 2015 Budget Midsession Review*, US Department of Labor, http://workforcesecurity.doleta.gov/unemploy/pdf/MSR.pdf.
7. Projected increase in Medicaid spending comes from *Growth in Means-Tested Programs and Tax Credits for Low-Income Households*, Congressional Budget Office, February 2013.
8. Medicaid statistics come primarily from Tables I.16 and III.3, *2014 CMS Statistics*, US Department of Health and Human Services, http://www.cms.gov/Research-Statistics-Data-and-Systems/Statistics-Trends-and-Reports/CMS-Statistics-Reference-Booklet/2014.html.
9. Returns with EITC come from the Internal Revenue Service, http://www.irs.gov/Individuals/Earned-Income-Tax-Credit-Statistics.
10. EITC and Child Tax Credit impact on poverty comes from Center on Budget and Policy Priorities, http://www.cbpp.org/research/policy-basics-the-earned-income-tax-credit, updated January 20, 2015.
11. IRS data on the Child Tax Credit come from Table 3.3: "All Returns: Tax Liability, Tax Credits, and Tax Payments, by Size of Adjusted Gross Income, Tax Year 2012," http://www.irs.gov/uac/SOI-Tax-Stats-Individual-Income-Tax-Returns-Publication-1304-(Complete-Report).
12. Eligibility for SSI payments comes from www.socialseccurity.gov, accessed May 21, 2013.
13. Statistics on the SSI program come from *Annual Report of the Supplemental Security Income Program*, Social Security Administration, 2012.

14. TANF quote comes from "TANF Fact Sheet," Office of Family Assistance, updated April 2009
15. Purposes of TANF come from "About TANF," US Department of Health and Human Services, accessed May 23, 2013.
16. Statistics on TANF come from Table A.1: "Federal TANF and State MOE Expenditures Summary by ACF-196 Spending Category, FY 2011," *Caseload Data 2012*, Office of Family Assistance, US Department of Health and Human Services, March 1, 2013; and *Characteristics and Financial Circumstances of TANF Recipients, Fiscal Year 2010*, Office of Family Assistance, US Department of Health and Human Services.
17. SNAP data come from *Characteristics of Supplemental Nutrition Assistance Program Participation and Cost*, the United States Department of Agriculture, http://www.fns.usda.gov/sites/default/files/pd/SNAPsummary.pdf.
18. SNAP budget information comes from Table 31-1, *Fiscal Year 2014 Budget of the US Government*.
19. Participant data for WIC come from *WIC Program Participation and Costs*, United States Department of Agriculture, June 6, 2014.
20. Cost of the School Lunch Program comes from "National School Lunch Program fact sheet," the USDA website, accessed May 29, 2013.
21. Description of Section 8 housing program primarily comes from HUD fact sheets for Housing Choice Vouchers and Project-Based Vouchers Program.
22. Detail of households receiving HUD assistance comes from *Fiscal Years 2012–2013 Annual Performance Plan*, US Department of Housing and Urban Development.
23. Information on Pell grants and other federal aid for higher education primarily comes from *Federal Student Aid Annual Report—FY 2012*, United States Department of Education.
24. Information on Title I grants comes from *Guide to US Department of Education Programs*, Office of Communications and Outreach, US

Department of Education, Washington, D.C., 2012. By the way, that guide lists sixty-nine separate programs.

25. Demographic information on Mamaroneck and Yonkers school districts comes from http://rocdocs.democratandchronicle.com/schools/district, accessed March 6, 2013.
26. Enrollment and financial data for Mamaroneck and Yonkers school districts come from school board reports. State aid data derived from New York State Education Department website, https://eservices.nysed.gov/publicsams, accessed March 4, 2013.
27. Spending gap for education in New York State comes from *Confronting the Opportunity Gap*, Alliance for Quality Education and the Public Policy and Education Fund, February 28, 2013.
28. Data on the "net price" of college come from http://trends.collegeboard.org/sites/default/files/college-pricing-2013-full-report.pdf.
29. Information on Head Start comes from Department of Health and Human Services, http://eclkc.ohs.acf.hhs.gov/hslc/mr/factsheets/docs/hs-program-fact-sheet-2012.pdf and http://www.acf.hhs.gov/programs/ohs/about/head-start, accessed June 7, 2013.
30. Information on Child Care and Development Fund comes from *Child Care and Development Fund Fact Sheet*, Office of Child Care, Administration for Children and Families, US Department of Health and Human Services.
31. Information on Community Development Block Grants comes from the HUD website, http://portal.hud.gov/hudportal/HUD?src=/program_offices/comm_planning/communitydevelopment, accessed June 7, 2013.
32. Number of Americans living in poverty and some 2011 income information comes from *Income, Poverty, and Health Insurance Coverage in the United States: 2011*, US Census Bureau.
33. Information on the Cato Institute comes from its website, http://www.cato.org/about.
34. Cato Institute study on welfare benefits comes from Michael Tanner and Charles Hughes's *The Work versus Welfare Trade-Off: 2013, An Analysis of the Total Level of Welfare Benefits by State*, Cato Institute.

35. CBO study on government benefits comes from *Effective Marginal Tax Rates for Low- and Moderate- Income Workers*, Congressional Budget Office, November 2012.
36. SNAP descriptive quote comes from Mark Strayer, Esa Eslami, and Joshua Leftin, *Characteristics of Supplemental Nutrition Assistance Program Households: Fiscal Year 2011*, Office of Research and Analysis, Food and Nutrition Service, US Department of Agriculture, Alexandria, VA: 2012.
37. TANF descriptive quote comes from "TANF Fact Sheet," Office of Family Assistance, updated April 2009.
38. Housing assistance descriptive quotes come from *Fiscal Years 2012–2013 Annual Performance Plan*, US Department of Housing and Urban Development.

Chapter 11

1. Charles Abrams quote from Wikipedia.
2. Cato Institute study on corporate welfare comes from Tad DeHaven's *Corporate Welfare in the Federal Budget*, Cato Institute Policy Analysis no. 703, July 25, 2012.
3. Figure on tax expenditures targeted to business comes from *Fiscal Year 2014 Analytical Perspectives: Budget of the United States*, Office of Management and Budget.
4. Estimate of cost of the TARP comes from *Report on the Troubled Asset Relief Program—March 2015*, Congressional Budget Office, March 18, 2015, http://www.cbo.gov/publication/50034.
5. Information on the support of the GSEs comes from *Conservator's Report on the Enterprises' Financial Performance, First Quarter 2013*, and *Quarterly Performance report of the Housing GSEs, First Quarter 2015*, Federal Housing Finance Agency, http://www.fhfa.gov/AboutUs/Reports/ReportDocuments/PerformanceReportofHousingGSEs-1Q2015.pdf.
6. Various quotes and information on Solyndra come from Solyndra press release dated March 20, 2009: http://www.solyndra.com/2009/

03/us-department/; and Solyndra press release dated August 31, 2011: http://www.solyndra.com/2011/09/solyndra-suspends-operations-to-evaluate-reorganization-options/. *Washington Post* article from http://www.washingtonpost.com/solyndra-politics-infused-obama-energy-programs/2011/12/14/gIQA4HllHP_story.html.

Chapter 12

1. Income data comes from Carmen DeNavas-Walt and Bernadette D. Proctor, *Income and Poverty in the United States: 2013*, Current Population Reports, US Census Bureau, US Government Printing Office: Washington, DC, 2014, pp. 60–249; and *The Distribution of Household Income and Federal Taxes, 2010*, Congressional Budget Office, December 2013. The graph data is from the Census Bureau.
2. Share of aggregate income data comes from Table H-3: "Mean Household Income Received by Each Fifth and Top Percent, All Races: 1967 to 2013," US Census Bureau.
3. Gini Index descriptive quote comes from the CIA *World Factbook*, accessed July 25, 2013.
4. Comparison of richest 10 percent of the population to the poorest 10 percent of the population by country comes from the CIA *World Factbook*, accessed April 16, 2015. The data are somewhat dated, and while believed to be representative, they may not be comparable across countries due to differences in certain definitions and data-collection methods.
5. Gross national income per capita and median household income information for selected countries are derived from *OECD Factbook 2013: Economic, Environmental and Social Statistics*, OECD Publishing, 2012; and "Household Income" in *Society at a Glance 2011: OECD Social Indicators*, OECD Publishing, 2011.
6. Pew Research Center data survey results and quote come from *The Lost Decade of the Middle Class*, Social and Demographic Trends, Pew Research Center, August 22, 2012.

7. Treasury report on income mobility comes from *Income Mobility in the US from 1996 to 2005*, Report of the Department of the Treasury, November 13, 2007.
8. Chetty, Hendren, Kline, and Saez study information comes from their *Where Is the Land of Opportunity? The Geography of Intergenerational Mobility in the United States*, January 2014. Further author information: Raj Chetty, Harvard University and NBER; Nathaniel Hendren, Harvard University and NBER; Patrick Kline, UC-Berkeley and NBER; Emmanuel Saez, UC-Berkeley and NBER.
9. IMF study on correlation between income equality and economic growth comes from Andrew G. Berg and Jonathan D. Ostry's "Inequality and Unsustainable Growth: Two Sides of the Same Coin?" IMF Staff Discussion Note, April 8, 2011.
10. Data on percentage of the workforce in agriculture comes from *The 20th Century Transformation of US Agriculture and Farm Policy/EIB-3*, Economic Research Service, US Department of Agriculture.
11. Household debt, consumer credit, and debt service ratio data come primarily from Table L.101, "Financial Accounts of the United States," Federal Reserve Board. Disposable personal income comes from Table 2.1: "Personal Income and Its Disposition," Bureau of Economic Analysis.
12. List of potential causes of income equality comes from Jon Bakija, Adam Cole, and Bradley T. Heim's *Jobs and Income Growth of Top Earners and the Causes of Changing Income Inequality: Evidence from US Tax Return Data*, April 2012.
13. Alfred Marshall quote comes from his *Principles of Economics, Complete and Unabridged*, 8th ed. I first saw a reference to this in Sherwin Rosen's "The Economics of Superstars."
14. Biographical information for Bill Gates and Mark Zuckerberg comes from Wikipedia.
15. Income information by level of education comes from Carmen DeNavas-Walt, Bernadette D. Proctor, and Jessica C. Smith, *Income,*

Poverty, and Health Insurance Coverage in the United States: 2010, Current Population Reports, US Census Bureau, US Government Printing Office: Washington, DC, 2011, pp. 60–239.

16. National high school graduation rate information is primarily US Department of Education data from *Building a Grad Nation: Progress and Challenge in Ending the High School Dropout Epidemic*, Annual Update, April 2014. *Building a Grad Nation* is a report by the combined efforts of Civic Enterprises, the Everyone Graduates Center at the School of Education at Johns Hopkins University, America's Promise Alliance, and the Alliance for Excellent Education. The Grad Nation campaign was launched by America's Promise Alliance (spearheaded by General Colin Powell and his wife, Alma Powell) with the goals of "achieving a 90 percent graduation rate nationwide by 2020, with no high school graduating less than 80 percent of its students, and regaining America's standing as first in the world in college completion" (from www.americaspromise.org).
17. Department of Education data on college attendance rates are taken from Table 211 of T. D. Snyder and S. A. Dillow, *Digest of Education Statistics 2011 (NCES 2012-001)*, National Center for Education Statistics, Institute of Education Sciences, US Department of Education, Washington, DC, 2012. The statistics here are calculated differently from those in the *Building a Grad Nation* report, and thus they are not directly comparable.
18. *Newsweek* list of top schools for low-income students comes from http://www.newsweek.com/high-schools/beating-odds-2014.
19. Comparison of graduation rates for various school districts in New York comes from the New York State Education Department.
20. Demographic information by zip code comes from American FactFinder, US Census Bureau, http://factfinder.census.gov/faces/nav/jsf/pages/index.xhtml.
21. Marital data comes from *Marital Status and Health: United States, 1999–2002*, Centers for Disease Control and Prevention.

22. Birth data comes from J. A. Martin, B. E. Hamilton, S. J. Ventura, M. J. K. Osterman, and T. J. Mathews, *Births: Final Data for 2011*, National vital statistics reports, vol. 62, no. 1; National Center for Health Statistics, Hyattsville, MD, 2013.
23. Charles Murray data and quotes come from his *Coming Apart: The State of White America 1960–2010*, Crown Forum, 2012. Quotes specifically come from pp. 57–59.

Chapter 13

1. John F. Kennedy quote from http://www.ushistory.org/documents/ask-not.htm.
2. Jonathan Haidt moral discussion comes from his *The Righteous Mind: Why Good People Are Divided by Politics and Religion*, Pantheon Books, 2012. Jonathan Haidt is a professor of psychology at the University of Virginia and a visiting professor of business ethics at New York University's Stern School of Business.
3. Examples of infanticide or elderly abandonment taken from Jared Diamond's *The World Until Yesterday: What Can we Learn from Traditional Societies?*
4. Information on giving levels at the Bronx Zoo comes from its website, http://bronxzoo.com/membership.
5. Information on giving levels at the Metropolitan Museum of Art comes from its website, http://www.metmuseum.org/give-and-join.
6. Scott Adams on taxing the rich comes from his "How to Tax the Rich," *Wall Street Journal*, January 29–30, 2011.
7. Information on CARE taken from its website, https://my.care.org/site/SPageServer?pagename=Landing_Partners_for_Change.
8. Mae West and Woody Allen quotes come from various sources (and slightly different versions of the quotes).
9. USGA handicap information comes from *The USGA Handicap System: With the USGA Course Rating System and USGA Handicap Decisions, Effective January 1, 2012–December 31, 2015.*

Chapter 14

1. Frederic Bastiat quote comes from Robert L. Heilbroner's *The Worldly Philosophers.*
2. Details of the report of the National Commission on Fiscal Responsibility and Reform can be found on its website, http://www.fiscalcommission.gov/.
3. Republican House budget plan information comes from *A Balanced Budget for a Stronger America*, Fiscal Year 2016 Budget Resolution, House Budget Committee, March 2015, http://budget.house.gov/uploadedfiles/fy16budget.pdf.
4. CBO analysis of President Obama's budget comes from *An Analysis of the President's 2016 Budget*, Congressional Budget Office, March 2015.
6. Historical deficit information comes from Tables 1.1 and 1.2, Office of Management and Budget.
7. CBO estimate of the impact of the recession on the deficit comes from "Letter from Douglas W. Emendorf, Director, Congressional Budget Office, to Honorable Chris Van Hollen," October 4, 2011.
8. CBO deficit projections come from *The 2015 Long-Term Budget Outlook*, June 2015, and supplemental information, Congressional Budget Office.
9. Capital gains information derived from the Table 1.4: "All Returns: Sources of Income, Adjustments, and Tax Items, by size of Adjusted Gross Income, Tax Year 2008," Internal Revenue Service.
10. US carbon emissions come from the Environmental Protection Agency, http://www.epa.gov/climatechange/ghgemissions/usinventoryreport.html.
11. CBO deficit-reduction studies come from *Options for Reducing the Deficit: 2015 to 2024*, November 2014, Congressional Budget Office; and *Options for Reducing the Deficit: 2014 to 2023*, November 2013, Congressional Budget Office.
12. Data on personal income tax receipts come from Table 2.1: "Receipts by Source: 1934–2020," Office of Management and Budget.

13. Health-care tax expenditure data come from Table 14-1, *Analytical Perspectives, Budget of the United States Government, Fiscal Year 2016*, Office of Management and Budget.
14. CBO cost estimate of President Obama's proposed tax changes "supporting middle class and working families" comes from *An Analysis of the President's 2016 Budget*, Congressional Budget Office, March 2015.
15. Al Gore quote comes from speech at New York University Law School, September 16, 2001, as referenced in Arthur B. Laffer and Stephen Moore's *Return to Prosperity.*
16. Figures on US corporate cash held overseas come from press release, Moody's Investors Service, March 18, 2013.
17. Estimate for corporate tax expenditures from Table 14-2A, *Analytical Perspectives, Budget of the United States Government, Fiscal Year 2016*, Office of Management and Budget.
18. Long-term budget projections come from "Summary Data for the Extended Alternative Fiscal Scenario," Separate File, Congressional Budget Office, http://www.cbo.gov/publication/45308.
19. My estimate for how much top tax rates would have to increase to raise $150 billion in tax revenue is derived from CBO estimates from *Options for Reducing the Deficit: 2015 to 2024*, Congressional Budget Office, November 2014.

Appendix

"I, Pencil" by Leonard E. Read, 1958

I am a lead pencil—the ordinary wooden pencil familiar to all boys and girls and adults who can read and write.[1]

Writing is both my vocation and my avocation; that's all I do. You may wonder why I should write a genealogy. Well, to begin with, my story is interesting. And, next, I am a mystery—more so than a tree or a sunset or even a flash of lightning. But, sadly, I am taken for granted by those who use me, as if I were a mere incident and without background. This supercilious attitude relegates me to the level of the commonplace. This is a species of the grievous error in which mankind cannot too long persist without peril. For, as a wise man observed, "We are perishing for want of wonder, not for want of wonders."[2]

I, Pencil, simple though I appear to be, merit your wonder and awe, a claim I shall attempt to prove. In fact, if you can understand me—no, that's too much to ask of anyone—if you can become aware of the miraculousness which I symbolize, you can help save the freedom mankind is so unhappily losing. I have a profound lesson to teach. And I can teach this lesson better than can an automobile or an airplane or a mechanical dishwasher because—well, because I am seemingly so simple. Simple? Yet, not a single person on the face of this earth knows how to make me. This sounds fantastic, doesn't it? Especially when it is realized that there are about one and one-half billion of my kind produced in the U. S. A. each year.

Pick me up and look me over. What do you see? Not much meets the eye—there's some wood, lacquer, the printed labeling, graphite lead, a bit of metal, and an eraser. Just as you cannot trace your family tree back very far, so is it impossible for me to name and explain all my antecedents. But I would like to suggest enough of them to impress upon you the richness and complexity of my background.

My family tree begins with what in fact is a tree, a cedar of straight grain that grows in Northern California and Oregon. Now contemplate all the saws and trucks and rope and the countless other gear used in harvesting and carting the cedar logs to the railroad siding. Think of all the persons and the numberless skills that went into their fabrication: the mining of ore, the making of steel and its refinement into saws, axes, motors; the growing of hemp and bringing it through all the stages to heavy and strong rope; the logging camps with their beds and mess halls, the cookery and the raising of all the foods. Why, untold thousands of persons had a hand in every cup of coffee the loggers drink!

The logs are shipped to a mill in San Leandro, California. Can you imagine the individuals who make flat cars and rails and railroad engines and who construct and install the communication systems incidental thereto? These legions are among my antecedents.

Consider the millwork in San Leandro. The cedar logs are cut into small, pencil-length slats less than one-fourth of an inch in thickness. These are kiln dried and then tinted for the same reason women put rouge on their faces. People prefer that I look pretty, not a pallid white. The slats are waxed and kiln dried again. How many skills went into the making of the tint and the kilns, into supplying the heat, the light and power, the belts, motors, and all the other things a mill requires? Sweepers in the mill among my ancestors? Yes, and included are the men who poured the concrete for the dam of a Pacific Gas & Electric Company hydroplant which supplies the mill's power!

Don't overlook the ancestors present and distant who have a hand in transporting sixty carloads of slats across the nation from California to Wilkes-Barre!

Complicated Machinery

Once in the pencil factory—$4,000,000 in machinery and building, all capital accumulated by thrifty and saving parents of mine—each slat is given eight grooves by a complex machine, after which another machine lays leads in every other slat, applies glue, and places another slat atop—a lead sandwich, so to speak. Seven brothers and I are mechanically carved from this "wood-clinched" sandwich.

My "lead" itself—it contains no lead at all—is complex. The graphite is mined in Ceylon. Consider these miners and those who make their many tools and the makers of the paper sacks in which the graphite is shipped and those who make the string that ties the sacks and those who put them aboard ships and those who make the ships. Even the lighthouse keepers along the way assisted in my birth—and the harbor pilots.

The graphite is mixed with clay from Mississippi in which ammonium hydroxide is used in the refining process. Then wetting agents are added such as sulfonated tallow—animal fats chemically reacted with sulfuric acid. After passing through numerous machines, the mixture finally appears as endless extrusions—as from a sausage grinder—cut to size, dried, and baked for several hours at 1,850 degrees Fahrenheit. To increase their strength and smoothness the leads are then treated with a hot mixture which includes candelilla wax from Mexico, paraffin wax, and hydrogenated natural fats.

My cedar receives six coats of lacquer. Do you know all of the ingredients of lacquer? Who would think that the growers of castor beans and the refiners of castor oil are a part of it? They are. Why, even the processes by which the lacquer is made a beautiful yellow involves the skills of more persons than one can enumerate!

Observe the labeling. That's a film formed by applying heat to carbon black mixed with resins. How do you make resins and what, pray, is carbon black?

My bit of metal—the ferrule—is brass. Think of all the persons who mine zinc and copper and those who have the skills to make shiny sheet brass from these products of nature. Those black rings on my ferrule are black nickel. What is black nickel and how is it applied? The complete story of why the center of my ferrule has no black nickel on it would take pages to explain.

Then there's my crowning glory, inelegantly referred to in the trade as "the plug," the part man uses to erase the errors he makes with me. An ingredient called "factice" is what does the erasing. It is a rubber-like product made by reacting rape seed oil from the Dutch East Indies with sulfur chloride. Rubber, contrary to the common notion, is only for binding purposes. Then, too, there are numerous vulcanizing and accelerating agents. The pumice comes from Italy; and the pigment which gives "the plug" its color is cadmium sulfide.

Does anyone wish to challenge my earlier assertion that no single person on the face of this earth knows how to make me?

No One Knows

Actually, millions of human beings have had a hand in my creation, no one of whom even knows more than a very few of the others. Now, you may say that I go too far in relating the picker of a coffee berry in far off Brazil and food growers elsewhere to my creation; that this is an extreme position. I shall stand by my claim. There isn't a single person in all these millions, including the president of the pencil company, who contributes more than a tiny, infinitesimal bit of know-how. From the standpoint of know-how the only difference between the miner of graphite in Ceylon and the logger in Oregon is in the type of know-how. Neither the miner nor the logger can be dispensed with, any more than can the chemist at the factory or the worker in the oil field—paraffin being a by-product of petroleum.

Here is an astounding fact: Neither the worker in the oil field nor the chemist nor the digger of graphite or clay nor any who mans or makes the ships or trains or trucks nor the one who runs the machine that does the knurling on my bit of metal nor the president of the company performs his singular task because he wants me. Each one wants me less, perhaps, than does a child in the first grade. Indeed, there are some among this vast multitude who never saw a pencil nor would they know how to use one. Their motivation is other than me. Perhaps it is something like this: Each of these millions sees that he can thus exchange his tiny know-how for the goods and services he needs or wants. I may or may not be among these items.

There is a fact still more astounding: The absence of a master mind, of anyone dictating or forcibly directing these countless actions which bring me into being. No trace of such a person can be found. Instead, we find the Invisible Hand at work. This is the mystery to which I earlier referred.

The Invisible Hand

By directing that industry in such a manner as its produce may be of the greatest value, he intends only his own gain...He is in this, as in many other cases, led by an invisible hand to promote an end which was no part of his intention...By pursuing his own interest he frequently promotes that of the society more effectually than when he really intends to promote it.

Adam Smith, *The Wealth of Nations*

It has been said that "only God can make a tree." Why do we agree with this? Isn't it because we realize that we ourselves could not make one? Indeed, can we even describe a tree? We cannot, except in superficial terms. We can say, for instance, that a certain molecular configuration manifests itself as a tree. But what mind is there among men that could even record, let alone direct, the constant changes in molecules that transpire in the life span of a tree? Such a feat is utterly unthinkable!

I, Pencil, am a complex combination of miracles: a tree, zinc, copper, graphite, and so on. But to these miracles which manifest themselves in Nature an even more extraordinary miracle has been added: the configuration of creative human energies—millions of tiny know-hows configurating naturally and spontaneously in response to human necessity and desire and in the absence of any human master-minding! Since only God can make a tree, I insist that only God could make me. Man can no more direct these millions of know-hows to bring me into being than he can put molecules together to create a tree.

The above is what I meant when writing, "If you can become aware of the miraculousness which I symbolize, you can help save the freedom mankind is so unhappily losing." For, if one is aware that these know-hows will naturally, yes, automatically, arrange themselves into creative and productive patterns in response to human necessity and demand—that is, in the absence of governmental or any other coercive master-minding—then one will possess an absolutely essential ingredient for freedom: a faith in free men. Freedom is impossible without this faith.

Once government has had a monopoly of a creative activity such, for instance, as the delivery of the mails, most individuals will believe that the mails could not be efficiently delivered by men acting freely. And here is the reason: Each one acknowledges that he himself doesn't know how to do all the things incident to mail delivery. He also recognizes that no other individual could do it. These assumptions are correct. No individual possesses enough know-how to perform a nation's mail delivery any more than any individual possesses enough know-how to make a pencil. Now, in the absence of a faith in free men—in the unawareness that millions of tiny know-hows would naturally and miraculously form and cooperate to satisfy this necessity—the individual cannot help but reach the erroneous conclusion that mail can be delivered only by governmental "master-minding."

If I, Pencil, were the only item that could offer testimony on what men can accomplish when free to try, then those with little faith would have a fair case. However, there is testimony galore; it's all about us and on every hand. Mail delivery is exceedingly simple when compared, for instance, to the making of an automobile or a calculating machine or a grain combine or a milling machine or to tens of thousands of other things. Delivery? Why, in this area where men have been left free to try, they deliver the human voice around the world in less than one second; they deliver an event visually and in motion to any person's home when it is happening; they deliver 150 passengers from Seattle to Baltimore in less than four hours; they deliver gas from Texas to one's range or furnace in New York at unbelievably low rates and without subsidy; they deliver each four pounds of oil from the Persian Gulf to our Eastern Seaboard—half-way around the world—for less money than the government charges for delivering a one-ounce letter across the street!

The lesson I have to teach is this: Leave all creative energies uninhibited. Merely organize society to act in harmony with this lesson. Let society's legal apparatus remove all obstacles the best it can. Permit these creative know-hows freely to flow. Have faith that free men will respond to the Invisible Hand. This faith will be confirmed. I, Pencil, seemingly simple though I am, offer the miracle of my creation as testimony that this is a practical faith, as practical as the sun, the rain, a cedar tree, the good earth.

Notes

- My official name is "Mongol 482." My many ingredients are assembled, fabricated, and finished by Eberhard Faber Pencil Company, Wilkes-Barre, Pennsylvania.
- G. K. Chesterton.

The Supplemental Poverty Measure

In order to address the concerns with the adequacy of the official poverty measure, the US Census Bureau, with support from the Bureau of Labor Statistics, released the first report describing research on the Supplemental Poverty Measure (SPM) in 2011. The SPM is meant to deal with weaknesses in the official poverty measure, namely that the current measure (1) excludes the impact of tax payments such as income taxes and social security taxes, as well as refundable tax credits such as the Earned Income Tax Credit; (2) excludes in-kind public benefits such as the Supplemental Nutritional Assistance Program (food stamps); (3) does not take into account expenses that are necessary to hold a job, such as transportation expenses and childcare; (4) does not take into account variations in medical costs; (5) has certain outdated household definitions; and (6) does not adjust for geographic differences in the cost of living. Thus, the SPM adds to household income the value of in-kind assistance, such as nutritional assistance, housing subsidies, and home-energy assistance, as well as the amount of any tax credits, and subtracts from household income the amount of any taxes paid, expenses related to work, medical out-of-pocket expenses (MOOP), and costs of childcare and child support, in order to obtain a more relevant measure of household resources. In addition, the SPM poverty thresholds are based on survey data for out-of-pocket spending on food, clothing, shelter, and utilities, whereas the current official thresholds are based on the cost of a minimum diet multiplied by three (that does sound a little too simplified, doesn't it?).

After all of that, the overall poverty rate does not differ much from the official rate, at 15.5 percent for the SPM compared to 14.5 percent for the official rate in 2013. On the income side of the ledger, there were a number of additions to account for government support programs and a number of subtractions to account for certain nondiscretionary costs. In addition, the dollar thresholds are higher under the SPM compared to the official thresholds, presumably to account for rising standards of living and people's actual spending habits. For example, the 2013 official poverty threshold for a two-adult, two-child household is $23,624, while the threshold for the same household if renting is $25,144 under the SPM. My quick-and-dirty analysis indicates that all of the increase in the poverty rate as measured by the SPM relative to the official measure is simply due to the higher dollar amount for the poverty threshold.

Just a couple of quick observations arising from the SPM compared to the official poverty estimates. The poverty rate for people under the age of eighteen drops by approximately 3.5 percentage points under the SPM, presumably because many government support programs are targeted to families with children, while the poverty rate for people sixty-five years and older increases by over 5 percentage points. The poverty rate increases in the Northeast and the West while declining in the Midwest, presumably reflecting the higher cost of living in the Northeast and West and the lower cost of living in the Midwest. The poverty rate for full-time, year-round workers increases from an official rate of 2.7 percent to 5.4 percent for the SPM, presumably reflecting the impact of taxes, work expenses, and the like, which are not captured in the official poverty statistics. And finally, the rate of those living at less than 50 percent of the poverty threshold declines from 6.5 percent under the official measure to 5.2 percent under the SPM (and from 9.3 percent to 4.4 percent for the under-eighteen group), presumably reflecting the impact of government support programs targeted to those with the lowest incomes and to families with children.

So there you have an alternative measure, giving different, but not dramatically different, overall indications of poverty, but perhaps giving a better indication of poverty across various groups of people. In any case, the overall incidence of poverty is not much changed, except that as with most things in life, the standard keeps getting higher.

Information on the supplemental poverty measure comes primarily from Kathleen Short, *The Research Supplemental Poverty Measure: 2011*, Consumer Income, Current Population Reports, US Census Bureau, US Government Printing Office: Washington, DC, November 2012, pp. 60–244; and Kathleen Short, *The Supplemental Poverty Measure: 2013*, Current Population Reports, US Census Bureau, US Government Printing Office: Washington, DC, October 2014.

Definitions of Food Insecurity

The United States Department of Agriculture (USDA) uses the concepts of *food security* or *food insecurity* when considering the issues of hunger or nutrition in the United States. The USDA makes a clear distinction between food insecurity and hunger, where "food insecurity—the condition assessed in the food security survey and represented in USDA food security reports—is a household-level economic and social condition of limited or uncertain access to adequate food," and "hunger is an individual-level physiological condition that may result from food insecurity."

The USDA has four labels to describe ranges of food security. *High food security* is defined as no reported indications of food-access problems or limitations. *Marginal food security* is defined as one or two reported indications, typically of anxiety over food sufficiency or shortage of food in the house with little or no indication of changes in diets or food intake. *Low food security* is defined as reports of reduced quality, variety, or desirability of diet, with little or no indication of reduced food intake. *Very low food security* is defined as reports of multiple indications of disrupted eating patterns and reduced food intake.

According to the USDA, at some time during 2011, 9.2 percent of households had low food security, and 5.7 percent of US households had very low food insecurity, so about 15 percent of households reported low or very low food security. As the USDA points out, "some households may be classified as food insecure or as having very low food security based on a single episode during the year." About one-third of households reporting very low food security reported the condition as frequent or chronic, so maybe slightly less than 2 percent of US households experience chronic conditions of very low food security. In fact, the USDA estimated that the average daily incidence of very low food security is between 0.8 percent and 1.1 percent of US households.

Information on the definition of *food insecurity* comes from the United States Department of Agriculture, http://www.ers.usda.gov/topics/food-nutrition-assistance/food-security-in-the-us, accessed July 28, 2013.

The Thrifty Food Plan

A fundamental part of the US food guidance system, the Thrifty Food Plan forms the basis for maximum food-stamp allotments. The TFP, last revised in 2006, provides a representative healthy meal plan at minimal cost and assumes that all food is consumed at home. Several standards form the basis for the TFP, including (1) the 1997–2005 Recommended Dietary Allowances (RDAs), Adequate Intakes (AIs), and Acceptable Macronutrient Distribution Ranges (AMDRs); (2) the 2005 Dietary Guidelines for Americans; and (3) the 2005 MyPyramid food-intake recommendations.

Grains account for 8 to 11 percent of TFP for a family of four, while vegetables account for 22 to 29 percent, fruits for 17 to 21 percent, milk products for 29 to 35 percent, meat and beans for 8 to 13 percent, and other foods (such as fats, oils, and sweets) for 3 to 6 percent. Compared to the previous TFP for a family of four, the 2006 TFP contains more vegetables, milk products, and fruits, with less meat, beans, grains and other foods. Compared to reported consumption, the revised TFP contains more vegetables, milk products, fruits, and grains, the same amount of meat and beans, and fewer other foods.

As of July 2013, the cost of the official USDA Thrifty Food Plan was $127.70 a week ($553.40 per month) for a family of four consisting of a couple and two young children. By comparison, the weekly expense of the moderate-cost plan was $200.80, and the cost of the liberal plan was $248.10.

Information regarding the Thrifty Food Plan comes from *Thrifty Food Plan, 2006*, Center for Nutrition Policy and Promotion, United States Department of Agriculture, April 2007. Cost data comes from http://www.cnpp.usda.gov, issued August 2013.

www.ingramcontent.com/pod-product-compliance
Lightning Source LLC
Chambersburg PA
CBHW071534200326
41519CB00021BB/6476

9780692481523